TERRITORIAL GOVERNANCE IN SOUTHEAST ASIA

This book considers decentralisation in Southeast Asia.

Focusing on Indonesia, Thailand, the Philippines and Malaysia, it looks back at the historical background of local governance in the region and examines the distinction between 'organic' and administrative local governments. It explores the concept of pluralism in relation to locality and localism and explores the extent to which decentralised governance is mandated by the constitution before looking at examples of autonomy in the region.

The book looks at processes and reservations such as sanctions, cancelling laws which are beyond powers or constitutional norms, dismissal of officials or fiscal measures. It looks at the way development communities internationally consider decentralisation of central importance and examines the impact of this. Finally it considers the way that the move to decentralise in the region has been followed by a measure of recentralisation.

Constitutionalism in Asia series

NUS National University of Singapore | Centre for Asian Legal Studies Faculty of Law

Constitutionalism in Asia series

Kevin YL Tan, Li-ann Thio and Jaclyn L Neo (Series Editors)

Asian constitutionalism is one of the most diverse, rapidly developing and challenging subjects of contemporary legal study. The continent is immensely diverse in its political ideology, religion, culture, language, economic development and colonial history. It has produced a great multitude of constitutional traditions, from authoritarian regimes to mixed communitarian and liberal constitutional models, and from regimes involving the military and monarchy to secular and theocratic constitutions. At the same time, its experience with courts and constitutions spans the gamut from rights-based to dialogical and good governance approaches, particularly where good government is sought through political process and public avenues rather than through the courts. With respect to judicial review and human rights, Asia provides a rich resource in examining how universal standards and local particularities interact. This series seeks to build on the growing academic interest in Asian constitutionalism by interrogating the normative, historical, empirical and conceptual dimensions of constitutionalism, through the lens of the Asian experience. It is expansive in scope and coverage and includes comparative studies between two or more Asian countries; comparisons between Asian and non-Asian jurisdictions; and critical single jurisdiction case studies. The series provides an excellent resource for scholars and students working in the field of Asian legal and constitutional studies, and comparative constitutional law more generally.

Territorial Governance in Southeast Asia

Andrew Harding

•HART•
OXFORD • LONDON • NEW YORK • NEW DELHI • SYDNEY

HART PUBLISHING
Bloomsbury Publishing Plc
Kemp House, Chawley Park, Cumnor Hill, Oxford, OX2 9PH, UK
1385 Broadway, New York, NY 10018, USA
29 Earlsfort Terrace, Dublin 2, Ireland

HART PUBLISHING, the Hart/Stag logo, BLOOMSBURY and the Diana logo are trademarks of Bloomsbury Publishing Plc

First published in Great Britain 2025

A catalogue record for this book is available from the British Library.

Library of Congress Cataloging-in-Publication data

Names: Harding, Andrew, 1950- author.

Title: Territorial governance in Southeast Asia / Andrew Harding.

Description: Oxford; New York: Hart Publishing, 2025. | Series: Constitutionalism in asia | Includes bibliographical references and index. | Summary: "This book advocates and defends the 3-decade-long decentralisation in Southeast Asia, arguing that it has on the whole been both successful and under-studied. Looking at 4 countries (Indonesia, Thailand, the Philippines and Malaysia), the book considers the issues of decentralised or territorial governance – a globally significant development – especially with regard to its relationship to societal pluralism, which is prevalent in Southeast Asia"—Provided by publisher.

Identifiers: LCCN 2024047038 (print) | LCCN 2024047039 (ebook) | ISBN 9781509961849 (hardback) | ISBN 9781509961887 (paperback) | ISBN 9781509961856 (Epub) | ISBN 9781509961863 (ebook)

Subjects: LCSH: Regional planning—Law and legislation—Southeast Asia. | Decentralization in government—Law and legislation—Southeast Asia. | Local government—Law and legislation—Southeast Asia. | Regionalism—Southeast Asia.

Classification: LCC KNC673 .H37 2025 (print) | LCC KNC673 (ebook) | DDC 342.59/042—dc23/eng/20241008

LC record available at https://lccn.loc.gov/2024047038

LC ebook record available at https://lccn.loc.gov/2024047039

ISBN: HB: 978-1-50996-184-9
ePDF: 978-1-50996-186-3
ePub: 978-1-50996-185-6

Typeset by Compuscript Ltd, Shannon

Credits

I READ RECENTLY a great suggestion that all books should have a list of credits, as they do with movies. After all they are in essence the work of more than one person. So here goes.

Principal moral support system, and constructive critic: Peter Leyland

Institutional support: Centre for Asian Legal Studies at the Faculty of Law, National University of Singapore, and its Director Jaclyn L Neo; Institute for Comparative Federalism at the European Academy in Bolzano, Italy, and the Institute's Director Francesco Palermo, for a month spent there as Federal Scholar in Residence in 2019

Indonesia whisperers/comments on drafts: Simon Butt, Ratu Durotun Nafisah, the late Keebet von Benda Beckmann

Malaysia whisperers/comments on drafts: Tricia Yeoh, Dian AH Shah, James Chin, Yap Kun Bek

Myanmar whisperers/comments on drafts: Nyi Nyi Kyaw, Marcus Brand, Kyaw Min San

Philippines whisperer/comments on drafts: Bryan DG Tiojanco

Thailand whisperers/comments on drafts: Rawin Leelapatana, Khemthong Tonsakulrungruang, Munin Pongsapan

Academic inspiration: In addition to all of those listed above, Bui Ngoc Son, Ran Hirschl, Jan-Michiel Otto, David Engel, Mark Sidel, Mara Malagodi, Tom Ginsburg, Alec Stone Sweet, Elisabeth Alber, Sören Keil, Karl Kössler

Research assistance and library facilities: Michael Cabinian; CJ Koh library, Singapore; Institute for Comparative Federalism, Italy

Publishing support: Hart Publishing, and book series editors Kevin Tan, Thio Li-ann, and Jaclyn L Neo

Collaborators, friends, colleagues, students, seminar and conference participants (at what seems a vast number of presentations and poster-sessions over too many years), anonymous proposal reviewers, lawyers, officials, and politicians who made perceptive or helpful comments: too many to list, but they have assisted me in my work with an extraordinary plethora of bits of information, questions, answers, citations, ideas, corrections, and discussions over coffee in a variety of places

Last but not least, constant forbearance and moral support, driving, and grip services: Sam Hew

Statements of law appearing in this book are correct, so far as I am aware, up to 19 June 2024.

Contents

PART III
SPECIAL REGIONAL AUTONOMY

PART IV
CONCLUSIONS

Table of Cases

Table of Legislation

Cambodia

Germany

Indonesia

Malaysia

Malaysia – Sabah

Malaysia – Sarawak

Myanmar

Philippines

Siam

Thailand

United Kingdom

Table of International Material

Introduction: A Sense of Place

One day in 2017 the inhabitants of Kampong Kerinchi, a reasonably prosperous suburb within the city limits of the Federal Territory of Kuala Lumpur, Malaysia, woke up to find that their area had been redesignated by City Hall as 'Bangsar South', its roads and avenues having all been renamed accordingly. They felt suddenly bereft of their sense of where they lived, and even, it was subsequently maintained with some passion, if not outrage, their 'identity'.

Kampong Kerinchi ('kampong' means village in Malay) is an area that predates Kuala Lumpur's urban sprawl, having been established in the 1870s, and its name is derived from a mountain in the southern part of the Indonesian province of West Sumatra, whose Minangkabau migrants settled in the village in the latter part of the nineteenth century. The continuation of this name, at odds with it being part of a large modern city, given its village-ness and foreign derivation, as well as the subsequent mingling of its original inhabitants with various newcomers, was a matter of some historical note for many of its inhabitants, who have a strong sense of local history. As many writers have noted, the Minangkabau have a uniquely matrilineal, democratic, adventurous, and outgoing culture.[1] On the other hand 'Bangsar', despite its easy association with the Malay word *bangsa* (nation), was in fact of purely colonial coinage, being a distinctly peculiar concoction of the names of two Frenchmen.[2] The name 'Bangsar South' was adopted only because the growing suburb of Bangsar had acquired a certain caché as a fashionable location, with its cafés, bars, restaurants, and bookshops, frequented mainly by the younger set.[3] The new name would certainly help to sell or rent out units at a high price.

The nominal association of 'Bangsar South' with what was in fact, bizarrely, a suburb at some distance from Kampong Kerinchi, suited the designs of developers, but the name change was followed by string of protests from residents, who stressed the historic nature and significance of the district's name, and their own sense of identification with it.

[1] F and K von Benda-Beckmann, *Political and Legal Transformations of an Indonesian Polity: The Nagari from Colonisation to Decentralisation* (Cambridge, Cambridge University Press, 2015) ch 14; and for Minangkabau culture in Malaya, see R Windstedt, *The Malays: A Cultural History*, 6th edn (London, Routledge and Kegan Paul, 1961) 56 ff.

[2] The two Frenchmen, who started a plantation there in colonial times, were Mr Bunge and Mr Grisar; the 'Bung' and the 'Sar' were put together to form 'Bangsar'.

[3] 'Bangsar: Where modern Malaysia goes to party' *Evening Standard* (11 January 2016) www.standard.co.uk/lifestyle/travel/bangsar-where-modern-malaysia-goes-to-party-a3153716.html.

They recruited their Member of Parliament to assist them in forcing the authorities to back down and revert to the previous name. In a 'proclamation ceremony' (no less) in January 2019 City Hall formally changed the name back to the original one, the original road names also being largely restored.[4] 'Bangsar South' (the name still clearly visible from the highway but not much otherwise) was then confined to one small part of the area that contains high-end restaurants and offices.

This story is interesting in that the sense of an historic identity was potent, even though it was essentially a somewhat vicarious identity, perhaps even arguably an example of Benedict Anderson's famous 'imagined communities'.[5] The lesson is perhaps that, even within dense modern urban development with its anonymising obliteration of difference, glitzy consumerism, and casual disregard of history, locality and identity do still have much relevance. How much more, one imagines, are they relevant in areas with a more obvious ethnic, religious or linguistic identity, or longer historical continuity? Amid the overwhelming diversity that characterises most of Southeast Asia, such communities as Kampong Kerinchi are actually the norm rather than the exception. Even in rapidly developing, socially mobile societies, place still matters.

Yet at the same time the imperatives of colonial and post-colonial history have forced such settled communities, together with ancient kingdoms, expanses of jungle, tracts of rice padi, and rapidly emergent cities, into somewhat disjointed 'Eastphalian' states.[6] These states exhibit an apparatus of government largely, and sometimes uncomfortably, based on Western models with colonial precedents and even colonial boundaries.[7] The entire effort of nation-building since its inception is still in most cases encompassed within the lifetime of a living person. Siam was renamed 'Thailand' in 1939. Modern independent Indonesia and the Philippines were both created in 1945, Burma/Myanmar in 1947, and Malaysia in 1963.

This book commenced with the conviction that localism is pervasive and important, and that governance at the level of subnational territories can confer great benefits when handled with sound judgement within a facilitating governance framework. Decision-making at the local levels impacts favourably on the general maintenance of good governance, the rule of law, and democracy, as well as service delivery. It concerns the everyday life of citizens in countless ways that national-level decision-making does not. Local decision-makers after all know their people and their territory best. They have local knowledge, they know

[4] 'Bangsar South now known as Kampung Kerinchi' *The Star* (1 January 2019) www.thestar.com.my/news/nation/2019/01/19/bangsar-south-now-known-as-kampung-kerinchi.

[5] B Anderson, *Imagined Communities: Reflections on the Origin and Spread of Nationalism* (London, Verso, 2006).

[6] S W Kim, D Fidler and S Ganguly, 'Eastphalia rising: Asian influence and the fate of human security' (2009) 26(2) *World Policy Journal* 53.

[7] W-C Chang, L Thio, KYL Tan and J Yeh, *Constitutionalism in Asia: Cases and Materials* (Oxford, Hart Publishing, 2014) ch 2 ('Constitutional Cultures in Asia').

what should be prioritised, what outcomes will likely occur, and what will work and what will not. Most importantly, they have at heart the interests of the local people, who are far more to them than a statistic on a file held in a ministry's airconditioned offices in the nation's capital. They are people with whom they generally deal face to face, or very close to that. This is the most powerful argument for subsidiarity, meaning that decisions should be taken at the level that is closest to those affected consistently with effective decision-making.[8] Subsidiarity entails a decentred form of territorial governance.

Localism and subsidiarity are two sides of a coin. It is the sense of localism that makes subsidiarity a desirable principle to follow. These two concepts inform this book at every level.

The book is concerned with 'territorial governance' – state governance of all kinds at all subnational levels. Its main task is to examine critically the condition of, and also arguments concerning, territorial governance as experienced in five states in Southeast Asia – Indonesia, Malaysia, Myanmar, the Philippines and Thailand. These five states correspond to the general description contemporary Southeast Asian states given above. They are also large states exhibiting many of the issues of territorial governance, such as the demand for local powers as a guard rail against authoritarian government and a catalyst of development, and for special autonomy for ethnic homelands. The book is also concerned with the project we call 'decentralisation', which (in Indonesia, the Philippines and Thailand at least) has been designed to satisfy demands for localism and subsidiarity by a transfer of powers to local government units, thereby creating new forms of territorial governance. Myanmar experienced decentralisation briefly during 2010–2021, but there is no project of decentralisation in Malaysia, which is the only formal federal system considered. The focus of this book is therefore on the systems of territorial governance as they now exist in five Southeast Asian states, rather than on the now largely historic process of decentralisation. The territorial governance discussed in this book is primarily governance at subnational levels that implies some form of local *self*-government, not central government conducted locally, which is normally called 'deconcentration'.[9] This latter concept is not, however, entirely irrelevant, as we will have to examine the balance between deconcentration and decentralisation; and deconcentration may well in practice involve a degree of localism, and even sometimes a degree of subsidiarity.

[8] 'Responsibility for service provision should be allocated on the basis of the principle of subsidiarity, that is, at the closest appropriate level consistent with efficient and cost-effective delivery of services. This will maximize the potential for inclusion of the citizenry in the process of urban governance.': UN Habitat, *The Global Campaign on Urban Governance, Concept Paper*, 2nd edn (2002) 20.

[9] 'A form of decentralisation involving distribution of functions to lower tiers of central administrative units on a sectoral or territorial basis while retaining accountability upward to the central institution': Asia Foundation, *State and Region Governments in Myanmar, New Edition* (Yangon, October 2018) ii.

Looking at the sources and literature on this subject, it is noticeable that coverage is patchy and that legal scholarship especially seems to have almost entirely passed over this important area of discussion. This book was therefore spurred also by curiosity to find out the facts about territorial governance as it now exists in Southeast Asia. It seeks to uncover this subject in its various guises and dimensions as a pervasive regional fact that merits comparative discussion. Its conclusion is that, despite many difficulties, decentred territorial governance as it has emerged in recent decades has been beneficial, and has potential to be even more beneficial. There has in fact been a revolution in territorial governance. Yet its occurrence has been halting and unaccompanied by close or comparative examination, at least in the field of legal scholarship.

In the course of exploring this subject we will examine in detail the purposes, structures, methods, and outcomes of territorial governance in the context of political and constitutional change across five key states whose populations together make up by far the greater portion of the Southeast Asian region's half a billion people. These states also offer us significant, although very different, systems of territorial governance as well as a range of pressing issues. Hence the region is an excellent laboratory for looking at the issues surrounding territorial governance generally. It shows a number of striking innovations that give us pause for thought about the implications of the five narratives, especially in terms of their lessons for the issue of diversity, in which the region abounds.[10]

The region's ethnic, religious and cultural diversity – and pluralism as a response to that diversity – emerge as important factors as is the case with many inquiries on Southeast Asia. To what extent, one wonders, is this diversity expressed in, or moderated by, modes of territorial governance? Is it a cause of, or a limitation on, territorial governance? If we see pluralism as a normative response to the facts of social diversity, is pluralism, this book asks, relevant to the various forms of territorial governance? The finding is that in many ways that are explored in the book pluralism (in all of its plural forms) is indeed highly relevant to territorial governance, and not just in the obvious instance of ethnic enclaves or homelands. It creates demand for autonomy or subsidiarity, both in the sense of providing a basis for local decision-making within the nation-state, and in the sense of giving voice and opportunity to localism. This theme underpins the narratives of territorial governance explored in this book.

This extended comparative inquiry therefore commences with the fact that territorial governance is a relatively unexplored, yet ubiquitous, fact of constitutional governance across the region. It is a fact whose importance is growing, and contains answers, or at least potential answers, to many of the region's problems of development, ethnic conflict, and governance deficit. It is worthy

[10] See ch 12.

of much further study from the perspective of several disciplines. This study does not attempt a holistic inquiry, but explores territorial governance as a legal, constitutional project whose dimensions are complex, question-begging, but ultimately transformative in important respects. It embraces five national narratives that have been little explored in comparison. It concludes with an argument that positions territorial governance positively with regard to development, democracy, and pluralism, emphasising the region's contribution in terms of innovative devices in the field of territorial governance. And of course, apart from what may be learned about territorial governance more generally, individual cases affecting half a billion people are inherently important and worth studying if only for that reason alone.

The first Part of the book (chapters one and two) deals with general issues and concepts, especially the constitutional entrenchment of territorial governance. Part II (chapters three to seven) offers in-depth case studies of each of the five systems of territorial governance. Part III (chapters eight to eleven) discusses four instances of special autonomy in Indonesia, the Philippines and Malaysia. Part IV draws conclusions from these case studies and discusses their general relevance.

Part I

General Issues

1

The Project

IN SOUTHEAST ASIA territorial governance is inevitably a matter of great importance. Indeed, throughout most of the region's history territorial governance, and not the abstract rule of statehood as we now conceive it, has been the main mode of governance. Even larger political units tended historically to correspond more to regions with a single urban centre, or provinces, than to the modern nation-states. This was often due as much to geography – jungle, mountains and rivers – as it was to local culture. At least 'local' culture may well in many cases have grown up as a result more of geography than of external infraction.[1]

In the absence of strongly centralised state-building until relatively recent times, and in the presence of a bewildering array of ethnicities and religious and linguistic communities, it is not surprising that communities in Southeast Asia have always had a strong sense of place, of real connection to the land.[2] This connection is social and can even be spiritual in nature. Engel and Chua in their study of Southeast Asian law and society research put it this way:

> concepts of personhood [are] closely linked to physical and social places, or what we call 'locality' and 'social terrain', respectively. Together, they suggest that, in Southeast Asia, who one is depends on where one is. Localities help to constitute personhood through the cultures, communities, and sacred things situated there. They determine the social status and identity of persons, families, and groups, thus shaping personhood both individually and collectively. Similarly, the social terrain determines how people interact with one another, thereby constituting one's personhood in relation to other people.[3]

Localism considered in this light is not region or province-wide but actually rather narrower in scope. The conjunction of identity and localism that we saw in the story of Kampong Kerinchi in the Introduction, and that we see in the quotation above lead to a question: is this conjunction perhaps not just a social

[1] W Wolters, 'Southeast Asia in the Asian setting: Shifting geographies of currencies and networks' in P Kratoska, R Raben and HS Nordholt (eds), *Locating Southeast Asia: Geographies of Knowledge and Politics of Space* (Singapore, NUS Press, 2005) ch 8.

[2] H Lansdowne, P Dearden and W Neilson (eds), *Communities in Southeast Asia: Challenges and Responses* (Victoria BC, CAPI, University of Victoria, 2002) Parts I and II.

[3] D Engel and L Chua, 'State and personhood in Southeast Asia: The promise and potential for law and society research' (2015) 2 *Asian Journal of Law and Society* 211.

fact but a possible way of dealing with the problems of social diversity? Given that Southeast Asia comprises a number of the world's most diverse societies, might this region of half a billion people, with its entrenched and extensive diversity, offer some cause for reflection on the relationship between pluralism and local governance? In this book we will explore this relationship in several different national and territorial-governance contexts. We will also explore more general aspects of territorial governance in the region. Localism is not after all confined to varieties of ethnic localism.

I. LOCALISM AND LOCAL KNOWLEDGE

It seems hardly understood in the literature in both constitutional law and politics that local decision-making, that is, decision-making by local and provincial government authorities, has enormous impacts on everyday life. These impacts are not simply those on spatial planning and physical development, amenities, facilities, communications, housing and the environment, which are already important enough. They are also impacts on local identity, as we have seen in the case of Kampong Kerinchi, and the sense of community well-being and confidence, which has no doubt been enhanced in that instance by its resistance to bureaucratic obliteration. Ironically, perhaps, it was Kuala Lumpur City Hall, a local government authority itself, not the Federal Government, that attempted to take away Kampong Kerinchi's identity. Localism has many levels of meaningful engagement.

Localism – this sense of place having consequences for decisions impacting on the locality – bears an obvious close relation to local knowledge. In the case of Kampong Kerinchi it was social and historical knowledge, but there are no limits to the scope or type of such knowledge. In fact, one of the most important arguments that has been advanced for decentralisation of government to local levels is based on the claims of local knowledge. This claim is of high importance and deserves some discussion. In a very broad sense, it virtually constitutes the claim for, and the essential virtue of, territorial governance itself, understood as local *self*-government.

What then is this claim for the importance of local knowledge? And what exactly do we conceive local knowledge to be?

The term 'local knowledge' is best known in connection with two very different scholars, the anthropologist Clifford Geertz[4] and the economist Friedrich Hayek.[5] Hayek discussed the nature of economic decision-making in relation to

[4] See C Geertz, *Local Knowledge: Further Essays in Interpretive Anthropology*, 3rd edn (New York, Basic Books, 2000).

[5] See F Hayek, 'The use of knowledge in society' (1945) 35(4) *American Economic Review* 519.

the problem of the need for rapid adaptation to change in the particular circumstances of time and place. He insisted that

> the ultimate decisions must be left to the people who are familiar with these circumstances, who know directly of the relevant changes and of the resources immediately available to meet them. We cannot expect that this problem will be solved by first communicating all this knowledge to a central board which, after integrating all knowledge, issues its orders. We must solve it by some form of decentralisation.[6]

This local knowledge of 'people, of local conditions, and of special circumstances' is impossible for officials at the centre to have or even to properly understand.[7]

Here we can bring in Geertz's use of 'local knowledge' in the sense of contextualisation of law, and indeed the very distinction between fact and law: 'Law … is local knowledge; local not just as to time, place, class, and variety of issue, but as to accent – vernacular characterisations of what happens connected to vernacular imaginings of what can'.[8] Thus, no matter what global ideas may apply as a matter of law, it is the contextual interpretation of these ideas in the locality that determines actual outcomes.[9]

Whereas Hayek uses local knowledge to analyse the making of economic decisions, Geertz uses it to understand law in society. Both perspectives are useful in considering territorial governance. Economic decision-making is not so different from administrative decision-making; vernacular understanding and description is an essential part of both types of decision, and the implementation thereof. In Southeast Asia the vernacular takes on more than casual or colourful importance. The prevalence of so many vernaculars makes locality the most fundamental of all social facts. And for those who conceive of law as manufactured by national-level officials, judges and legislators, local knowledge is an extremely important check and limitation on their task. This in itself is a lesson for those concerned with territorial governance.

In territorial governance terms, decision-makers must, like the anthropologist, 'contrive to place such singularities in an informing proximity', and 'move along (across, over, amid, through, between) cases, instances, and granular observations to broader … more elevated perceptions'.[10] Thus the acquisition of local knowledge is not just a matter of smoothing the rough, awkward edges of centrally-derived policy. It should also contribute to better policy by looping back to the centre. Local knowledge may well justify decentralisation of decision-making to the territorial level, but it also spells a need for careful design of central-local relations.

[6] ibid 526.

[7] ibid 522.

[8] Geertz (n 4) 215.

[9] A Harding, 'Global doctrine and local knowledge: Law in Southeast Asia' (2002) 51(1) *International and Comparative Law Quarterly* 35.

[10] Geertz (n 4) xi.

A hypothetical example will illustrate the point.

A local authority has to choose between a large non-local contractor offering standardised construction at a low price, and a local contractor offering customised construction at a slightly higher price. By choosing the latter, a local authority may be bending centrally determined procurement rules, but considers it will in the end get flexibility, efficiency, and sensitive consideration of local requirements and conditions, for example regarding the scheduling of work, local weather, employment and subcontracting, and an understanding of traffic flows, without too much extra cost.

This is an example of the exercise of local knowledge. The central official will probably accept the lowest tender, but to do so may not be in the public interest as judged locally. The chances are that local residents will be happier with the localised, and hence customised, product. Without recognition of the claim to local knowledge, such a choice would likely not be possible. The outcome serves efficiency as well as democracy.

II. DECENTRALISATION AS AN INTERNATIONAL PROJECT

Despite the disputed extent to which decentralisation of powers ought to occur,[11] its persistence and growth are remarkable, as is evidenced in its espousal by the international community, which has increasingly become a major advocate and actor in decentralisation projects. It is not too far-fetched to say that decentralisation is these days a very important part of what we mean by 'development'. The United Nations Development Programme, for example, is unambiguous in its support for the linkage of decentralisation with development:

> For development and governance to be fully responsive and representational, people and institutions must be empowered at every level of society – national, provincial, district, city, town and village. From UNDP's perspective, [decentralisation and governance for development] comprises empowering of sub-national levels of society to ensure that local people participate in, and benefit from, their own governance institutions and development services.[12]

The United Nations' Sustainable Development Goals recognise this point when they refer, as they do at Goal 16(6) to development of 'effective, accountable and transparent institutions *at all levels* [emphasis added]'. Socio-legal scholar Luis Eslava in his study of Bogota goes so far as to assert that 'decentralisation

[11] See eg EJ Malesky and FE Hutchinson, 'Varieties of disappointment: Why has decentralisation not delivered on Its promises in Southeast Asia?' (2016) 33(2) *Journal of Southeast Asian Economies* 125.

[12] UNDP, *Decentralised Governance for Development: A Combined Practice Note on Decentralisation, Local Governance and Urban/Rural Development* (2004) 2.

has been the official channel through which local jurisdictions have been transformed into the new foci of development'.[13]

This book does not claim that Southeast Asian territorial governance is unique. Indeed, it is clear that similar developments are easily seen across much of the world, both 'developed' and 'developing'. What needs stressing, however, is that this is a story that has not until now really been told, let alone appreciated for its significance for Southeast Asia or for the study and general theory of decentralisation or territorial governance.

Since the early 1990s there has occurred a largely unappreciated trend towards decentralisation of governance across most of the world, including Southeast Asia.[14] Decentralisation has conferred autonomy on provincial and local governments. Democratic elections have proliferated at the subnational level, extending the reach of democracy and constitutional government. Over three decades decentralisation has become practically ubiquitous at a global level.[15] In virtually every country, subnational autonomy extending to provincial and local government has increased, and in many cases this development has been constitutionally sanctioned or even mandated.[16]

As this book shows, Southeast Asia has decentralised governance in the nation-state to a degree that is quite surprising, given the region's reputation for creating authoritarian, or 'illiberal' states.[17] Africa, South Asia and South America, too, as 'developing areas', have seen a good deal of decentralisation, reflected even more obviously in the literature than Southeast Asian stories of decentralisation – a fact this book has the ambition, so far as possible, to alter. North America and Europe have also seen a measure of, or at least a demand for, decentralisation of various kinds, even though their systems of territorial governance were initially established many decades ago and have undergone little change.[18] These systems have in turn influenced the design of territorial

[13] Emphasis added; L Eslava, *Local Space, Global Life: The Everyday Operation of International Law and Development* (Cambridge, Cambridge University Press, 2015) 54.

[14] M Turner (ed), *Central-Local Relations in Asia and the Pacific: Convergence or Divergence?* (London, Macmillan, 2000); A Harding and M Sidel (eds), *Central-Local Relations in Asian Constitutional Systems* (Oxford, Hart Publishing, 2014).

[15] G Marks, L Hoogh and A Schakel, *The Rise of Regional Authority* (Abingdon, Routledge, 2010) ch 2. As an index of this process these authors (at 67) identify, across 42 countries over 50 years to 2010, 337 reforms strengthening regional autonomy, and 56 that weaken it.

[16] C Fombad, 'Constitutional entrenchment of decentralisation in Africa: An overview of trends and tendencies' (2018) 62(2) *Journal of African Law* 175. See also J Hatchard, M Ndulo and P Slinn, *Comparative Constitutionalism and Good Governance in the Commonwealth: An Eastern and Southern African Perspective* (Cambridge, Cambridge University Press, 2004) ch 9 'Devolution of powers to local communities'. And see ch 2.

[17] Thio Li-ann, 'Constitutionalism in illiberal polities' in M Rosenfeld and A Sajó (eds), *Oxford Handbook of Comparative Constitutional Law* (Oxford, Oxford University Press, 2012).

[18] T Groppi, 'Local authorities as guarantors of the rule of law: Recent developments in the Council of Europe' (*International Journal of Constitutional Law Blog*, 17 May 2024); J Newman, D Richards, A Westwood and P Diamond, 'Local democracy is essential for effective decentralisation in England' (*LSE Blog*, 9 May 2023).

governance in countries that were colonised.[19] Devolution of powers and 'regionalism' in Europe represent obvious, more recent, examples of decentralisation responding to issues of autonomy, pluralism, and identity.[20]

Despite the colonial origins of much of territorial governance in Southeast Asia, the region has, in line with Ran Hirschl's argument concerning megacities,[21] exhibited a degree of experimentation and innovation that is virtually unknown in Western states (European regional autonomy possibly excepted). There is a possibility here of real constitutional contributions from the global South to the global North.[22]

The spread of this decentralising tendency, as we may call it, requires explanation. To decentralise executive and legislative power may after all reflect any one or more of several objectives, and may be initiated by different actors, from local representatives and activists, through national policy-makers, to international organisations. Is decentralisation, though, a search for administrative efficiency, or enhanced, competitive development, or democratic legitimacy? Is it a reflection of the growing power of megacities, with other localisms in the tailwind; or merely an insurance provision for political parties that may lose control of the centre? Or is it rather a response to identity politics in plural societies, designed perhaps to avoid or resolve inter-communal conflict and thereby contribute in some way to nation-building? In Southeast Asia, this book argues, there are factors of local identity and culture that exercise considerable traction in terms of the territorial governance systems. After all, one objective of demanding autonomy is not simply to make local policy decisions, but to adopt modes of governance, (possibly, as we shall see, including traditional ones), that are preferred locally. One of the major questions, therefore, raised by the research for this book was, to what extent is traditional local governance reflected in the design of decentralisation? This will be seen as a significant factor in ways that will be uncovered and explained as we proceed through the case studies and the arguments.

Localism itself has local variants. It is likely that we will find a mix of motives when we examine individual cases. We will consider who drives change in territorial governance, and why they do so. Legislative and administrative projects rarely in the event mirror with any precision the motives of those who originated them. If so, we have to adjust our sights to look at the consequences, not just the motives. This leads us directly to the thorny issue of assessing success and failure.

[19] Fombad (n 16) 185.

[20] Marks et al (n 15).

[21] R Hirschl, *City, State: Constitutionalism and the Megacity* (Oxford, Oxford University Press, 2020) 103.

[22] This is discussed further in ch 12.

III. SUCCESS AND FAILURE: THOSE 'TWO IMPOSTERS'[23]

Decentralisation projects of various kinds are rarely described as wholly successful. On the one hand, although there are some examples of what is referred to as 'recentralisation',[24] examples are virtually non-existent of decentralisation being abandoned as a bad job in some kind of rapidly centripetal withdrawal, citing the project's lack of success. Typically, decentralising reform projects involve different stages of implementation, some changes of direction, significant adjustments, and controversial turf-wars over powers and money. They can also be proxies for national political conflicts. Success or failure may well, in the end, be in the eye of the beholder rather than judged by a set of performance indicators. To judge by the literature, one observer's notion of failure may well be the same as another's notion of success. It all depends on one's expectations and priorities. Apart from this, direct lateral comparison across a number of cases is hazardous when decentralisation takes so many different forms and has so many different outcomes as well as starting points – that is, the pre-existing systems of territorial governance. In this sense, even the extent of actual decentralisation of power in a given system may be difficult to judge.

Nonetheless, despite the ambiguity inherent in assessing the practical outcomes of decentralisation, its benefits in terms of empowerment of localities and the democratisation of local governance are, in general terms, these days virtually uncontested, at least in principle, even if they are not so easy to pin down with precision in practice.

The main questions then are, not whether decentralisation should take place, but how far it should go, and what control mechanisms are appropriate in terms of central-local relations and accountability of local entities. At the very least we can agree, as one commentator has put it, that 'local councillors should not be dependent on national politicians for getting windows fixed in city hall'.[25] There must be some level at which the exercise of local autonomy simply has to make sense.[26] The era of centralised planning in which the progress of every truckload of produce, or every hospital extension, or the granting of every licence, is mandated by a bureaucrat at the centre, is long gone. Where government intrudes at all on these issues it is often a local or

[23] 'If you can meet with Triumph and Disaster, and threat those two imposters just the same', as Rudyard Kipling wrote in his famous poem *If*.

[24] See further, ch 12, where the suitability of this term is doubted.

[25] K Eaton, 'Political obstacles to decentralization: Evidence from Argentina and the Philippines' (2001) 32(1) *Development and Change* 101.

[26] Of modern states perhaps only some micro-states like the Vatican or Tuvalu are without some level of decentralised governance. In Southeast Asia even Singapore (land area 730 sq km) devolved some limited powers to Town Councils in 1989; and Brunei (population 430,000) has mechanisms for government consultation with village heads.

provincial authority. To centralise every function, to make every decision at the centre, is risible, dangerous, bureaucratic (in the worst sense of the term), and seriously dysfunctional according to modern standards.

Keeping in mind, therefore, that success and failure may both be imposters, in this inquiry we will nonetheless attempt in brief to assess as far as possible the outcomes or consequences of decentralisation, as well as the functionality of territorial governance as it has evolved. Whether such outcomes represent success or failure, to repeat, depends entirely upon what is considered important.

This is not of course to argue that the progress of decentralisation has been a story of unalloyed improvement, nor that territorial governance is always efficient or responsive. Indeed, the process of decentralisation has often been disruptive, confused, and praiseworthy only in certain of its aspects. The process has often led to unforeseen outcomes and intractable problems, as we will find in Part II. This study is intended as evaluative as well as descriptive and analytical, and one is therefore forced to confront evaluation. Here it is necessary to rely on literature from various disciplines, and such assessments will be brief and general. But the important point in the context of evaluation is that decentralisation has had impacts going either far beyond, or falling well short, of the intentions of the legislator. Despite the problems of both process and outcome to which decentralisation has given rise, the finding of this book is that decentralisation, or territorial governance as it has come about, represents in many ways an improvement when compared to the highly centralised polities of the recent past. It has in short advanced the cause of democracy and delivered more and better development for local populations. Of the five countries Malaysia alone has not experienced decentralisation (this is explained in chapters four and eleven), while Myanmar, now in the throes of a tragic civil war, experienced it between 2010 and 2021 (this is discussed in chapter five).

A more modest objective in this study is to relate territorial governance in Southeast Asia to ideas and findings about the subject more generally. The interesting aspect of this line of inquiry is that in Southeast Asia territorial governance reflects elements of local identity and relates as much to culture, custom, and traditional governance as it does to the modern demands of politics, economics, and administration. In this sense the subject is highly worthy of legal speculation. To what extent does the system of territorial governance affect or determine the nature of public law in the nation-state as a whole? This is one of the underlying themes of the book.

IV. TERRITORIAL GOVERNANCE AND SCHOLARSHIP

A principal motivation for this study, as we have seen, is that the phenomenon of territorial governance in the Southeast Asian region deserves examination but has hardly been explored comparatively. Its stories have been, to some extent, contested locally, but not communicated to the wider world. The 'silent revolution', as Charles Fombad has called it in relation to African decentralisation,[27] has its parallel in Southeast Asia; yet many people will be surprised to hear it. The subject has also rarely been linked with legal or constitutional study, as though territorial governance is a mere detail, a footnote perhaps to administrative law, that has no impact on the general account of democracy, nation-building, political accountability, and good governance in a given nation-state. This is despite evidence that territorial governance has clear impacts on national, not just local, democracy, as will be seen in Part II. Very plausibly, the entrenchment of democracy, to be something more than a once-in-five-years event, needs to be built from the ground up rather than from the top down. Indeed, if local power can be exercised in an unaccountable manner, it is hard to see how a national democracy can survive at all in any meaningful way. It would have to be in essence some kind of an exception to the normal rule.

It was noticeable in researching for this book that journals on topics such as decentralisation, regionalism, and federalism appeared to have many studies on Africa or South America, for example, but very few indeed on Southeast Asia. Such studies as were unearthed were mainly descriptive, assuming, contrary to most of what is discussed in this book – one that concerns democracy and pluralism – that decentralisation is really only about achieving administrative and fiscal efficiency.

Territorial governance has, it seems, largely been a topic for consideration by political scientists interested in why and how decentralisation occurs, how successful or legitimate it has been, or (with reference to regional autonomy) how it helps in managing issues of ethnic or religious identity;[28] or by public administration and development scholars interested in maximising administrative efficiency and effectiveness, or else the process of fiscal balancing.[29] At the same time, it was also noticeable that legal scholarship too has neglected to take account of territorial governance, and not just in Southeast Asia but generally. Constitutional law tomes, for example, make scarcely any reference to decentralisation or to any aspect of territorial governance; even central-local relations barely feature in this literature.[30] Yet territorial governance is of constitutional importance in terms of both origins and consequences, and

[27] Above n 16, at 177.

[28] R Toniatti and J Woelk (ed), *Regional Autonomy, Cultural Diversity and Differentiated Territorial Government: The Case of Tibet – Chinese and Comparative Perspectives* (Abingdon, Routledge, 2017).

[29] J-M Otto and G Frerks, 'Decentralisation and development: A review of development administration literature' (Van Vollenhoven Institute, Leiden, Research Report 96/2, 1996); MH Nelson (ed), 'Local Government in Asia' chs 6–10 in *Thai Politics: Global and Local Perspectives, KPI Yearbook No.2 (2002/3)* (Bangkok, King Prajadhipok's Institute, 2004).

[30] For example, M Rosenfeld and A Sajo (ed), *The Oxford Handbook of Comparative Constitutional Law* (Oxford, Oxford University Press, 2012) has 1396 pages and 64 chapters, of which one is on federalism, but there is no other coverage of territorial governance; local government does not feature.

its heavy impact on democracy, the rule of law, the balancing of powers, and also on the system of administrative law.[31] There is of course a persistent interest in the theory and practice of federalism, which has largely bypassed Asia. East of India, only Malaysia has a formally federal system, and even this is a highly centralised form of 'quasi-federalism'.[32] More recently the constitutional aspects of regional autonomy, which involves special rules for devolved entities, have merited the attention of legal scholars.[33] Part III of this book deals with regional autonomy and its relationship with pluralism.[34]

V. SOUTHEAST ASIAN DIMENSIONS OF TERRITORIAL GOVERNANCE

Let us now pay attention, with reference to territorial governance, to the broader context of Southeast Asia. This section provides a brief sketch of matters that are gone into in greater detail later in the book.

With increasing prosperity and articulation of government and the state in Southeast Asia, more and more decisions are taken, and more and more services and programmes are provided, by local and provincial governments. These decisions and services are often the ones that most directly affect the lives of citizens. For example, spatial and development planning, housing, the environment, transport, and public health, are deeply impacted by local government. Increasingly provincial and local governments are even taking responsibility for delivery of previously centralised services such as education, health care, and social welfare.[35] Large cities, which are drivers of all aspects of development (save agriculture) and are also large consumers of the benefits of development, have been granted unprecedented autonomy as they have grown beyond their traditional constitutional status as well as their legal boundaries.[36]

Such developments are not of course unique to Southeast Asia, but, as all work on the region seems to emphasise, the really important aspect of

[31] NM Davidson, 'Localist administrative law' (2017) 126 *Yale Law Journal* 564.

[32] See A Harding and J Chin (ed), *50 Years of Malaysia: Federalism Revisited* (Singapore, Marshall Cavendish, 2014). Currently, peace talks in Myanmar (see ch 5) and proposals in Philippines (see ch 6) are embracing the possibility of moving towards federalism in both of these states. Myanmar is already described by some observers as a quasi-federation: M Brand, 'Achieving "genuine federalism"? Myanmar's inexorable path towards constitutional devolution and decentralised governance' ch7 in A Harding and Khin Khin Oo (eds), *Constitutionalism and Legal Change in Myanmar* (Oxford, Hart Publishing, 2017).

[33] See eg P Leyland, 'The multi-faceted constitutional dynamics of UK devolution' (2011) 9(1) *International Journal of Constitutional Law* 251; F Palermo and C Kössler, *Comparative Federalism: Constitutional Arrangements and Case Law* (Oxford, Hart Publishing, 2017) 20ff.

[34] Y Ghai and S Woodman (eds), *Practising Self-Government: A Comparative Study of Autonomous Regions* (Cambridge, Cambridge University Press, 2013).

[35] See eg A Harding and P Leyland, *The Constitutional System of Thailand: A Contextual Analysis* (Oxford, Hart Publishing, 2011) ch 4.

[36] See further ch 12.

the nation-states in question is their ethnic, religious, and linguistic diversity, which was noted above. This diversity affects the manner in which the nation-state deals with almost every issue, and we will find that territorial governance is no different in this respect. Accordingly, one preoccupation of this book that might not have been a preoccupation if any other part of the world had been chosen, is with the impact of history and culture on territorial governance. In particular we can ask from where the structures of local government have been derived. Are they based on colonial models of territorial governance, or have those been eclipsed by the newly decentralised system? In designing local-government structures do the nation-states rely on traditional names, boundaries, offices, or structures? Do they reflect in some ways political culture, or traditional modes of territorial governance? Or do they merely provide off-the-peg local governments that do not differ at all from one place to another? Or, as in Indonesia, is there a tension within the decentralisation process between these two different notions of local governance?[37] Some attention is given in Part II to the evolution of the modern system of territorial governance. However, sources on the actual geographical design of local government districts are extremely sparse.

Although we tend to think of territorial governance as organised and controlled from the centre in a kind of cautiously retractable beneficence, it is well to remember that modern constitutionalism in the West grew out of territorial governance, not the other way around. In the West democracy itself started as an exclusively urban phenomenon; in Europe cities were generally democratic and often quite autonomous in some respects, both in the ancient world and in the medieval period. Cities sat in the councils of the Holy Roman Empire.[38] By 1871 Germany had united 39, and Italy 13, states, some of which had been independent cities. Prior to that the words 'Germany' and 'Italy' were only geographical expressions, to use Metternich's phrase.[39]

Following the unification of nation-states out of petty kingdoms (or sometimes republics), entities that are now generally deemed provinces of the nation-state, local government in Europe generally grew somewhat inductively, rather than being organised in the logical manner embodied by Bonapartism. Standardisation of local government in England, for example, was only achieved in the late nineteenth century.[40]

[37] F and K von Benda-Beckmann, *Political and Legal Transformations of an Indonesian Polity: The Nagari from Colonisation to Decentralisation* (Cambridge, Cambridge University Press, 2012); JAC Vel and AW Bedner, 'Decentralisation and village governance in Indonesia: The return to the nigari and the 2014 Village Law' (2015) 47(3) *Journal of Legal Pluralism and Unofficial Law* 493; J Vel, Y Zakaria and A Bedner, 'Law-making as a strategy for change: Indonesia's new Village Law' (2017) 4(2) *Asian Journal of Law and Society* 447.

[38] B Stolberg-Rilinger, *The Holy Roman Empire: A Short History* (Princeton, Princeton University Press, 2018) ch 2.

[39] CJH Hayes, *Modern Europe to 1870* (New York Macmillan, 1970) ch xvi.

[40] D Wilson and C Game, *Local Government in the United Kingdom*, 4th edn (Basingstoke, Palgrave Macmillan, 2011) ch 4.

In Asia on the other hand, while state-building was, in the pre-colonial period, a matter mainly of conquest of smaller kingdoms by bigger ones, much as had occurred in Europe, government at local levels has largely been directed from the centre. The concept of the state tended towards the idea of a centre radiating influence outwards in concentric circles of progressively diminishing influence; this is the galactic state formed in the shape of a mandala.[41] Local autonomy therefore tended to reflect a weak centre rather than either a strong periphery or a wealthy city.

To the extent that Southeast Asian territorial governance has been anything other than the assertion of central power locally it was really villages, the face-to-face communities, that counter-balanced the impersonal state, acting as a focus for clan-based resistance and local identity, rather than for deliberate decentralisation.[42] This tendency of village resistance has continued somewhat into the modern era.[43] Colonialism, continuing and reinforcing the trend of centralisation, generally suppressed, or tried to suppress, localism, or tolerated it only by necessity or as a façade for indirect rule.[44] In British-ruled territories in the twentieth century local government was usually organised by the colonial administration, and was often then used as a sandpit for developing national democracy prior to the granting of independence.[45] In the Dutch East Indies in the early twentieth century there was a deliberate attempt at modest decentralisation to urban municipalities, but these were defined on the Dutch pattern rather than relying on the existing forms of village – the *desa* or *kampong*. To this extent they were administrative rather than organic – described indeed by Van Vollenhoven as 'Western enclaves in an Eastern society'.[46]

[41] F Fukuyama, *The Origins of Political Ordering: From Prehuman Times to the French Revolution* (New York, Farrar, Strauss and Giroulx) ch 7. In the idea of a 'galactic state', which is much concerned with the geo-body of the state, consciousness lies at the centre and satellites surround it: S Tambiah, 'The galactic polity in South East Asia' (2013) 3(3) *HAU: Journal of Ethnographic Theory* 503. Gilbert Rozman presents an interesting argument that central-local relations in East Asia (China, Taiwan, Japan, and Korea) can be reformulated on the basis of a localist interpretation of Confucianism. He finds evidence that Confucianism, rather than encouraging centralisation, actually sought to balance the power of the state with institutions lying between the state and the family. The implication is that they have not in fact done so in recent times: G Rozman, 'Center-local relations: Can Confucianism boost decentralisation and regionalism?' ch 7 in DA Bell and Hahm Chaibong (eds), *Confucianism for the Modern World* (Cambridge, Cambridge University Press, 2003).

[42] Fukuyama, ibid ch 6.

[43] J Scott, *The Art of not Being Governed: An Anarchist History of Upland Southeast Asia* (New Haven, Yale University Press, 2009). Currently in Myanmar, villages and townships have provided a basis for People's Defence Forces fighting against the military and providing their own, spontaneous local government: see ch 5.

[44] See eg on Indonesian history, von Benda-Beckmann and von Benda-Beckmann (n 37) ch 6.

[45] See eg in Malaya; see A Harding, 'Local democracy in a multi-layered constitutional system: Malaysian local government reconsidered', ch 8 in Harding and Sidel (n 14) 143; Malaysian democracy started with local elections in the early 1950s. Similarly, US democratisation in the Philippines under the Taft administration started with local government: see ch 6.

[46] J-M Otto, 'Indonesian opposition in the colonial municipality: A Minahasser in Bandung' (2015) 2 *Asian Journal of Law and Society* 169.

Insofar as there are typically or uniquely Southeast Asian types of local government, these are probably therefore more likely to be found at the level of villages than at the level of larger subnational units. The region does not in general have anything quite like India's *panchayat* republics, which were deliberately promoted as an indigenous form of governance during decolonisation,[47] but it does have a traditional concept of village government, as in the case of *barangay* in the Philippines,[48] Thailand's *tambon*, Java's *desa*, and West Sumatra's *nagari*.[49] In this last case Franz and Keebet von Benda-Beckmann have shown how decentralisation has since 1999 resulted in a strong revival of traditional modes of local-government.[50] This is an example of survival of organic local government (*nagari*) resisting the standardisation inherent in the administrative variety (the *desa*) imposed from the centre.[51]

Village governance has not been the subject of any concerted comparative study in Southeast Asia so far, but largely these traditionally-named units with their traditionally-named officials and (sometimes) deliberative councils or consultative mechanisms (we will see several examples in Part II), seem to function practically as administrative units within the overall democratic structure of governance rather than continuing in operation as traditional or pre-modern forms of local governance in a new constitutional setting. The *nagari* appear to be an exception, representing both a rebellion against the standardisation (termed *desa*-fication[52]) inherent in the Indonesian decentralisation project, and an expression of unique Minangkabau *adat*-based culture. Interestingly enough, although the 2014 Village Law allows villages to become *adat* villages, few outside West Sumatra have actually done so.[53]

Where traditional culture does normally come into the picture is in the use of local autonomy and community rights to preserve such culture and identity (as in Indonesia, above, and Thailand, below). In the tension between the impersonal state and local identity, this use of local autonomy in Southeast Asia is one of the major purposes of seeking to pursue or preserve autonomy.

In Burma, as in India, the British attempted to use the village as a basis for administration, and the village head as a mediational device. Furnivall writes of Burmese resistance in the face of British attempts to convert traditional, organic villages with their own headmen into constitutionalised, administrative units. The administrative system was not based on what was naturally there, but rather

[47] A Thiruvengadam, *The Constitution of India: A Contextual Analysis* (Oxford, Hart Publishing, 2017) 96–98.

[48] See further ch 6.

[49] See further chs 3 and 7.

[50] von Benda-Beckmann and von Benda-Beckmann (n 37) ch 7.

[51] ibid 267.

[52] ibid.

[53] Vel et al (n 37).

attempted to distort it into something suited to the needs of British administration rather than the expression of Burmese custom and tradition.[54]

In Southeast Asia state-building was of course necessarily to some extent achieved at the cost of local autonomy. In pre-modern Thailand, for example, the Siamese state that ultimately modernised the country during the Bangkok period was constructed out of small kingdoms (*mo'an*) corresponding roughly to modern provinces. Since the prevailing historical narrative is one of gradual centralisation of power, eventually embracing the Malay/ Muslim border provinces in the South and the Lanna kingdom in the North, there was nothing corresponding to modern local self-government. However, Siam's detailed 1727 *Edict on the Method of Provincial Administration* embodies ideals of good governance, and a response to the rapacious ambitions of provincial governors. It ensures that the governor would report to the King regularly on all relevant matters; that he would not take local women for wives or servants without their parents' consent; not sit in judgment without being accompanied by a legal officer; and generally that he would exercise powers for the peace of the district and the happiness of the people.[55] The accretion of power at the centre has now had to be balanced by decentralising reforms, not just in the interests of efficient decision-making, but to preserve identity, customs, and culture in a diverse country.[56]

This aspect of the book goes some way to answering the question, why Southeast Asia? The answer is that, as with so many other issues, the region is not only typical of what happens elsewhere and sometimes even derivative therefrom, but also offers some problems, insights, and solutions that are unique. It will tell the stories that the region offers in an attempt to understand the region, its nation-states, its laws, and its societies in all their rich colours, from the aspect of territorial governance.

VI. TERRITORIAL GOVERNANCE AS A LEGAL TOPIC

In spite of the advance of decentralisation across Southeast Asia, local-government law (that is, public law as it relates to local government) has been almost entirely neglected in the region as an object of study.[57] Comparative

[54] JS Furnivall, *Colonial Policy and Practice: A Comparative Study of Burma and Netherlands Indies* (Cambridge, Cambridge University Press, 1957) 194ff; see further ch 5.

[55] HG Quaritch Wales, *Ancient Siamese Government and Administration* (New York, Paragon, 1934: 1965) 126–30.

[56] See ch 6.

[57] There are notable exceptions. The first is the Philippines, where the Local Government Code 1991 has received a good deal of attention: D Gatmaytan, *Local Government Law and Jurisprudence* (Diliman, University of Philippines College of Law, 2014); see also AQ Pimentel, *The Local Government Code Revisited* (Central Book Supply, 2011); R Casis (ed), *The Local Government Code: An Assessment* (Diliman, Law Complex Printery, University of the Philippines, 1999). The second is Malaysia: Kanesh Sundrum's four-volume series *Kanesh on Local Government Laws*

work has hardly been undertaken at all. The subject of local-government law is not generally taught in law schools in Southeast Asia (it is also uncommon elsewhere), even though many legal practitioners (a number of them were consulted during the research) will spend their careers dealing with issues of local democracy and various forms of public participation; planning law and other spatial or land issues such as compulsory acquisition, transport and infrastructure; licensing; educational rights; and even social issues such as the care of children or the elderly, and public health; and many other important local-government issues that impact immediately, and sometimes drastically, upon the lives of citizens as well as the local economy.[58] These issues also have constitutional dimensions in terms of territorial governance and decentralisation reforms; division or balancing of powers; democracy (electoral rights, public participation, and freedom of information, for example); good governance (fiscal and policy transparency and accountability); and the role of administrative and judicial dispute-resolution.

While lack of law-school preparation for local-government-related legal practice may be understandable if not supportable, and is by no means confined to Southeast Asia, the lack of interest in territorial governance on the part of legal scholarship is less excusable. An examination of recent collections of work on Asian constitutionalism revealed virtually no, or only incidental, reference to local government, or actually any form of territorial governance, beyond some slight reference to federalism, and the odd case that happens to feature a local government authority. These tomes, impressive as they are, appear to assume that constitutionalism stops at the belt road surrounding the capital conurbation with its public bureaucracies, assemblies, courts, lawyers and law schools, there being nothing of interest beyond. Yet one does not need to spend much time in Southeast Asia to realise that very different perspectives are available on almost everything when viewed from a different geographical vantage point or by a different community. Given the extent and scope of law-making, administration, and democratic institutions and process at the local level across the region, this is a rather odd state of affairs. Then again, the lack of development of administrative-law scholarship more generally across the region is also a matter of concern, and this too impacts on our ability to understand territorial governance.

When we move to constitutional law, we need to ask whether territorial governance is even recognised as a topic at any level. The nub of interest

(Kuala Lumpur, Current Law Journal, 2021–23). These works are intended primarily for legal practice.

[58] A study of planning law in Kuala Lumpur revealed that lawyers hardly deal with planning matters at all except for occasional instances of judicial review and planning appeals, relevant work going mainly to architects: A Harding and A Sharom, 'Access to environmental justice in Malaysia (Kuala Lumpur)' ch 5 in A Harding (ed), *Access to Environmental Justice: A Comparative Study* (The Hague, Martinus Nijhoff, 2007) 136. So it may be that the neglect of this area is actually to the detriment of the legal profession.

here is whether territorial governance represents an entrenched constitutional principle, that is, a democratic *right to local self-government*, or the mandating of a developmental process for decentralisation. We will find there are two models here. They are dubbed the 'constitutional mandate' model, corresponding to local self-government as a right; and the 'legislative' model, under which local self-government is not mandated by the constitution but is purely a matter of legislative choice, such as an organic law on local government. These issues are pursued in chapter two.

VII. DECENTRALISATION AND THE DEVELOPMENTAL STATE

In Asia one might expect (and it has been hinted above) that the state-centric nature of Asia's dominant-party systems, and its post-war subordination of all sources of power to the overriding objective of development, characteristic of the Asian developmental state,[59] make territorial government a matter of insignificant detail. This book, to the contrary, shows that in Asia democratic local self-government has proceeded almost everywhere, irrespective of the exigencies of the developmental state. Indeed, local self-government under decentralisation calls into question whether the Asian developmental state is any longer a relevant concept in explaining development in Southeast Asia. Since the early 1990s state after state in Asia has decentralised decision-making and service-delivery in ways that have probably contributed significantly to political, social, and economic development.[60] Democracy and good governance cannot fail to have impacted in some ways on constitutional government and democracy as a national way of life. Cities in particular have grown to be powerful agents impacting internationally as well as on national political systems.[61]

At the same time, it does need to be recognised that in Asia from the 1950s political power and administrative capacity were centralised to a great degree in pursuit of development goals. Asian developmental states (as they were called by Chalmers Johnson and Alice Amsden) centralised power especially during the 1960s, 1970s and 1980s.[62] These states were lauded for having done so by the

[59] C Johnson, *Japan, who Governs? The Rise of the Developmental State* (New York, WW Norton, 1995).

[60] Although 1990 may be seen as a turning point, it should also be recognised that some states had mounted extensive decentralisation projects during the 1970s and 1980s, and even in some cases the 1960s: D Rondinelli, 'Implementing decentralisation programmes in Asia: A comparative analysis' (1983) 3 *Public Administration and Development* 181.

[61] Hirschl (n 21); J Lin, *Governing Climate Change: Global cities and Transnational Law-Making* (Cambridge, Cambridge University Press, 2018); ASEAN Smart Cities Network, at asean.org/asean/asean-smart-cities-network/.

[62] Johnson (n 59); A Amsden, *Asia's Next Giant: South Korea and Late Industrialisation* (New York, Oxford University Press, 1989); M Woo-Cummings (ed), *The Developmental State* (New York, Cornell University Press, 1999); Kevin YL Tan, 'The role of public law in developing Asia' (2004) *Singapore Journal of Legal Studies* 265.

World Bank in 1993.[63] As Kevin Tan argues, states need to acquire power before they can create development; this factor is key to understanding development, and it fits with the traditional Southeast Asian culture of respect for, as opposed to distrust of, government.[64] For many indeed the Asian developmental state is still with us. But it is nonetheless little recognised that in more recent times these developmental states, looked at from the aspect of territorial governance, have been disaggregated to a surprising extent in a trend that contradicts the prevailing narrative of centralisation. This aspect of development seems not to have been extensively examined. Has decentralisation succeeded in redefining development in Southeast Asia, and in disaggregating power to the advantage of democratic participation? This question will be central to this book's inquiry, and the finding is that it has in general terms done exactly this.[65]

We will see that decentralisation has indeed contributed much to nation-building across Southeast Asia by allowing voice, expression and continuity to local identities, which proliferate as deep elements of culture amongst the region's teeming and extremely diverse populations.[66] One objective of territorial governance in the region, in addition to the generally well-understood objectives globally, has been to provide large opportunities for local difference, whether ethnic, cultural or religious, to be expressed through the exercise of local autonomy. Examples of this phenomenon will be examined in both Part II and Part III.

The region has naturally suffered the downsides as well as the upsides of development. Rapid development leads to a greater disparity between rural and urban areas, despite the overall increase in prosperity, creating political tensions that can be seen most obviously in Thailand,[67] but seem to be present in some form almost everywhere. The common Asian phenomenon of the flight from rural to urban areas leaves many urbanites with insecure economic or social status in cities, and it leads to pressing social issues in both rural and urban areas; urban authorities in particular have difficulty responding to this need and are often in conflict with the centre.[68]

These factors, contributing as they do to the push for decentralisation, actually pose an analytical difficulty. If the developmental states have ruthlessly centralised power in the interests of rapid development, as is argued by those who advance their claims to success, why is it that these same states have in

[63] World Bank, *The East Asian Miracle: Main Report* (1993) at documents.worldbank.org/curated/en/975081468244550798/Main-report. The report looked at eight high-performing Asian economies.

[64] Tan (n 62) 272.

[65] See ch 12.

[66] L Chua and D Engel, 'State and personhood in Southeast Asia: Promise and potential for law and society research' (2015) 2 *Asian Journal of Law and Society* 211, at 219.

[67] J Glassman, '"The provinces elect governments, Bangkok overthrows them": Urbanity, class and post-democracy in Thailand' (2010) 47(6) *Urban Studies* 1301.

[68] A Harding and M Sidel, 'Analysing central-local relations in Asian constitutional systems: Decentralising power in 21st-century Asia' ch 1 in Harding and Sidel (n 14).

the last three decades decentralised power to the extent that they have done – with only some significant retraction, and apparently not very differently when compared with other parts of the world? It is of course more than just a linguistic point that decentralisation requires centralisation as a precondition. Southeast Asia has in general experienced progressive centralisation of power throughout most of its history, as will be elaborated in the country studies in Part II. In some measure the recent decentralisation appears to be a reaction to the hyper-centralisation of the decades following World War II, Indonesia and the Philippines being striking examples of movement from a highly centralised system of militarised dictatorship to one in which territorial governments at all levels enjoy broad powers and are democratically elected.[69] Decentralisation is in fact a process that requires considerable political will, vertical mobilisation, and devotion of resources at the centre and also spreading downwards from the centre to the locality. It requires in short that powerful central agencies give up some of their power. We will see that decentralisation has not in general been a matter of central agencies being forced to surrender power to ambitious local players. Nor has it happened in a fit of absent-mindedness. Rather it has been a top-down enterprise that represents a considerable and deliberate disaggregation of Southeast Asia's centralised developmental states since the early 1990s. Most cases of decentralisation in the region commenced during that decade.[70] We may therefore see this development as part of the region's democratisation process over the last 30 years or so.

VIII. DEFINING THE PROJECT

We come then to the project itself and how the book defines and delimits its subject matter. Let us recap on the relevant issues.

First of all, how are 'territorial governance' and 'decentralisation' defined?

Territorial governance is public governance of any kind that exists at the subnational level and that amounts in some sense to local self-government. It embraces federalism, provincial or regional governance, and local governance. Territorial governance may in some cases involve a process of decentralisation of powers from the centre. But it may have simply evolved, as in Malaysia for example, without any overt attempt to decentralise; or may exist as a mere possibility for the future, as in Myanmar.[71]

Terminology surrounding decentralisation is notoriously loose, but this book is clear as to what is, and crucially what is not, covered by 'decentralisation'. We will not in general (except by way of contrast and explanation)

[69] See chs 3 and 6.
[70] Philippines from 1991; Indonesia since 1999; Thailand since 1997.
[71] See chs 4 and 5.

be concerned with central government agencies operating locally, or with local agencies implementing centrally-determined policies as agents (often this is termed 'deconcentration', or 'administrative decentralisation'), but with democratically elected, autonomous, self-government by subnational units.[72] Decentralisation, therefore, deals with the process of granting or devolving powers to these units. It is motivated by the idea of subsidiarity, which necessitates re-examination of decision-making processes and how they affect areas beyond the capital city. It also embraces localism in the way we saw earlier.

This book is not about federalism as such, although in some cases the existence (in Malaysia) or possibility (in Myanmar and the Philippines) of federalism will be relevant in discussing the shaping of territorial governance, including local government. Chapter eleven is devoted to the issue of federalism in Sabah and Sarawak as a case of special autonomy within Malaysian federalism. The concern in Part III is with the asymmetric devolution of powers to regions where there is or has been inter-ethnic or inter-religious conflict (for example, Aceh, Papua, and Bangsamoro); and the possibility of such devolution in the case of Thailand's Muslim southern border provinces is considered in chapter seven.

Territorial governance, even when clearly defined, is a topic with many aspects to it, and can be approached from many disciplinary perspectives. Scholars of political science, public administration and public finance, economics, sociology, and even history and anthropology, may have much of interest and relevance to say about it. That which belongs to these types of literature is taken account of, so far as is possible, in this book. But the purpose is not to offer a multi-disciplinary overview as such of territorial governance in Southeast Asia. Rather the book seeks to analyse it from the perspective of public law. How does territorial governance affect our understanding of the rule of law, constitutional government, administrative law, democratic rights, and the balancing of powers? These matters have been considerably, and sometimes deeply, affected by the evolution of territorial governance, despite the connection being almost entirely absent in the literature. Our understanding of both public law and territorial governance are, it is apparent, in need of some mutual adjustment.

Accordingly, the purpose is to try to answer three related questions by reference to a particular region of the world, Southeast Asia, by a combination of national case studies and comparative inquiry.

The first is, does territorial governance in Southeast Asian reflect in any way traditional, pre-modern forms of local governance, or does it simply take the form of modern standardised agencies imposed territorially? To put this another way, are local authorities 'organic' (evolving out of traditional forms

[72] Malaysia is a possible exception here, as it does not have local elections. However, local government is a facet of state government, and there is debate about restoring local elections.

of local governance) or 'administrative' (conforming to a centrally conceived framework)?

Second, does constitutional law in Southeast Asia provide for territorial governance in the form of something like a right to local self-government, embodying the entrenched existence and/ or development of autonomous local powers and democratic processes?

Third, and following from these two questions, how is the relationship between territories and the centre provided for constitutionally or statutorily? Are local governments subject to having their powers taken away or controlled in certain circumstances? Or can their exercise of powers be delimited by central administrative action such as the cancelling of decisions, appeals, punitive sanctions, or budgetary constraints? How real, in other words, is local autonomy, given the need for a system of central-local relations?

Although one can find modes of territorial governance across all the states comprising the region of Southeast Asia, this book deals with five large countries that offer different but interesting perspectives on the subject matter. For the sake of concentration of the argument and organisation of the evidence, it does not deal with the one-party socialist states (Vietnam and Laos), which have different constitutional structures and political assumptions from the other Southeast Asian states – although here too one can find a surprising amount of genuine devolution of powers as a result of reform processes in recent decades.[73] Singapore and Brunei, which are too small to contribute much to the discussion, are excluded, as is Cambodia.

By looking at these five cases of large and diverse nation-states, we see three instances of operation of decentralisation over three decades; one stable system of territorial governance that has changed little during that period; and one process of decentralisation arrested *in medias res*. Given the vast array of powers exercised by different levels of government in these rather different structures, this study interweaves the case studies with a thematic discussion of the relevant issues in territorial governance that have been adumbrated in this chapter.

[73] Bui Ngoc Son, 'Central-local relations and the constitutional discourse on political decentralisation in 21st-century Vietnam' ch 4 in Harding and Sidel (n 14).

2

Constitution

I. TERRITORIAL GOVERNANCE: TWO MODELS OF CONSTITUTIONAL STATUS

WHAT ARE THE legal instruments that provide for territorial governance? To what extent is territorial governance mandated and directly governed by national constitutions? Do these constitutions provide for anything like a *right* to local self-government? Do they prevent the abridgement of local powers? And beyond these questions, in what way does a national ideology, or a sense of what the nation is, inform the approach taken to territorial governance? This chapter explores these questions in relation to the five Southeast Asian states discussed in Part II.

The questions posed are important ones. While it is true that administrative law, and beyond that, local government law, generally deal with local and other subnational levels of government, constitutional law, as Hirschl puts it, is 'public law's main highway',[1] so that we may expect it is the constitution that will ordinarily dictate the fundamental principles applied to territorial governance, even if not providing all the detail. We can also assess the scope and importance of territorial governance in a given system by reference to its constitutional status. What is in question is not simply whether territorial governance attains the majestic status of a constitutional topic, but, more importantly, whether it achieves the embeddedness of real local autonomy within the national system of governance.

The same is true of the process of decentralisation. One might question the suitability of providing constitutionally that there *be* a decentralisation process, as this would correspond to a programme rather than an established, entrenched system of territorial governance. Nonetheless, constitutions are in fact, in many cases, programmatic, especially when they are drafted after regime change, and even more so if they reflect a prior political agreement as to the way forward. Decentralisation is programmatic in this sense in the constitutions of Indonesia (1945, as amended in 2000),[2] the Philippines (1987)[3] and Thailand

[1] R Hirschl, *City, State: Constitutionalism and the Megacity* (Oxford, Oxford University Press, 2020) 16.

[2] See ch 3.

[3] See ch 6.

(1997, 2007, and 2017).[4] In the case of Myanmar, decentralisation featured in the 2008 Constitution, and decentred territorial governance will likely feature prominently in any new constitution that may be drafted.[5] In the remaining instance of Malaysia, territorial governance is entrenched, in the sense that federalism is a highly important feature of national governance. But there is no provision for any decentralisation programme as such, either in the constitution or otherwise.[6]

In chapter one two models for the basis of territorial governance were outlined, namely the 'constitutional-mandate' model and the 'legislative-mandate' model. The distinction between these, it will be recalled, is that under the constitutional-mandate model, there is a constitutional right of some kind to local self-government; whereas under the legislative-mandate model local self-government is not required by, and so not entrenched in, the constitution, but is purely a matter of legislative choice, such as might be provided by an organic law on local government or the like. In Part II we will deal extensively with the content of such laws. Here we are concerned only with their status. The distinction is important, because, for example, it would be possible under the first model, but not the second, to claim a *right* to local democratic elections, to resist the abridgement of local powers, or to prevent the undue restriction of local finance.[7] Under the legislative-mandate model, local autonomy is in no sense entrenched. Given that constitutional argument would be impossible under this model, the best hope in such a case for those resisting incursion on local powers would lie in judicial review of administrative discretion exercised under statute law.

To be clear, under the legislative-mandate model, it is a matter entirely within the power of the legislature to change the status or incidents of territorial governance; to abridge the conditions of democracy and accountability under which it operates; to denude it of powers or finance, or summarily take over local powers; or even, in an extreme if unlikely case, to abolish territorial governance completely.[8] All of this could be done without any constitutional infringement, just by passing a law, or making use of powers already granted under existing law. Under the constitutional-mandate model, such measures could be held unconstitutional. The distinction is not purely theoretical. As we will see in the case of Malaysia, the local government system has been deprived of democratic accountability via an apparently constitutionally valid statutory

[4] See ch 7.

[5] See ch 5.

[6] See ch 4.

[7] A good example is afforded by the Philippines Supreme Court case of *Pimentel v Aguirre* GR No 132988 (2000).

[8] It is not entirely inconceivable. Hitler used his Enabling Act 1933 to abolish the German lander, a crucial first step in establishing the Third Reich's extreme dictatorship, centralising power in Berlin at the expense of the federal structure.

abolition of local elections in 1976, consolidating a position first established via exercise of emergency powers in 1965.[9] And in the Philippines we will see that local powers have been constitutionally protected.

From this we may conclude that in order to provide real local autonomy it is not enough to make constitutional *mention* of territorial governance: there must be a constitutional *right* to territorial self-government, and there must be credible guarantees of its autonomy. In the constitutional-mandate model territorial governance is guaranteed in this manner, and must conform to certain constitutional norms, such as that adequate financial provision be made for the exercise of local powers; and that local governments must be democratically elected.[10] The constitutional mandate may go further than this, to prescribe the kind of decentralisation programme discussed above, which would usually include an obligation to create a territorial governance system that conforms to constitutionally prescribed norms. It is only under conditions of this kind that it may be claimed that citizens enjoy a constitutional right to local self-government. And it is only under these conditions that a system of territorial governance is likely to thrive as a vital and effective element in the polity.

Conceivably constitutions can go further than has been indicated, by specifying the detailed content of the right to local self-government, as does the Philippines' Constitution of 1987, which is discussed below. For example, it may be provided that alteration of local government boundaries, and the creation or abolition of local governments, cannot be effected except with the consent of the local electorate.[11] A specific share of national revenue or the right to raise revenue independently may be specified. There may even be a right to the recognition, in some manner, of local identity such as local culture, customs, or language.[12]

These two models do not simply represent differing analyses of the constitutional texts. Constitutional design results in territorial governance being conceived either as a convenient way of implementing national policy at the local level (labelled earlier as 'deconcentration'), or as a means whereby localities can decide and prioritise according to their own judgement of their particular needs. The concept of local self-government indicates a form of territorial governance corresponding with the latter as opposed to the former perspective. Of course, it is possible, if unlikely, for the legislative-mandate model to produce an outcome corresponding roughly to the description of territorial governance in the constitutional-mandate model, containing appropriate guarantees for local self-government; such outcome will not, however, enjoy constitutional status

[9] See p 76.

[10] C Fombad, 'Constitutional entrenchment of decentralisation in Africa: An overview of trends and tendencies' (2018) 62(2) *Journal of African Law* 175.

[11] See eg the Constitution of the Philippines 1987, Article X.

[12] See the Constitution of Indonesia 1945, s 18B; Constitutional Court Decision 4/PHPU.D-XI/2013 (on the *noken* customary voting system).

and could at any time be altered to the disadvantage of local governments, creating a sense of dependency. To conclude, the constitutional status of territorial governance is likely to either reflect political will to create and preserve the right to local self-government; or to treat territorial governance simply as a mechanism for delivering centrally decided policy – or, worse, as just a topic that needs to be parked in some convenient place in the constitutional text, along with, say, harbours, posts, and libraries.

II. ENTRENCHMENT

Having drawn a clear distinction between these two models, and in pursuit of the logic of the notion of constitutional mandate, we can now ask how territorial governance is or may be constitutionally entrenched. Entrenchment can of course occur in different ways and to different extents. One can look at the number of levels of territorial governance that are mandated, as well as the extent of the powers and resources constitutionally granted to its different levels. Important in this respect will be provision for central-local or intergovernmental relations.

As Charles Fombad reminds us in examining constitutional entrenchment in Africa's 'silent revolution' in decentralised government,[13] the extent and nature of entrenchment is of considerable significance, not just in the assessment of the system of territorial governance, but in the actual progress of decentralisation. It will be the conclusion of this book, as argued in later chapters, that, in this context at least, constitutional design in Southeast Asia does matter in the way that Fombad maintains it will. The obvious advantages of entrenchment lie in ensuring that the process of decentralisation is implemented in a mandatory fashion, and is not interrupted or countermanded by ill-considered recentralisation; in providing clarity of the roles played by each level of government; and in making local government units ultimately less dependent on central government.[14] Less obviously, perhaps, the entrenchment of territorial governance, if one believes in building democracy and constitutional government from the ground up, assists in ensuring that democracy and constitutional government become a national, not just a local, fact. Beyond that, the extent of entrenchment may be assumed to be a good indicator of the seriousness with which decentralisation has been undertaken; entrenchment is, as Fombad insists, the 'strongest possible indication of a government's commitment to sharing powers with subnational units'.[15] This claim is shown in Part II of this book to be made out with respect to Southeast Asia.

[13] Fombad (n 10). See also A Harding, 'The constitutional dimensions of decentralisation and local government in Asia', ch 3 in A Bedner and B Oomen (eds), *Real Legal Certainty and its Relevance: Essays in Honour of Jan-Michiel Otto* (Leiden, Leiden University, 2018).

[14] Fombad, ibid 196–97.

[15] ibid 177.

Ultimately, nonetheless, entrenchment can only be as deep as the process of constitutional amendment allows.[16] But requiring constitutional amendment in order to reverse or interfere with territorial governance does offer useful protection in flagging the constitutional nature of the issues implied in the system of territorial governance.[17] In fact, since the advent of decentralisation there has in fact been no constitutional as opposed to legislative amendment that has abridged local autonomy in Southeast Asia.[18]

III. THE BASIC STRUCTURE DOCTRINE

A further related question that arises in relation to entrenchment is whether territorial governance is protected by the basic structure doctrine (BSD). Under this doctrine, a constitutional amendment may be invalidated if it violates the constitution's basic structure.[19] If the system of territorial governance is a part of that basic structure, then it would be entrenched sufficiently deeply that *even a constitutional amendment* duly passed according to the process provided in the constitution would be ineffective to violate the basic principles of that system. Those principles would include not just the continued existence of territorial governance, but also its real autonomy.[20] For example, if the right of local electorates to refuse consent to a boundary change is not part of the basic structure, then local government areas could be drastically reduced in number, or local elections could be abolished by constitutional amendment, deeply impacting the right to local self-government.

We usually think of the justification for the BSD as emanating from popular expectation at the moment of constitution-making. If the constitutional moment at which the constitution was crystallised is to be construed as one that created an expectation of a particular structure of territorial governance, then the BSD should in principle apply to that structure.

In federal systems, there is arguably a popular expectation of the kind justifying the BSD. Yet it is not the same expectation as in a unitary state, because the constitutional moment also involves a surrender of sovereignty of its subjects to the federation that the constitution creates. Thus in addition to popular expectation there is a supra-constitutional treaty obligation of some kind to observe the rights of the subjects of the federation, not just those of the people generally.[21]

[16] R Albert, *Constitutional Amendments: Making, Breaking and Changing Constitutions* (Oxford, Oxford University Press, 2019) Pt 2.

[17] ibid 13–15, 196–97.

[18] Arguably Thailand's 2017 Constitution makes less solid provision for local autonomy than did its predecessors of 1997 and 2007: see p 124.

[19] *Kesavananda Bharati v State of Kerala* (1973) 4 SCC 225.

[20] This was recognised by Sikri CJ, ibid at [391].

[21] See further ch 11. And Sikri CJ, ibid.

Malaysia is the sole federal system considered in this book, and the above discussion is somewhat speculative. Nonetheless, Malaysia's founding document, the Malaysia Agreement 1963, has received the status of a constitutional document by virtue of a constitutional amendment in 2022.[22] The significance of this Agreement is discussed further in chapter eleven, and there is plausibly an argument that the federal structure should be seen as part of the basic structure of the constitution, despite some judicial authority to the contrary.[23]

However, once we move beyond federalism, the matter becomes even more debateable. The fact is that decisions on the BSD have hardly addressed the structure of government (often referred to as 'political constitutionalism') as opposed to rights and judicial independence (often referred to as 'legal constitutionalism'). It might even be argued that the structure of government (other than federalism) should not even in principle be protected by the BSD, because the state should be free to redesign the structure of government.[24] It is therefore a moot point whether the BSD applies at all to levels of territorial governance in a unitary state. The answer probably depends on the importance allocated to those levels in the constitution. In a unitary state it seems likely that, if the constitutional-mandate model applies, a serious abridgment of local self-government by constitutional amendment might be held to be unconstitutional. Yet, while there are many BSD cases supporting rights and judicial independence, there seems to be no court decision to date applying the BSD to territorial governance as such. Apart from the question whether the BSD applies in principle, its application in the context of territorial governance remains a matter of speculation.

IV. THE LEGISLATIVE-MANDATE MODEL

We can now look further at the two models of territorial governance, starting with the legislative-mandate model. This model is represented in Southeast Asia only by Malaysia. In the case of the legislative-mandate model, territorial governance is either not recognised at all in the constitution, or is mentioned only as a subject for legislation, and there is no constitutional provision for local self-government. Even the limited entrenchment afforded by recognition as a subject is, however, at least an acknowledgement that localism has some kind of quasi-constitutional status, even if there is nothing amounting to a duty to observe subsidiarity or a right to local self-government. Such shallow entrenchment may nonetheless expressly require the enactment of one or more organic laws dealing with territorial governance, such as a local government

[22] See p 41.

[23] See p 186ff.

[24] See eg the Kenyan case of *Attorney-General v David Ndii* [2022] KESC 11 (KLR); [2023] 1 LRC 1.

law; or it may imply a need to enact such a law by using such phrase as 'as enacted by law'.

In Malaysia federalism, as we have seen, is an entrenched feature. Local government is a state function and is recognised by the Federal Constitution in a number of respects. The constitution provides, notably, for a National Council on Local Government (NCLG), and allows the federation to enact legislation on local government for the sake of uniformity. And it has done so with the Local Government Act 1976.[25] However, there is no right to local democracy, and in fact local-government elections were suspended as an emergency measure in 1965 and then abolished on a permanent footing in 1976.[26] The demand for restoration of local-government elections is nonetheless persistent, and the framework can be recreated, in spite of the abolition of elections, for holding elections whenever they are reintroduced by law.[27] As matters rest, local-authority members are appointed by state governments, while the federal government appoints the *Datuk Bandar* (Mayor) of the Federal Territory of Kuala Lumpur. An attempt to execute local quasi-elections in the state of Penang by consulting the electorate on local-government appointments was ruled unlawful by the courts as a colourable device to circumvent the abolition of local elections.[28]

One can at least, however, say that in this case, given the constitutional status of the NCLG, it would be difficult to proceed on the basis that the continuance of local government (as opposed to democratically elected local governments) is entirely a matter of parliamentary discretion. Its existence as a state function guarantees that local government must continue to exist, even if heavily controlled by the state governments. The powers of states over local government also raise the issue whether the NCLG is even a constitutionally validly created entity.[29]

While territorial governance is recognised, these provisions go little further than saying that there shall be territorial governance with competences. Nothing is said about local self-government or any guaranteed extent of its powers or their protection. The situation of the states is of course a different matter, as we have seen.[30]

[25] A Harding, *The Constitution of Malaysia: A Contextual Analysis* (Oxford, Hart Publishing, 2012) 155.

[26] See p 71.

[27] Harding (n 25) 160–61. Local elections were held between 1953 and 1965.

[28] *Government of the State of Penang and Anor v Government of Malaysia and Anor* [2014] 7 Current Law Journal 861.

[29] A Harding, 'A baseline study of local government in West Malaysia', NUS Working Paper No 14/2022, 28. Since the NCLG was established by a constitutional amendment, only use of the BSD could invalidate it.

[30] Another good example of the legislative-mandate model is Cambodia, whose constitutional provision on territorial governance is quoted below, adding, in Article 146 of its 1993 Constitution that '[p]rovinces, municipalities, districts, *khan*, *khum* and *sangkat* shall be governed in accordance with organic law'. There are three levels of territorial government, and each is governed by its own organic law as provided by Article 146. The organic laws provide for local elections at all three levels, although local democracy is not actually demanded by the constitution.

V. THE CONSTITUTIONAL-MANDATE MODEL

The constitutional-mandate model is clearly the more consequential of the two models. We can look now at three examples in which territorial governance is taken more seriously than in the legislative-mandate model, is fully entrenched, and involves a constitutional right to elected local self-government.

A. Myanmar

Myanmar's 2008 Constitution is now in effect in abeyance following the military coup of 1 February 2021. The possibility remains, however, that a future constitution based on agreements heavily implicating both federalism and decentralisation could take the 2008 Constitution as a starting point. The history of extreme centralisation is not encouraging in this respect, as we shall see in chapter five.

The 2008 Constitution provides for elected state and regional assemblies.[31] Myanmar has altogether no less than five levels of government. The states and regions, of which there are seven in each category, have similar constitutional status to each other as well as to the union territory of Naypyidaw, the five Self-Administered Zones, and the single Self-Administered Division.[32] States are defined by ethnicity, or the 'national races' in Myanmar discourse, whereas regions comprise the Burman ethnic majority.[33]

B. Philippines

The Philippines has historically been a decentralised state, due to a combination of a political culture of localism and deliberate policy during the period of American rule (1898–1946), which ensured that local self-government along the Jeffersonian pattern was entrenched even before national democracy came about. The Philippines was one of the earliest states in Asia to engage in decentralisation, with US-facilitated projects in the 1960s. During the post-Marcos period (1986 to date) there has been a strong emphasis on local government reform as an antidote to the Marcos period's centralisation.[34] This developed into one of the world's most ambitious decentralising initiatives. Hutchcroft

[31] 2008 Constitution of Myanmar, s 13.

[32] M Crouch, 'Ethnic rights and constitutional change: The recognition of ethnic nationalities in Myanmar/ Burma' ch 6 in A Harding and M Sidel (eds), *Central-Local Relations in Asian Constitutional Systems* (Oxford, Hart Publishing, 2014). See further ch 5.

[33] Crouch, ibid 110.

[34] PD Hutchcroft, 'Paradoxes of decentralisation: The political dynamics behind the passage of the 1991 Local Government Code of the Philippines' ch 6 in MH Nelson (ed), *Thai Politics: Global and Local Perspectives, KPI Yearbook No.2 (2002/3)* (Bangkok, King Prajadhipok's Institute, 2004).

contrasts the 'centralising ethos' of Thailand's prefectural reforms in the late nineteenth century with the lack of any such history in the Philippines.[35] The Philippines Constitution of 1987 therefore takes local government very seriously as a constitutional subject.

Article X entrenches local autonomy and allows local authorities to create their own sources of revenue subject to limitations 'consistent with the basic policy of local autonomy'. It requires[36] a local government code (in fact enacted by Congress in 1991[37])

> which shall provide for a more responsive and accountable local government structure instituted through a system of decentralisation with effective mechanisms of recall, initiative, and referendum, [and] allocate among the different local government units their powers, responsibilities, and resources.

Of special interest in view of the ubiquitous problem of local government finance, is section 7 of Article X:

> Local governments shall be entitled to an equitable share in the proceeds of the utilisation and development of the national wealth within their respective areas, in the manner provided by law, including sharing the same with the inhabitants by way of direct benefits.[38]

A local-plebiscite requirement applies to preserve the continued existence of these local authorities as well as their boundaries. Local authorities are empowered to 'group themselves to consolidate or coordinate their efforts, services, and resources for purposes commonly beneficial to them'. And the President is required to

> provide for regional development councils or other similar bodies composed of local government officials, regional heads of departments and other government offices, and representatives from non-governmental organisations within the regions for purposes of administrative decentralisation to strengthen the autonomy of the units therein and to accelerate the economic and social growth and development of the units in the region.

Thus the Philippines' Constitution in effect recognises a right to the continuous existence of local authorities, to local autonomy in terms of powers and finance, and to a supportive and developmental national policy on local government. There have been several proposals to convert the Republic into a federation. Each of the proposed models would render the Republic even more

[35] ibid 313.

[36] 1987 Constitution, Article X, s 3.

[37] Local Government Code 1991 (Republic Act 7160).

[38] There is a useful comparison here with Germany's Basic Law, Article 28, which guarantees autonomy to municipalities in terms of both competence and financial resources. Relatively few European constitutions have provisions guaranteeing local government autonomy: S Bartole, 'Internal ordering of the unitary state' ch 28 in M Rosenfeld and A Sajo (eds), *The Oxford Handbook of Comparative Constitutional Law* (Oxford, Oxford University Press, 2012) 616.

decentralised than it already is; but it is not presently entirely clear how this development, if it ever comes to pass, would affect local government.[39]

C. Thailand

Unlike the Philippines, Thailand has historically been highly centralised as a prefectural state since the late nineteenth century, when Bangkok asserted its power over the Lanna Kingdom in the North and the Malay/ Muslim border provinces in the South.[40] However, neither this predisposition, nor the oscillation between military and civilian government that has continued since the end of the absolute monarchy in 1932, has interfered with a process, under the recent successive democratic constitutions (1997, 2007, 2017), of progressively decentralising powers and providing for local democracy at every level.

Decentralisation is seen as encouraging the practice of democracy under the Thai mantra of 'the democratic regime with the King as head of state'.[41] The development of local government (and also provincial government) is a state duty,[42] the process for fulfilling which has been continuously implemented since the enactment of the Decentralisation Plan and Process Act 1999, required by provisions of the 1997 Constitution. This development of local government involves electoral democracy[43] as well as what the current Thai Constitution of 2017 prescribes as local autonomy in the form of 'self-government according to the will of the people in the locality'.[44] In addition, it embraces democratic participation and freedom of information, with an emphasis on utilities and services.

The 2017 Constitution also specifically provides for the preservation of local communities, heritage, cultures and customs, which is a particularly important factor in the most ethnically diverse areas of Southeast Asia such as Northern Thailand.[45] This is expressed as both a democratic right of local communities, and as a duty of both the state and citizens.[46] Local elections were held in 2020, following the surrender of power following military rule. Thus in Thailand territorial governance may be said to be constitutionally mandated.

[39] See eg 'The PDP Laban model of PH federalism: An executive summary' (Institute for Autonomy and Governance, 28 September 2017) iag.org.ph/index.php/blog/1503-the-pdp-laban-model-of-ph-federalism-an-executive-summary.

[40] A Harding and P Leyland, *The Constitutional System of Thailand: A Contextual Analysis* (Oxford, Hart Publishing, 2011) 123. See further ch 7.

[41] See further ch 6. Local elections, suspended during military rule 2014–19, were held in 2020.

[42] 2017 Constitution, ss 76, 250.

[43] ibid s 252.

[44] ibid s 249.

[45] C Barry (ed), *Rights to Culture: Heritage, Language, and Community Rights in Thailand* (Silkworm Books, Chiang Mai, 2013).

[46] ibid ss 43, 50, 57, 76.

D. Indonesia

The Indonesian Constitution of 1945 establishes the Republic as a unitary state,[47] which 'shall be divided into provinces and those provinces shall be divided into regencies (*kabupaten*) and municipalities (*kota*), each of which shall have regional authorities which shall be regulated by law'.[48] There are therefore three layers of territorial governance. These regional authorities 'shall administer and manage their own affairs according to the principles of regional autonomy and the duty of assistance' (*tugas pembantuan*).[49] Each of these levels is required by Article 18 to have its own elected regional assembly and executive officers (governors, regents, and mayors). Interestingly, they are also to 'exercise wide-ranging autonomy, except in matters specified by law to be the affairs of the central government', which expresses a form of subsidiarity. However, the 'structure and administrative mechanisms of regional authorities' are to be regulated by national law. Central-local relations are also regulated by national law, which must have 'regard to the particularities and diversity of each region'. The State 'recognises and respects units of regional authorities that are special and distinct', as well as traditional communities along with their traditional customary rights as long as these remain in existence and are in accordance with the societal development and the principles of the Unitary State.

Two laws passed in 1999, the Regional Autonomy Law and the Fiscal Balancing Law, which commenced the decentralisation process, had to be provided for constitutionally to ensure their validity, and this was done in the 2000 amendment to the Indonesian Constitution, providing Articles 18, 18A, and 18B.[50] Under these provisions new regional autonomy laws were also enacted in 2004 and 2014, as is discussed further in chapter three. It is clear from these Articles that in Indonesia there is a constitutional right to democratic local self-government. All of these entities are guaranteed the wide-ranging autonomy of their governments, under elected leadership, and have their own elected representative bodies and legislative powers. The relative powers of central, provincial, regional, and city governments are regulated by law with due regard to 'regional uniqueness and diversity'. In a country with more than 300 officially identified ethnic groups, six official religions and more than 17,000 islands, this reference to uniqueness and diversity is no mere constitutional verbiage. The diversity is further recognised by provision in Article 18B that the state (as is the case in Thailand) recognises and respects *adat* (customary) law communities and

[47] 1945 Constitution, Article 1.

[48] 1945 Constitution, Article 18(1).

[49] Article 18(2). '*Tugas pembantuan*' means, literally, 'assistance task', or co-operation, that is to say, it is seen as a duty owed by local entities to the central government to render assistance.

[50] For further discussion, see S Butt and T Lindsey, *The Constitution of Indonesia: A Contextual Analysis* (Oxford, Hart Publishing, 2012) 158ff.

their traditional rights. Village governments are not constitutionally entrenched but are provided by statute.[51]

The reforms did not stop there. A major innovation introduced under the 2000 2nd amendment to the 1945 Constitution is the House of Regional Representatives (*Dewan Perwakilan Daerah*, or DPD), a national body established to give the regions special representation in the national legislative process.[52]

The Indonesian Constitution therefore clearly entrenches territorial government at a deep level and is a strong example of the constitutional-mandate model. The detailed working of the structure adumbrated here is examined in chapter three.

VI. SOVEREIGNTY, INDIVISIBILITY, AND THE GEO-BODY OF THE STATE

Having laid out the two models of constitutional mandate and legislative mandate, and having discussed the issue of entrenchment, we can now turn to the issue of national ideology and constitutional provision for territorial governance. The question here is, how does the constitution perceive the very spatial existence of the nation-state it creates? While constitutional law is now revealed to be a subject that has neglected the spatial aspect of its subject matter,[53] one does nonetheless find constitutional provisions that speak of the nation's spatial existence, or its 'geo-body'.[54] Implicit in this idea is the nation-state seen as equivalent to a human body, where damage to or incursion upon any part of it becomes a violation of its integrity, dignity, and even functionality. We will see, however, that constitutional texts that imply this metaphor seem not to have been sufficiently thought through in the context of territorial governance. The importance of this issue lies in the fact that forms of national ideology will, as we shall see, either encourage or discourage territorial self-government.

A. Indonesia

The Indonesian Constitution merely provides for a unitary state. But at Article 18(1) it also provides that '[t]he Unitary State of the Republic of Indonesia shall be divided into provinces and those provinces shall be divided into regencies (*kabupaten*) and municipalities (*kota*), each of which shall have regional authorities which shall be regulated by law'. Although semantically

[51] ibid 165.
[52] ibid 58.
[53] Hirschl (n 1) ch 1.
[54] T Winichakul, *Siam Mapped: A History of the Geo-Body of a Nation* (Honolulu, University of Hawaii Press, 1994).

one might question how unitary a state can be that *shall* (not may) also be divided, this provision seems clear enough. There is of course a long history of suspicion of federalism in Indonesia, which has been viewed as a neo-colonial attempt to break up the Republic.[55] Given that Timor Leste seceded from Indonesia in 2002; that two territories (Aceh and Papua), as we shall see in chapter 9, enjoy regional autonomy; and that subnational units enjoy considerable powers; one might question how 'unitary' the state really is practice. However, what seems clear from an analysis of Indonesian decentralisation is that it has halted, not inflamed, demands for secession.[56] And so on a practical level, there seems to be no cause for ideological concern for the state's geo-body.

B. Malaysia

In the case of Malaysia, the only federation under discussion in this book, the position is more complex. In a federal system the notion of a national geo-body is perplexing. If it exists, it is likely to attach to the states individually, not collectively. And this is what is apparent in Malaysia's Federal Constitution.

Until a constitutional amendment in 2022, Article 1(2) of the Federal Constitution, making no reference to indivisibility or the like, merely stated that '[t]he States of the Federation shall be', and then listed the 13 states. However, this provision had earlier (1974) been amended so as to remove the separate listing of Sabah and Sarawak, which claim special status under the Malaysia Agreement 1963 and the Federal Constitution of 1957, as amended in 1963. Under the 2022 amendment, the states are now (as before 1974) listed in two categories, namely the States of Malaya, and the Borneo states (ie, Sabah and Sarawak, listed, interestingly, as 'territories', not states). We will see in chapter eleven that this amendment is not merely symbolic: it may have practical, as opposed to psychological, consequences. It provides something like a theoretical platform on which to place demands for devolution of powers, currently framed as demands for recognition of the rights of these two 'territories' under the Malaysia Agreement.[57]

Thus in Malaysia, unlike the cases listed above, the concept of territorial integrity applies not to the nation-state itself, but rather to the states that constitute the Federation. This is confirmed in Article 2(b), where it is provided that 'a law altering the boundaries of a state shall not be passed without the consent of that state (expressed by a law made by the legislature of that state) and of the Conference of Rulers'. This protection has not, however, in practice,

[55] P Holland, 'Regional government and central authority in Indonesia' ch 14 in T Lindsey (ed), *Indonesia: Law and Society* (Annandale, NSW, Federation Press, 1999) 201.

[56] See further ch 3.

[57] For the arguments concerning the Malaysia Agreement 1963, see, further ch 11.

prevented the federal government from securing portions of the states of Selangor, Negri Sembilan, and Sarawak for the creation of federal territories, albeit by agreement.[58] Nor has it prevented what is alleged to be a 'sea-grab' of territorial waters, as alleged in current litigation, that belong to Sabah and Sarawak, by virtue of the Territorial Sea Act 2012.[59] From the perspective of Sabah and Sarawak, the concept of the geo-body is a fundamental, existential one.

C. Myanmar

Myanmar is the most interesting and extensive example for us to examine in this context, as the issue of its geo-body is even more pressing than elsewhere in the region, due to its history of inter-ethnic, and therefore inter-regional, conflict. Provisions relating to sovereignty and the nation's and the states' geo-bodies (do they have one and what is its extent?) are likely to be very prominent ones in any future constitution-making episode, but it is instructive to see how the 2008 Constitution deals with the issue.

Myanmar is described as an 'independent sovereign nation', known as the Republic of the Union of Myanmar,[60] in which the 'sovereign power of the Union is derived from the citizens and is in force in the entire country'.[61] This union is 'constituted' by the states, regions, union territories and other subnational units – language that smacks of federation.[62] The state is also 'where multi-national races collectively reside'.[63] The Union's 'consistent objectives' include (notably as the first ones listed), 'non-disintegration of the Union', 'non-disintegration of national solidarity', and 'perpetuation of sovereignty'. The stated essential purpose of the state is therefore – and this is unusual – to protect its own geo-body. This geo-body is of course the very matter that is in dispute. The text goes on to deal with the seven regions and seven states of the country, and it is, interestingly, their names that are afforded special protection;[64] although other provisions[65] ensure that their boundaries too

[58] Federal Constitution, Article 1(4).

[59] This matter is in fact the subject of litigation currently before the courts in relation to Sabah, which claims that the federal Territorial Sea Act 2012 violates Sabah's territorial rights. This is in effect a claim of violation of the state's geo-body: 'Sabah NGO challenging Territorial Sea Act in court', Borneo Post, 15 September 2023, at 'Sabah NGO challenging Territorial Sea Act in court' (theborneopost.com, 15 September 2023) www.theborneopost.com/2023/09/15/sabah-ngo-challenging-territorial-sea-act-in-court/.

[60] Constitution of the Union of Myanmar 2008, ss 1–2.

[61] ibid s 4.

[62] ibid ss 8–9. See further ch 5.

[63] ibid s 3.

[64] ibid s 9.

[65] ibid ss 52–54.

cannot be altered without their consent. They are provided to be of equal status, and most importantly of all, 'no part of the territory constituted in the Union such as Regions, States, Union Territories and Self-Administered Areas shall ever secede from the Union'.[66] It is rare for a constitution to specifically mention secession. There are obviously good reasons to be coy about this issue: allowing secession might encourage either its occurrence, or else its use as a threat, while prohibiting it, on the other hand, looks like coercion. This too will be an issue in constitution-making in future, as it was in 1947.[67]

Unlike Malaysia, it is the geo-body of the *Union*, not that of the states and regions, that is regarded as sacred and inviolate. For the states and regions, it is in essence their identity, rather than their geo-body, that appears to require protection. This is obviously of prime importance for the states, which are defined by their ethnic identities; it is this issue that will define the geo-body of Myanmar in a future constitution, one that is likely to be federal. At some level a future constitution will likely also have to define the territorial integrity of the states once their geography has been defined. This is discussed further in chapter five.

D. Philippines

The Constitution of the Philippines, an archipelagic state, simply defines at Article I the extent of the Philippines' sovereignty and jurisdiction by reference to territory, including the sea. There is no reference to indivisibility, but instead, to the contrary, at Article II, section 25, to the state ensuring the autonomy of local governments. There is therefore no latent ideological conflict in the text. In chapter ten we examine regional autonomy in Bangsamoro and its impact, not just on Bangsamoro, but on the national governance system. But we will see that the 1987 Constitution of the Philippines makes explicit provision for regional autonomy. Some commentators believe nonetheless that the mere existence of asymmetric autonomy in Bangsamoro violates the constitutional order.[68]

E. Thailand

Thailand's Constitution of 2017 affords a good example of the geo-body concept. It provides in its very first section that 'Thailand is one and indivisible Kingdom'. There is no indication, however, what exactly this means. Territorial governance is merely referred to in Chapter XIV as 'local administration'.

[66] ibid s 10.
[67] See p 91.
[68] See p 105.

One might of course think that any apparent contradiction between territorial integrity and territorial governance is easily explained, despite the linguistic obfuscation in the texts, simply by distinguishing division due to secession and insurgency on the one hand, and division due to internal territorial governance on the other. Indivisibility provisions, one may argue, are directed towards national sovereignty, not towards decentralised forms of territorial governance. In fact, however, there is evidence that the national sovereignty principle represented by 'indivisibility' provisions and the like is often deliberately set in *opposition* to attempts at decentralisation (or further decentralisation), precisely on the basis that they tend to destroy national sovereignty. In relation to Thailand, for example, some critics view decentralisation as a threat to the very integrity of the Kingdom established in section 1 of the 2017 Constitution, mentioned above. These critics would no doubt take section 1 quite literally and very seriously, seeing in decentralising power to territorial units a violation of the principle in section 1.

> The conservative notion of local governance is intertwined with the Thai elites' preference for the model of 'deconcentration', i.e., the establishment of provinces, districts, *Tambon* (sub-districts), and villages, as agents of the central government, rather than 'decentralisation'; the difference between the two lies in the extent of local autonomy … When local politicians commenced 'to exert local influence' over matters such as policy-making and appointments, traditionally reserved for officials in the military and centralised bureaucracy, the accusation of threats to the [democratic regime with the King as head of state] was invoked in consequence, thus, in turn, prompting royalist coups especially in 1958, 1971, 1976, 1991, 2006, and 2014 suspending both parliamentary democracy and decentralisation.[69]

This view is confirmed by the fact that both the military government of 2014–19 and its post-election but military-led successor have been reluctant to allow further decentralisation,[70] even for the troubled Southern border provinces.

Those advocating nationalism the world over have naturally emphasised centralisation, being opposed to local variation and local democracy, just as much as they are opposed to foreign interference, and seeing national sovereignty as a trump card to be played against decentralisation or territorial rights. Thus the issue of indivisibility is not just a problem of interpretation of constitutional texts. Rather it is an ideological flashpoint. In the eyes of nationalists, local autonomy tends to destroy unity and leads to adherence to values lying beyond loyalty to the nation-state, which is presumed to be an unquestionable

[69] A Harding and R Leelapatana, 'Towards recentralisation? Thailand's 2014 coup, tutelage democracy, and their effects on local government', *50 Shades of Federation*, referring to F Ferrara, *The Political Development of Modern Thailand* (Cambridge, Cambridge University Press, 2015) 271, at 'Towards Recentralisation?: Thailand's 2014 Coup, Tutelage Democracy and their Effects on Local Government' (50 Shades of Federalism) 50shadesoffederalism.com/case-studies/towards-recentralisation-thailands-2014-coup-tutelage-democracy-and-their-effects-on-local-government/.

[70] See p 134ff.

given. In this formulation, the notion of territorial governance is seen as more or less treasonable.

The implications of constitutional texts dealing with spatial aspects of constitutionalism seem then, in light of what we have noted in these constitutional texts, not to have been sufficiently considered. At what point of decentralisation of powers is the principle of national sovereignty or indivisibility breached? Traditional or long-established forms of territorial governance are probably not regarded as dangerous to sovereignty, but on the other hand ambitious forms of decentralisation may be seen by some as precisely threatening sovereignty. Others may hold a contrary view, that the decentralisation of powers tends to increase support for the legitimacy of a nation-state that would accord a high degree of trust in, and respect for local, ethnic, cultural, linguistic, or religious difference. This book does not discover any evidence for the notion that decentralisation increases the risk of secession by encouraging a sense of local identity. Indeed, as we will see especially in relation to Indonesia, decentralised powers and regional autonomy seem to have *prevented* rather than encouraged secession.[71]

VII. CONCLUSION

Entrenchment does not inevitably ensure that territorial governance will be more autonomous than it would otherwise be. Yet in practice we will see in further analysing the territorial governance systems further that there is in fact a direct correlation between entrenchment and genuine autonomy. It might of course be simply a matter of the political will for decentralisation being expressed both in the constitution and in political or administrative practice. However, the seriousness engaged in entrenchment of independent and legitimate, democratically accountable, structures of territorial governance also tends to concentrate the power of advocacy in the event of assault on powers exercised territorially. Constitutional entrenchment seems, unsurprisingly perhaps, to entrench in practice, not just in theory.

In the remainder of this book we will explore and critique the content of territorial governance in terms of issues going far beyond the level entrenchment, namely, the various layers of territorial governance, the type and extent of autonomous powers, their protection in terms of central-local relations, and the nature of local democracy as well as local distinctiveness. The important finding of this chapter is that the constitutional foundation is a critical factor in defining territorial governance's ethos, importance, and ultimately also its content.

[71] See p 63.

Part II

Case Studies

THIS PART OF the book set outs case studies of the five countries forming the basis for the discussion. They present three cases of decentralisation (Indonesia, Philippines and Thailand); one of federalism (Malaysia); and one involving historically, and hypothetically for the future, elements of both (Myanmar). The objective in this Part is to provide a sufficiently detailed account of each of these cases to enable analysis to be undertaken and conclusions reached in the final Part IV of the book. It will also form a backdrop for the related inquiry into special autonomy in Part III. In this Part we will pay attention to the nature of territorial governance in the five countries, inquiring into the extent of the autonomy achieved, central-local relations, local democracy and accountability, and the ever-present issue of pluralism. We will also be prompted to reflect on general issues relating to territorial governance and innovations that have emerged in response to the demand for new forms of territorial governance.

3

Indonesia

'Buah jatuh tak jauh dari pohonnya': The fruit does not fall far from the tree.
Indonesian proverb.

I. DISAGGREGATING THE UNITARY STATE

At the time of President Suharto's resignation in 1998 and the resulting call for *reformasi* it had long been the case that in a large and very diverse country such as Indonesia some kind of decentralisation would become irresistible. The matter had been debated during virtually the entire period of Indonesia's independence from 1945.[1] Now was the moment for real reform to occur.

The question was, crucially, what extent of decentralisation was appropriate? Federalism was not a strong candidate as an alternative to the extreme centralisation of Suharto's authoritarian rule, primarily because it would tend to encourage secession on the part of a number of provinces, but also because it had negative, colonial associations.[2] Nonetheless, both federalism and abolition of the provinces were mentioned early in the debates.[3] Three provinces had already seen the emergence of a violent secessionist movement or rebellion (Aceh, Irian Jaya[4] and Timor Leste; and earlier, in the 1950s, West Sumatra

[1] For the history of territorial governance prior to 1999, see PKM Roosmalen, 'Netherlands Indies town planning: An agent for modernisation (1905–1957)' in C Freek Colombijn et al (eds), *Cars, Conduit, Kampongs: The Modernisation of the Indonesian City, 1920–1960* (Leiden, Brill, 2014) 87; P Holland, 'Regional government and central authority in Indonesia' ch 14 in T Lindsey (ed), *Indonesia: Law and Society* (Annandale, NSW, Federation Press, 1999); L Schmit, 'Decentralisation and legal reform in Indonesia: The pendulum effect' ch 8 in T Lindsey (ed), *Indonesia: Law and Society*, 2nd edn (Annandale, NSW, Federation Press, 2007) 154ff; A Booth, 'Before the "big bang": Decentralisation debates and practice in Indonesia, 1949–1999' ch 2 in H Hill (ed), *Regional Dynamics in Decentralised Indonesia* (Singapore, ISEAS-Yusoff Ishak Institute, 2014). For the post-1999 period, see Schmit, ibid 157ff; E Aspinall and G Fealy, 'Introduction: Democratisation, decentralisation and the rise of the local' in E Aspinall and G Fealy (eds), *Local Power and Politics in Indonesia: Decentralisation and Democratisation* (Singapore, Institute of Southeast Asian Studies, 2003).

[2] Holland, ibid 201.

[3] D Horowitz, *Constitutional Change and Democracy in Indonesia* (Cambridge, Cambridge University Press, 2013) 71ff; M Lane, *Decentralisation and its Discontents: An Essay on Class, Political Agency, and National Perspective in Indonesian Society* (Singapore, ISEAS, 2014) 19ff.

[4] As it was then called, now Papua. See ch 9.

and South Sulwesi). There was also a persistent demand almost everywhere for more local or regional autonomy, to counteract the centre's dictatorial tendencies during the New Order period under Suharto, under which there had been oppressive military or bureaucratic interventions, and the regions' abundant natural wealth had been channelled to the centre.[5] The existing system of territorial governance[6] required regional governors to be centrally appointed while acting, somewhat awkwardly, as both agents of central government and representatives of regional autonomy.

Suharto's fall created the opportunity to satisfy this long-standing demand, allowing the possibility of pushing back against dictatorship by exercising local autonomy, obtaining a fair share of the profits from natural resource exploitation, and reviving local governance or religious traditions that expressed local identity. Additionally, international bodies such as the World Bank and the IMF had called for decentralisation as a means of liberalising the Indonesian economy.[7] The so-called *Tim Tujuh* (Team of Seven), comprising mainly US-trained academics, had been engaged by Suharto to advise on government structures, and pressed his successor, Habibie, to legislate for strong decentralisation of powers.[8] Radical reform was, in short, irresistible.

Matters moved quickly, and in 1999 two laws, the Law on Regional Government[9] and the Law on Fiscal Balance Between the Central and Regional Governments,[10] were passed, some of the first of the *reformasi* measures to come into effect in 2001. There seemed to be more haste than speed in these reforms, and the early years of decentralisation proved somewhat chaotic, with poor and inconsistent drafting of the laws, changes taking place before legal authority had been granted, and insufficient coordination between the legal and fiscal elements.[11] Nonetheless, the change in allocation of powers was dramatic, transforming, as Butt and Lindsey maintain, 'one of the world's most authoritarian and centralised states into one of its most democratic and decentralised'.[12]

The Indonesian Constitution of 1945, prior to the Second Amendment in 2000, envisaged an extremely centralised state with virtually no local autonomy.

[5] S Butt and T Lindsey, *The Constitution of Indonesia: A Contextual Analysis* (Oxford, Hart Publishing, 2012) 160.

[6] See Law 5/ 1974 on Regional Government.

[7] V Hadiz, *Localising Power in Post-Authoritarian Indonesia* (Stanford, California, Stanford University Press, 2010) 19; F von Benda Beckmann and K von Benda Beckmann, *Political and Legal Transformations of an Indonesian Polity: The Nagari from Colonisation to Decentralisation* (Cambridge, Cambridge University Press, 2013) 156ff.

[8] Horowitz (n 3) 60ff.

[9] Law 22/ 1999.

[10] Law 25/ 1999.

[11] G Bell, 'The new Indonesian laws relating to regional autonomy: Good intentions, confusing laws' (2001) 2(1) *Asian-Pacific Law and Policy Journal* 1; Schmit (n 1) 157ff; F von Benda Beckmann and K von Benda Beckmann, 'Recentralisation and decentralisation in West Sumatra' ch 12 in C Holtzappel and M Ramstedt (eds), *Decentralisation and Regional Autonomy in Indonesia: Implementation and Challenges* (Singapore, ISEAS, 2009).

[12] Butt and Lindsey (n 5) 161.

Article 37(5) even states: 'Provisions relating to the form of the unitary state of the Republic of Indonesia may not be amended'. Yet under the reforms little was now left to the national government of the formally unitary state beyond the largely unavoidable and typical powers of central authority: foreign affairs, defence, judicial affairs, monetary and fiscal policy; but also overall development planning and religion. Not only did the reforms limit the powers of central government, but they virtually also pushed the provinces brusquely aside in order to devolve most powers, including health, education, land, environment, infrastructure and transport, down to the lower levels of regencies (*kabupaten*) and municipalities (*kota*). Of the funding leaving Jakarta, amounting to not less than 25 per cent of revenue, only 10 per cent went to the provinces, but 90 per cent to the lower levels.[13] Large amounts of resources (physical, human and fiscal) were transferred to local governments. The provinces were left only in effect with roles of agency and coordination. Such an outcome might seem counter-intuitive, but the underlying purpose was to bypass the provinces, which were seen as foci of possible secession, in the midst of a real fear around the turn of the century that the republic could break up entirely.[14]

This strategy proved successful in at least one sense, in that decentralisation appeared within a short space of time to satisfy the general demand for greater local autonomy, arouse keenness to exercise the new powers, and, crucially, dampening the ardour for secession in several areas.[15] However, the new laws, in order to be challenge-proof in a new era of constitutional jurisdiction,[16] had then to be given constitutional authority, and accordingly the 1945 Constitution was amended in 2002 (the 4th Amendment) to provide that authority.[17]

Under the constitutional amendments, the regional authorities, comprising provinces, regencies[18] and municipalities, were to 'administer and manage their own affairs according to the principles of regional autonomy and the duty of assistance (*tugas pembantuan*).'[19] Provincial governors (*gubernur*) and other heads (*bupati* or regents, and *walikota* or mayors) were to be elected, as were assemblies for each level of territorial governance. Regional authorities were to exercise 'wide-ranging autonomy, except in matters specified by law to be

[13] Horowitz (n 3) 73.

[14] ibid 72; JF McCarthy and C Warren, 'Communities, environments and local governance in reform era Indonesia' in JF McCarthy and C Warren (eds), *Community, Environment and Local Governance in Indonesia: Locating the Commonweal* (Abingdon, Routledge, 2009) 5.

[15] Although not in Aceh and Papua, for which see ch 9.

[16] S Butt, *The Constitutional Court and Democracy in Indonesia* (Leiden, Brill, 2015).

[17] See ch 2. New Articles 18A and 18B were added, as well as 22C and 22D constituting a new chapter VIIA on the *Dewan Perwakilan Daerah* (DPD, or Council of Representatives of the Regions), for which see below. The amendments proceeded on the assumption that the 1999 laws might be struck down by the newly established Constitutional Court, unless they had constitutional backing in the manner that the amendments achieved. The point was that the new laws could be regarded as unconstitutional in light of Article 18.

[18] Sometimes rendered 'districts' or 'counties'.

[19] Article 18(2). The duty of assistance is owed by lower to higher-level authorities.

the affairs of the central government'. Central-regional relations were to have 'regard to the particularities and diversity of each region', while their relations in finance, public services, and the use of natural and other resources were to be 'regulated and administered with justice and equity according to law'. Under Article 18B of the Constitution the state recognised and respected units of regional authorities that are special and distinct, as well as 'traditional communities along with their traditional customary rights as long as these remain in existence and are in accordance with the societal development and the principles of the Unitary State of the Republic of Indonesia'.

II. AN ASSEMBLY OF REGIONAL REPRESENTATIVES

One other important aspect of these reforms was the introduction, pursuant to the new Articles 22C and 22D of the Constitution, of a unique device in the annals of territorial governance, namely an elected assembly of local representatives, the *Dewan Perwakilan Daerah* (DPD). The idea was to reinforce decentralisation by creating a national body with power to ensure effective legislation and implementation in relation to decentralisation. The membership of the DPD must consist of the same number of elected representatives from each province. Currently there are 136 members, four from each of the now 34 provinces.[20]

The place of the DPD in the Indonesian constitutional system requires some explanation. The body with highest constitutional authority in Indonesia is the *Majlis Permusyawaratan Rakyat* (People's Consultative Council, or MPR), which although it does exercise legislative powers has alone the power to amend the constitution, and to inaugurate and also impeach the President and Vice-President.[21] Until the 4th Amendment in 2002 the MPR consisted of elected and appointed members, especially members of the military. The effect of the amendment was to reconstitute the MPR so as to comprise the members of the Parliament (the *Dewan Perwakilan Rakyat*, or DPR) and the DPD.[22] Currently the MPR has 711 members, comprising the 575 members of the DPR and the 136 members of the DPD. The proportion of DPD to DPR members must not exceed one third (in fact it is currently rather less than that), so as to ensure that the DPR, and not the President or the provinces, control the highest body in the land. Nonetheless the replacing of appointed with regionally elected members signifies the importance of territorial governance in Indonesia in the twenty-first century.

[20] Butt and Lindsey (n 5) 59, 62ff.
[21] 1945 Constitution, Article 2.
[22] Butt and Lindsey (n 5) 59.

For all that, the DPD itself has limited powers under Article 22D of the Constitution to advise the DPR on legislation relating to regional autonomy, being unable itself to pass laws. It may propose bills to the DPR, and may oversee the implementation of laws, but only those related to regional autonomy; central-local relations; formation, expansion and merger of regions; management of natural other economic resources; and financial balancing between the centre and the regions.

This system has been described as neither bicameral nor unicameral.[23] It is in a sense tricameral, but Butt and Lindsey point out that the MPR rarely exercises its powers, that the DPD cannot legislate, and that DPR laws override local legislation, so that the legislature is essentially in practice unicameral.[24] It is perhaps better to see the system as sui generis, but for our purposes affording considerable scope for the regions to exercise some control at least over the legislative process regarding matters affecting them, as well as constitutional amendments. This already goes further than some democratic countries in which the upper house is appointed, or does not specifically represent territorial units, or in which there is no body advising parliament on regional issues. While the model is very much the outcome of Indonesia's recent history, it should prompt more general consideration of the ways in which important territorial perspectives might be brought to bear so as to influence national-level legislation. Two important factors tending to enhance territorial governance are that candidates for election to the DPD must not belong to a political party,[25] and that the Constitutional Court has insisted that DPD candidates must be domiciled in the relevant province.[26]

III. SECOND THOUGHTS?

What followed as the reforms of 1999 unfolded in practice was an enthusiastic but increasingly inconsistent and questionable exercise of local powers. Powers and functions appeared to overlap to a considerable extent as between the three tiers of governance. Budgetary allocations did not always fall consistently alongside legal obligations.[27] There were problems with staffing and expertise at the lower levels of government.[28] Indonesia has also enjoyed a considerable degree

[23] ibid 54.
[24] ibid 60ff.
[25] Constitution, Article 22E(4).
[26] Decision No.10/PUU-VI/2008 which states that any DPD member shall be living within the regional province that he or she represented. See, further, S Butt, 'Indonesia's Constitutional Court and Indonesia's Electoral Systems', ch 9 in A Harding and A Chen (eds), *Constitutional Courts in Asia: A Comparative Perspective* (Cambridge, Cambridge University Press, 2018).
[27] Schmit (n 1) 157ff.
[28] Adi Abidin, 'When the burden is shouldered alone: Experiences in autonomy at regencies and municipalities', ch 1 in Holtzappel and Ramstedt (n 11).

of territorial stability since the secession of Timor Leste in 2002,[29] a factor tending to displace the need to avoid secessionist tendencies with the need to consider efficiency and certainty. It did not therefore take very long for second thoughts to appear concerning the extent of decentralisation undertaken in the 1999 laws, or at least the powers of central government to control the exercise of decentralised powers. Despite the apparent largesse in devolving power to the regions, events since the reforms of 1999–2002 have resulted in a measure of what is sometimes termed 'recentralisation', evidenced in laws passed in 2004 and 2014.[30]

President Yudhoyono declared in 2006 that regional autonomy had 'gone too far', that it had scared off investors rather than attracting them, and had failed to result in improved public services.[31] Local governments had been issuing logging licences almost with abandon, leading to illegal logging and hyper-deforestation.[32] An NGO report in 2007 showed that local governments did not prioritise spending in areas like health and education.[33] Lack of legal certainty also bugs a number of areas of activity in which powers have been decentralised, especially the environment and foreign investment, both areas that have national as well as territorial impacts. Although this lack of certainty is clearly an issue, it is not necessarily to be listed as a demerit of decentralisation as such. As Butt and Lindsey show, legislative conflicts and especially uncertainties over who can legitimately exercise power are endemic in the Indonesian legal system generally, and not simply an outcome of decentralisation.[34]

The Law of 2004 drew back somewhat on the autonomous powers of regencies and municipalities, and the Law of 2014 that replaced it did so to an even further extent, restoring to provinces the status in the hierarchy of government that they had had before decentralisation. This indicates that the initial fears of serial secession attempts had subsided. The account of the structure of territorial governance that follows is based on the Law of 2014, but in this discussion we shall see how the law changed between 1999 and 2014 so as to supervise to a certain extent the exercise of local powers. For various reasons that will be mentioned, the intention of the law on the books may not represent in practice the actual situation with the exercise of decentralised powers. The basis for this 'recentralisation' is not precisely the *retransfer* of substantive local functions to the centre, but rather the *recalibration* of intergovernmental relations so as to facilitate provincial and central control over the exercise of local powers. This

[29] This is subject to a consideration of special regional autonomy in Aceh and Papua in ch 5.

[30] Law on Regional Administration, No 32/ 2004; Law on Regional Administration, No 23/ 2014. It will however be argued in ch 12 that 'recentralisation' is a misnomer for what has occurred in Indonesia and elsewhere.

[31] *Jakarta Post* (24 August 2006).

[32] Hadiz (n 7) 99.

[33] *Jakarta Post* (9 December 2007).

[34] S Butt and T Lindsey, *Indonesian Law* (Oxford, Oxford University Press, 2019) ch 2; S Butt and N Parsons, 'Reining in regional government – local taxes and investment in decentralised Indonesia' (2012) 34(1) *Sydney Law Review* 91.

process also involves the establishment of a hierarchy in which the authorities carrying out most functions (regencies and municipalities) are answerable to higher authorities in terms of their actual exercise of power. The Law of 2014 also attempts to provide a greater degree of legal certainty compared with the Law of 2004. This recalibration of powers is nonetheless as we shall see blurred by the uncertain extent of supervisory powers, especially when it comes to the critical issue of review of local legislation.

IV. THE LEGAL FRAMEWORK OF TERRITORIAL GOVERNANCE

In its Preamble the Law of 2014 states that the Law of 2004 Act is 'no longer compatible with the development of the state, political subdivision, and the demands of the regional administration that need to be replaced'.

The Law of 2014, while expressly endorsing the principles of regional autonomy and decentralisation, affirms the overall control of the central government with regard to regional governments. In several of its provisions it refers to deconcentration of most central government administration to provincial governors, making them representatives of the central government in carrying out its functions at the regional level.[35] The principle of *tugas pembantuan*[36] also implies that regional governments act as agents of central government;[37] and central government develops and supervises the performance of regional governments.[38] One important clarification is that central government deals with cross-border issues (national and provincial borders), while provinces deal with cross-border issues at the lower level (regencies and municipalities).[39] Another is that, in an extensive Appendix, it defines in considerable detail the allocation of functions between the three levels of government.

Powers are formally divided into absolute, concurrent and general government affairs.[40]

Absolute powers are those conducted by the central government alone, and these remain as stated above, but they may also be delegated (that is, under deconcentration) to other agencies, including provincial governors.[41]

Concurrent powers are now defined with greater clarity than before in the Appendix to the Law of 2014,[42] and may be exercised by any of the three tiers of government. They are divided into obligatory and optional affairs, implying

[35] Law of 2014; eg Article 1, especially 1(9).
[36] Article 1(11).
[37] See also Article 93. Similarly, Article 38(1) of the Law of 2004 had imposed an obligation on regional governments to coordinate and implement central government functions at the local level.
[38] Article 7(1).
[39] Article 12.
[40] Article 9.
[41] Article 10(2).
[42] Article 15(1).

a distinction between duties and powers. Duties are further divided into those relating to basic services and those not related to basic services. The former include health and education; infrastructure and planning; housing; public order; and social affairs. The latter include employment; issues relating to protection, registration and regulation of the population (women and children, civil registration, and family planning); food; land, forestry, and environment; transport and communications; cultural issues; and investment and small enterprises. The optional component includes fishing and marine matters; energy and mineral resources; trade and industry; and tourism.[43]

General government affairs are not defined clearly but relate to second order issues such as the *Pancasila*,[44] fostering unity in diversity, resolving conflicts, facilitating coordination, and constitutional implementation.[45]

The impact and even the precise intention of the Law of 2014 is, however, obscured in many respects by uncertain provisions, and by the unlikelihood, in some cases, of their practical implementation.

For example, although the Law of 2014 appears as an attempt at increasing supervision, it does not, unlike the Law of 2004,[46] allow the central government to exercise local powers. Article 17 requires regional governments to follow 'norms, standards, procedures and criteria' ('NSPK') laid down by the central government, on pain of invalidation of the relevant policy.[47] Yet it is questionable whether such policies can, constitutionally, be invalidated by the central government; and given the uncertainties even over the power of central government to invalidate local legislation, Article 17, while having some impact and force, especially when read with Article 16 (on NSPK relating to concurrent powers) looks less than threatening.[48]

Executive heads are elected for five-year terms and are responsible to their electorates via the elected assembly. The power to dismiss a provincial governor for cause lies, however, with the President, and the power to dismiss a regent or mayor for cause lies with the provincial governor. The procedure is exceedingly tortuous and creates a significant chill effect regarding the exercise of these powers. Dismissal may only occur on specific grounds set out in the Law of 2014[49] on the recommendation of the regional assembly (the *Dewan Perwakilan Rakyat Daerah*, or DPRD), where it passes a motion supported by at least two thirds of those present who must be at least three quarters of the total membership. Even then the assembly must refer its decision to the Supreme Court, which must examine and try the matter within 30 days. If the Supreme Court approves

[43] Article 12.
[44] ie Indonesia's national ideology: see Butt and Lindsey (n 34) 38ff.
[45] Article 25.
[46] At Article 10(5).
[47] Article 17(3).
[48] Butt and Lindsey (n 5) 66.
[49] Articles 79–82.

the decision the assembly must make another decision (under similar conditions to the decision to refer to the Supreme Court) to refer the matter to the President, who must then dismiss the person within 30 days. This does not apply however to the commission of serious criminal offences such as corruption, where dismissal may simply be effected by the President.[50] In addition to this power the central government, the provincial governors, and the elected assemblies can implement various sanctions against executive heads short of dismissal in cases of, for example, failure to submit regular reports.[51]

V. CENTRAL-LOCAL RELATIONS AND THE INVALIDATION OF LOCAL LEGISLATION

The overarching difficulty of Indonesian decentralisation emerging over the last two decades is one of central-local relations, and specifically controls over the legislative powers of provinces, regencies and municipalities. The failure to resolve this issue efficiently has created much confusion.

The starting point is the DPRDs, which are now governed by the Law of 2014, and are the elected legislative assemblies of the provinces, regencies and municipalities, which approve budgets and provide executive accountability, as well as making local laws (*Peraturan Daerah*, or '*Perda*'). Provincial assemblies are typically between 35 and 100 in number, while the lower-level assemblies are typically 20 to 50 in number.[52]

These assemblies enjoy wide powers, as we have seen, to enact with the agreement of the relevant executive head, *Perda* that may include the creation of minor criminal offences.[53] Executive heads are also able to make laws implementing *Perda*. *Perda* may also, intriguingly, 'contain local content material in accordance with law', a provision that, given the diversity of cultures across Indonesia, has much potential to embrace and express pluralism in territorial governance, and certainly appears to have been construed in that way.

Such was the enthusiasm with which the new legislative powers were exercised at the local level following the reforms, that it proved necessary to institute an administrative system of what the Constitutional Court has referred to 'abstract executive preview' for scrutinising *Perda*, of which, given the number of territorial units and the breadth of powers conferred on them, run to many thousands a year. This system is currently provided by the Law of 2014,[54] which extends the system of reviewing local legislation. Laws adopted by a provincial assembly and regulations adopted by a governor must be submitted to the minister within

[50] Article 83.
[51] Articles 68–77.
[52] See Part IV of the Law of 2014, and the constitutional provisions cited above.
[53] Articles 236–38.
[54] Articles 249–51. Previously it was contained in Articles 144–45 of the Law of 2004.

seven days of adoption, while those adopted by local assemblies and regulations adopted by the regent or mayor must be submitted to the governor (who in this matter acts as the representative of the central government[55]). This requirement is routinely ignored, being backed by the light sanction of a mere reprimand.[56]

Legislation of these kinds may be invalidated by the minister or the governor, as the case may be, on a number of grounds. The legislation must not be contrary to the provisions of higher legislation, or the public interest, or 'decency'. Contrary to the public interest for these purposes are laws disrupting harmony between the various groups, or access to public services, peace and public order, or economic activity to improve the welfare of the community; also laws that discriminate on the basis of race, religion or belief, or gender.[57] Obviously, laws that are unconstitutional are invalid as conflicting with higher law. Sanctions apply in relation to failure to submit a law, or implementing a law that has been invalidated.[58]

Under the above process large numbers of *Perda* were invalidated over the last two decades,[59] but in two decisions in 2017[60] the Constitutional Court struck down these provisions in the Law of 2014, so far as they applied to *post-enactment* review, in relation to, in the first case the minister, and in the second case the provincial governors. Such review, it said, could only be done by a judicial authority via judicial review. These cases have been shown to be highly problematical from a number of points of view, both in terms of their formal reasoning and their practical consequences.[61]

Since these cases, the only option for the central government has been to apply to the Supreme Court for judicial review, as the Constitutional Court itself has no power over legislation below the level of national laws. The basis and incidence of exercise of this power of review remain obscure and contested, and the performance of the Supreme Court in judicial review matters has been both inconsistent and self-limiting. The result is that the intractable and perennial problem of legal uncertainty has been somewhat exacerbated rather than clarified. The issue therefore remains, as it was at the outset, how to deal with a tsunami of laws, many of which are in conflict with other laws, or are just inherently objectionable on other grounds.[62] Butt's critique of this issue concludes

[55] Article 251(2).

[56] Article 249.

[57] Article 250(2).

[58] Article 252.

[59] S Butt, 'Regional autonomy and legal disorder: The proliferation of local laws in Indonesia' (2010) 32 *Sydney Law Review* 177, 189.

[60] Constitutional Court of Indonesia, Decision No 137/PUU-XIII/2015 (delivered on 5 April 2017) [City/ County *Perda* Review case]; and Constitutional Court of Indonesia, Decision No 56/PUU-XIV/2016 (delivered on 14 June 2017) [Provincial *Perda* Review case].

[61] S Butt, 'The Indonesian Constitutional Court: Reconfiguring decentralisation for better or worse?' (2019) 14 *Asian Journal of Comparative Law* 147.

[62] One reason, it is suggested, for the proliferation of such 'bad' laws is the relative inexperience of local law-makers (see Butt, ibid). This situation may well improve with time, as more regional heads and representatives gain experience in these matters.

with the suggestion that only a system for intergovernmental 'collaborative lawmaking' before laws are passed will be able to resolve the problem. The example of adopting a convention to deal with legislative conflicts in the context of the UK's devolution process, now expressed in statutory form,[63] might offer some food for thought as how this issue might eventually be resolved. Meanwhile, however, there has been increasingly stringent application of pre-enactment review, which potentially poses a threat to the present equilibrium in central-local relations. While the government's intention was to prevent 'bad' local laws, it has employed executive powers (mostly through ministerial regulations) to establish very detailed NSPK governing how concurrent powers must be exercised.[64] This type of regulation potentially strengthens central government influence, and gives little room for local autonomy. Further, there is what seems an unnecessary dualism in *Perda* pre-enactment review that complicates the process, as draft *Perda* are, since 2022, subject to review by both the Ministry of Home Affairs and the Ministry of Law and Human Rights.[65] The implementation of *Perda* review after the 2017 court decisions risks creating confusion and restricting autonomy, rather than fostering intergovernmental collaboration.

VI. THE DISCONTENTS

There is no doubt that decentralisation has been dysfunctional in many respects, and the problems arising have been a cause for concern, albeit concern subsiding somewhat as the process of decentralisation has struggled and perhaps succeeded in finding the right balance and the right process for intergovernmental relations and local functionality.

Yet if one examines these problems carefully, it appears that in some cases the problem is attributable to prior political and legal-cultural conditions which, while causing disappointment, can hardly, as we have seen with legal uncertainty, be laid at the door of decentralisation as such. In other cases the problems seem to be soluble issues of transition, adjustment, and bedding-down, which have in fact ameliorated over time. And there is a case to be made that, despite the many problems, decentralisation has in general gone rather better than many feared at the outset.[66] As Mietzner put it, writing in 2014, even before the implementation of the Law of 2014:

> … the surprising thing about post-Suharto decentralisation is not that it has faced seemingly overwhelming difficulties; this was always to be expected in a country with a per capita income of below $1,000 (in 2001) and a long history

[63] See eg Scotland Act 2016, s 2.
[64] Law of 2014, Article 16.
[65] Law on Lawmaking, No 13 of 2022, Articles 58, 63.
[66] A study by Schmit in 2007 (n 1, 149) concludes that the results of decentralisation were 'better than could have been expected'.

> of patrimonialism. From a historical perspective, the really astonishing feature of decentralisation 13 years after it was launched is how stable centre–periphery relations have become.[67]

Even severe critics have not gone so far as to suggest a reversion to the status quo ante of the New Order dictatorship. At this stage, a quarter of a century after decentralisation commenced, such an outcome is probably unthinkable.

Some serious problems were nonetheless noted early in the process. The World Bank, for example, emphasised certain structural problems. It noted the need to improve the legal and regulatory framework for decentralisation, especially sectoral laws; to solve intergovernmental fiscal issues giving rise to inadequate local revenues and inequalities between regions; and to 'close the accountability gap' by creating new monitoring, evaluation and audit processes.[68] Obtaining and keeping suitable staff has also been identified as one of these structural issues.[69] But other more general criticisms have been raised.

First, decentralisation was linked to secession tendencies, as though it were damaging to the unity of Indonesia. As we have seen, this is a common criticism from a nationalist perspective, beyond Indonesia.[70] It is suggested that a more accurate assessment is that, on the contrary, decentralisation, if we add in the special regional autonomy for Aceh and Papua, which are discussed in chapter nine, has forestalled secessionist tendencies in many areas, and these have actually not been revived with the restoration in 2014 of a significant place in the constitutional hierarchy for Indonesia's provinces.

Second, it is noted that local authorities display great differences in endowments, leading to inequality and a general deficiency of revenue. These inequalities existed before decentralisation, and the development of the law and administration on fiscal balancing and monitoring has been constantly refined over 25 years to improve this situation. Deficiency of local revenue is virtually a standing condition of territorial governance almost everywhere. Local governments have attempted to secure extra streams of revenue, sometimes leading to conflict with the centre.[71] A related criticism is that of bureaucratic expansion or overreach, leading to reduced spending on essential services.

Third, criticism has focused on administrative malfunction, corruption, and abuse of power, often caused by, or leading to discord within, local authorities, especially between the legislative and executive branches; between local authorities; and between different levels of government. Decentralisation has

[67] M Mietzner, 'Indonesia's decentralisation: The rise of local identities and the survival of the nation-state' ch 3 in Hill (n 1) 62.

[68] World Bank, *Cities in Transition: Urban Sector Review in an Era of Decentralisation in Indonesia* (Jakarta, 2003).

[69] Adi Abidin (n 28).

[70] See p 40ff. See also McCarthy and Warren (n 14).

[71] Butt (n 59) 189.

been criticised for creating 'little kings' at the local level, resulting from local elite capture, and for encouraging identity politics.[72] As Schmit puts it

> '[u]nchanging continuities' are at work. Where corruption merely becomes decentralised instead of eradicated … it is all just the same old story: under 'traditional' Indonesian authority patterns familiar at the national level are merely being reproduced at the provincial and local level.[73]

In one early instance noted by Hadiz, virtually an entire provincial assembly was indicted for corruption. In another ten *bupati* in one province were prosecuted for illegal logging and embezzlement.[74]

This raises the question of how to proceed. As with secessionist tendencies, this factor is not the creation of decentralisation, but rather a pre-existing condition. How to deal with it is a large question on which whole books have been written, and the problem clearly goes far beyond the matter of decentralisation.[75] There may well be an argument that reducing the individual nodes at which decisions are made is part of the remedy, but then so is the enhancement of democracy and good governance at all levels of government, as enjoined by Goal 16 of the UN Sustainable Development Goals, which envisages the building of 'effective, accountable and inclusive institutions *at all levels*'.[76] What does not appear preferable to enhancing checks and balances is to further increase supervision, which will inevitably involve greater concentration of power, and decrease accountability. It is difficult to see how such measures would improve the situation. The corruption of the previous dictatorship is precisely the situation that decentralisation was designed, in part at least, to rectify.

More generally, decentralisation needs to be sufficiently flexible in its implementation to allow for a certain degree of local contextualisation. For example, in a relatively small island province like Bali, a strong case can be made for pushing decentralisation, both upwards to the provincial level and downwards to villages.[77] Environmental problems are rendered worse, it is alleged, by giving power to lower-level authorities to attract investment having environmental consequences beyond their boundaries.[78]

[72] D Bourchier, 'The romance of *adat* in the Indonesian political imagination and the current revival' in JS Davidson and D Henley (eds), *The Revival of Tradition in Indonesian Politics: The Deployment of Adat from Colonialism to Indigenism* (Abingdon, Routledge, 2007) 114; H Schulte-Nordholt and G van Klinken (eds), *Renegotiating Boundaries: Local Politics in Post-Suharto* Indonesia (Leiden, KITLV Press, 2007); Carnegie, *The Road from Authoritarianism to Democratisation in Indonesia* (New York, Palgrave Macmillan, 2010) ch 3.

[73] Above n 1, 153.

[74] Hadiz (n 7) 175.

[75] See eg S Butt, *Corruption and Law in Indonesia* (Abingdon, Routledge, 2012). See also B Hofman, K Kaiser and G Schulze, 'Corruption and decentralisation' ch 3 in Holtzappel and Ramstedt (n 11).

[76] For the SDGs, see sdgs.un.org/goals.

[77] Agung Wardana, *Contemporary Bali: Contested Space and Governance* (Singapore, Palgrave Macmillan, 2019) 51.

[78] ibid ch 3.

VII. VILLAGES: PLURALISM AND THE DUAL SYSTEM

Decentralisation has not only brought about autonomy at the level of regencies and municipalities, but in a way that speaks very directly to pluralism and custom, it has also allowed for the adoption of variations on standard models. This is nowhere more apparent than at the village level, where there has been a move towards reviving traditional institutions. In this sense we can see the Law on Villages of 2014[79] as completing the process commenced in 1999. A major reason for the enactment of this law was the demand for revival of traditional village governance, which the New Order government had tried to suppress. In chapter one a distinction was drawn between organic and administrative local institutions, and this distinction is precisely reflected in Indonesian village governance.

In 1979, during the New Order period, a Village Law was passed that sought to standardise villages along the Javanese pattern for the sake of efficiency and development. This reform cut against traditional village governance in way that created resentment. This was especially true of West Sumatra, whose Minangkabau village culture had been especially significant in the past, prior to the standardisation of villages ('*desa*-fication', as it has been called[80]) and there was keenness to revive the traditional *nagari*, or traditional local administrative units, which do not remotely conform to the Javanese model.[81] This process of reviving the *nagari* is discussed in detail and illuminatingly by Franz and Keebet von Benda Beckmann in their masterwork on the *nagari* of West Sumatra, published in 2013.[82]

In Bali, to provide another example, as discussed by Agung Wardana, there is a distinction between *desa dinas* (roughly, administrative villages) and *desa adat* (roughly, customary or cultural villages, but they are also referred to in Bali as *desa katraman*). These existed alongside each other during the colonial period, performing administrative and cultural functions.[83] Even the 1979 reforms were unable to obliterate *desa adat*, but they were in effect marginalised. The Law on Villages of 2014 created an opportunity to redress the balance, so that 'downward decentralisation does not mean to return to the pre-colonial village structure in the hands of *adat* villages, but rather, enhancing the power to be able to work in balance with its *dinas* counterpart'.[84]

[79] Law No 6/ 2014.

[80] von Benda Beckmann and von Benda Beckmann (n 7) 267.

[81] von Benda Beckmann and von Benda Beckmann (n 11) 302; C Geertz, 'Form and variation in Balinese village structure' (1959) 61 *American Anthropologist* 991.

[82] For discussion of this work in relation to village governance reform, see J Vel and A Bedner, 'Decentralisation and village governance in Indonesia: The return to the *Nagari* and the 2014 Village Law' (2015) 47 *Journal of Legal Pluralism and Unofficial Law* 493.

[83] Wardana (n 77) 46ff.

[84] ibid 51.

The Law on Villages gave greater autonomy to villages, along with a right to receive funding in the sum of Rp 1 billion annually.[85] However, the main innovation of this law is its Article 6, which allows a village to choose to be a *desa dinas* or a *desa adat*. In practice most villages, even in Bali and West Sumatra, where traditional village governance structures are most distinctive, have decided to remain as *desa dinas*. This is due not to a rejection of the continuing relevance of tradition and custom, but rather to the logistical problems a new designation would create, and the fact that the dualistic system, balancing administrative and cultural matters, under conditions of relative village autonomy, is generally thought to work satisfactorily in practice.[86] As Carol Warren indicates, decentralisation has empowered the *desa adat* to 'widen its domain beyond that previously understood by strictly "religious" and "adat" issues and to take leadership in village governance'.[87]

VIII. CONCLUSION

The original concept of decentralisation was both inspiring and flawed. It was inspiring in that it envisaged Indonesians, citizens of a vast and highly diverse republic, being able for the first time to be self-governing in their localities. At the general election of February 2024 Indonesians were able to vote at four levels – for their President and Vice-President; for their members of parliament; and for their representatives at both provincial and regency/ municipal levels. They had had the benefit – not unalloyed benefit, it is true – of autonomy for a quarter of a century, and a decade or longer at the village level. During this period territorial governance under decentralisation has entrenched democracy, guaranteed a good measure of autonomy compared to the previous half century, and facilitated development that responds to local needs. Most importantly, the republic's dissolution has not occurred, and apart from Timor Leste, which had been forcibly taken over by Indonesia only in 1975, and which seceded in 2002, not a single province has seceded. As Ostwald et al have expressed it, 'decentralisation has been accompanied by a cauterisation of many of the centrifugal forces that Indonesia faced at the end of the Suharto period'.[88] Democracy, moreover,

[85] This was around US$85,000 at 2014 rates.

[86] Agung Wardana and Darmianto, 'Traditional village institutions and the Village Law' (*Inside Indonesia*, 12 May 2017).

[87] C Warren, '*Adat* in Balinese discourse and practice: Locating citizenship and the Commonweal' in Davidson and Henley (n 72) 170. The adat revival is especially important for those areas with an indigenous population: Syahriza Alkohir Anggoro and Tunggul Anshari Setia Negara, 'The struggle for recognition: Adat law trajectories under Indonesian politics of legal unification' (2022) *International Journal on Minority and Group Rights* 1.

[88] K Ostwald, Y Tajima and K Samphantharak, 'Indonesia's decentralisation experiment: Motivations, successes, and unintended consequences' (2016) 33(2) *Journal of Southeast Asian Economies*, Special Focus: (De)centralisation in Southeast Asia 139, 153.

is now taken for granted at the level of local self-government, and autonomy has allowed many local governments to create new policy and process, civic consultation fora, public transparency campaigns, local watch initiatives, and annual accountability reporting. They have also been able to draw on a variety of resources in support of local governance, such as local government associations and innovation centres.[89]

It was entirely predictable that the strong downward thrust of decentralisation in 1999 would earn a backlash, and the Laws of 2004 and 2014, together with the Law on Villages of 2014, have probably secured a better equilibrium of powers between the various levels of government than existed under the 1999 laws. In territorial governance one can see the relative chaos of the early period turning into relative order in a smooth transition. After a decade of the current legislation on regional autonomy, one might now conclude that decentralisation as a project is completed, for better or for worse, and the era of entrenched territorial governance has begun. However, the passing of a Civil Service Law in 2023[90] heralds the occupation of civilian offices by active military personnel, a clear reversion to the *dwi fungsi* (dual function, military/ civilian) of the New Order period, and raising a prospect that some local and provincial offices could soon be occupied by the military without popular election. And the election of General Prabowo, whose party policy involves reversion to the original 1945 Constitution (that is, without the amendments on regional autonomy), as Indonesia's next President in 2024 offers the distinct possibility of further reduction in local autonomy.[91]

[89] Schmit (n 1) 150. For success stories based on studies in Solo and Surabaya, see T Bunnell, MA Miller, NA Phelps and J Taylor, 'Urban development in a decentralised Indonesia: Two success stories?' (2013) 86(4) *Pacific Affairs* 857.

[90] Law 20/2023. The impact on regional government of the Omnibus Law on Job Creation, No 6/2023 is also a matter of uncertainty at the present time.

[91] S Butt, 'Parting gifts to Prabowo imperil democracy' (*Indonesia at Melbourne*, 20 May 2024) indonesiaatmelbourne.unimelb.edu.au/legislatures-parting-gifts-to-prabowo-imperil-democracy/.

4

Malaysia

'Clapping with one hand cannot produce sound':
Malay proverb

I. MALAYSIAN FEDERALISM

MALAYSIA PRESENTS A different case from the others considered in this book, in that it is the only federal system amongst the five countries, and it has not experienced decentralisation. It is, moreover the only one of these countries having a Westminster-style constitution. Indonesia, Philippines and Thailand[1] present variations on the theme of recent (that is, within the last quarter century) decentralisation of a centralised, unitary, and highly militarised state. Myanmar[2] presents several as yet undecided issues of territorial governance going to the fundamental nature of the state itself. In each of these other cases federalism was either never mooted or was specifically rejected during the process of decolonisation or modernisation. The priority was to establish a strongly centralised government as a counter-balance to ethnic, religious, and linguistic diversity, and thereby to achieve rapid development.[3] The Malaysian case, in spite of federalisation (a process that began in 1895[4] and was completed in 1963 with the accession of Sabah and Sarawak[5]) has been one of progressive centralisation from a historical base of highly diffused territorial governance. This process of centralisation has thus far been unmoderated by any decentralisation project, except for a brief experiment in the middle of the colonial period,[6] and has taken place over a period of 150 years (starting with the first British intervention in 1874), not just a few decades. Centralisation was accelerated during approximately the same period in which the other states, apart from Myanmar, decentralised (that is, the 1980s

[1] See chs 5, 8, 9.
[2] See ch 7.
[3] A Harding, *The Constitution of Malaysia: A Contextual Analysis* (Oxford, Hart/Bloomsbury Publishing, 2022) 44ff, ch 3.
[4] ibid 6ff; J Sidhu, *Administration in the Federated Malay States* (Kuala Lumpur, Oxford University Press, 1980).
[5] See, further, ch 12.
[6] Harding (n 3) 11.

and 1990s), and it was carried out in the interests of rapid development.[7] It has also encountered, as we shall see, cultural obstacles preventing the emergence of a unitary state. Moreover, since the Malaysia Agreement 1963, the presence of Sabah and Sarawak in the federal structure, enjoying a form of special autonomy, has presented the most pressing issue in territorial governance, and has in some ways arrested the unrelieved progress of centralisation. These two states are separated from West or Peninsular Malaysia (otherwise, historically, 'Malaya') by a large tract of the South China Sea, and exhibit considerable differences, compared to Malaya, in ethnicity and other demographic markers. The issue of special autonomy for Sabah and Sarawak is discussed, along with the other cases of special autonomy, in chapter eleven in Part III.

The process of centralisation having reached its maximum extent by 2008,[8] subsequent developments which are discussed below have tended to relax somewhat the tight grip in which state and local government were held during most of the long rule of the dominant Barisan Nasional ('BN') coalition from 1957 to 2018. This has not been without controversy and conflict, but the outcome has been adherence to the division of powers. As Francis Loh argues, 'federal-state controversies do not necessarily arise as a result of the opposition-led state governments. Rather most of these problems pertain to the centralisation of power and resources that have gone unchecked for more than fifty years'.[9] It is a notable feature that Malaysian federalism accords comparatively little autonomy to the states, except for Sabah and Sarawak. Currently there is strong demand from these two states for greater state autonomy, heralding possible fundamental changes that may affect the other states too in a federal structure that has remained remarkably stable since 1963, but is now held up for careful reexamination.[10]

Another distinguishing feature of Malaysian territorial governance is that, unlike the other countries discussed here, there are no local elections. Local government being a state matter, councillors are appointed by the state governments. Here again, however, the centripetal tendency appears to have gone

[7] Sultan Nazrin Shah, *Striving for Inclusive Development: From Pangkor to a Modern Malaysian State* (Oxford, Oxford University Press, 2019) chs 7and 8; Francis Loh Kok Wah, 'Centralised federalism in Malaysia: Is change in the offing?' in ML Weiss (ed), *The Routledge Handbook of Contemporary Malaysia* (Abingdon, Routledge, 2015) 75.

[8] This date is chosen because of the emergence in the general election of that year of a two-party or two-coalition system and the electoral success of the then opposition parties in taking control of some of the state governments. BN rule came to an end as a result of the general election of 2018, following which a period of political fragmentation has made territorial governance much more important than it was previously. See, further, A Hean Leng and A Whiting, 'Federalism and legal unification in Malaysia' in D Halberstam and M Reimann (eds), *Federalism and Legal Unification: A Comparative Investigation of Twenty Systems* (Dordrecht, Springer, 2014) 298; A Harding and J Chin (ed), *50 Years of Malaysia: Federalism Revisited* (Singapore, Marshall Cavendish, 2014).

[9] Loh (n 7) 79; also W Case, 'Semi-democracy and minimalist federalism in Malaysia' in Baogang He, B Gilligan and T Honugochi (eds), *Federalism in Asia* (Cheltenham, Edward Elgar, 2007).

[10] See, further, T Yeoh, *States of Reform: Governing Selangor and Penang* (Penang, Penang Institute, 2012).

as far as it could, and there is a persistent if not widespread demand for the restoration of local democracy.[11] The current state of territorial governance in Malaysia, with reference to federalism and local government, will be described and critiqued in this chapter.

II. DEVELOPMENT OF THE SYSTEM OF TERRITORIAL GOVERNANCE

After the collapse of the Malacca Empire in the early sixteenth century, when Malacca was taken over by the Portuguese, the empire fragmented into a number of states, each of which had its own traditional Ruler (known as 'Raja' or later generally 'Sultan'). British intervention involved initially the establishment of crown colonies in Penang (1786), Singapore (1819) and Malacca (1824).[12] From 1874 onwards a residential system, under treaties concluded with the various Malay Rulers, was established in the nine Malay states, which made up the remainder of Malaya. Under this system the Ruler retained control over matters concerning religion and custom, while the British Resident, on whose advice the Ruler would act, was responsible for all other matters except custom and religion.[13] Both the powers of the states and the nine Malay monarchies are therefore to this day deeply connected with culture and religion.[14]

The residential system began the process of centralisation. Under British rule some states (the 'Federated Malay States' or FMS) agreed to federalisation under a central government in Kuala Lumpur, while others (the 'Unfederated Malay States' or UMS) refused.[15] By the end of World War II independence was in view, and the eleven states of Malaya (the nine Malay states plus Penang and Malacca) signed the Federation of Malaya Agreement in 1948. The federal system was in essence a fallback measure following the rejection of a Malayan Union in 1946.[16] The sticking point for adopting a unitary state was that, despite an obvious need for a strong central government as a prior condition for independence, abolition of the Ruler's powers, which would be necessary under a unitary state, was an outcome at odds with Malay governance traditions, which strongly embrace

[11] A Harding, 'Local democracy in a multi-layered constitutional system: Malaysian local government reconsidered' ch 8 in A Harding and M Sidel (eds), *Central-Local Relations in Asian Constitutional Systems* (Oxford, Hart Publishing, 2015); DP Chacko, *Reintroduction of Local Government Elections in Malaysia* (Petaling Jaya, Bersih and Adil Network Sdn Bhd, 2021).

[12] These colonies formed the Straits Settlements from 1867. For a summary history of constitutional developments in the colonial period, see Harding (n 3) 6ff.

[13] R Emerson, *Malaysia: A Study in Direct and Indirect Rule* (New York, Macmillan, 1937); J Gullick, *Rulers and Residents: Influence and Power in the Malay States 1870–1920* (Singapore, Oxford University Press, 1992).

[14] A Harding and H Kumarasingham, 'The Malay monarchies in constitutional and social conception' (2022) 9 *Asian Journal of Law and Society* 399.

[15] The FMS comprised Negri Sembilan, Pahang, Perak, and Selangor. The UFMS comprised Johor, Kelantan, Kedah, Perlis and Terengganu. See Sultan Nazrin Shah (n 7) ch 1.

[16] Khong Khim Hoong, *Merdeka! British Rule and the Struggle for Independence in Malaya 1945–57* (Petaling Jaya, INSAN, 1984) ch 4; Harding (n 3) 14ff.

both monarchy and localism.[17] Thus in Malaya the monarchy system and federalism are very much intertwined: neither can be abolished or abridged without abolishing or abridging the other. It was this federal entity of 1948 that achieved independence under the 1957 Constitution of the Federation of Malaya. In this Constitution, only 'a measure of autonomy' (to use the expression adopted by the Reid Commission, which drafted the 1957 Constitution[18]) was accorded to the states, indicating that the system may have been federal in name but was in reality highly centralised, or as some have maintained merely 'quasi-federal' in nature.[19] The creation of a bicameral legislature in 1957 envisaged that state representatives would have a majority in the upper house, and would therefore be able to protect states' rights. However, over time the proportion of members appointed by the federal government has reduced this bulwark for states' rights virtually to vanishing point.[20]

In 1963 Sabah, Sarawak and Singapore, pursuant to the Malaysia Agreement 1963 ('MA63'), joined with the existing federation to form a new Malaysian federation.[21] Singapore left the federation in 1965, so that since then the federation has comprised 13 states. Thus, over two decades between 1945 and 1965 more centralisation was achieved in what is now Malaysia than in the previous four-and-a-half centuries; and even more was to come as the federal power began to assert itself over the states. Sabah and Sarawak, however, enjoy somewhat greater powers under MA63 than do the states of the original Federation of Malaya, so that the federal system has in effect two tiers, the first consisting of Sabah and Sarawak and the second consisting of the other eleven states.[22]

As a result of this history, we can summarise the system of territorial governance as follows. Under the Federal Constitution there are three levels of government: federal, state (with special autonomy for Sabah and Sarawak), and local. Unlike the other countries considered in this book, Malaysia has only one level of local government. City councils (18), municipal councils (38), and district councils (94) have congruent powers. There are also three federal territories (Kuala Lumpur, Labuan, and the administrative capital, Putrajaya).[23]

[17] A Milner, *Kerajaan: Malay Political Culture on the Eve of Colonial Rule* (Tucson, University of Arizona Press, 1982).

[18] *Report of the Federation of Malaya Constitutional Commission 1957* (Kuala Lumpur, Government Printer, 1957, para 15.

[19] Ang and Whiting (n 8) 304.

[20] A Harding, 'The *Dewan Negara* and constitutional reform: Upper houses in comparative perspective' (2021) 1 *Journal of the Malaysian Parliament* 1.

[21] I have worded this sentence with a deliberate nod to the ambiguity, discussed in ch 12, between joining an existing federation and creating a new one. The historical facts can be construed either way.

[22] BH Shafruddin, *The Federal Factor in Government and Politics of Peninsular Malaysia* (Singapore, Oxford University Press, 1987) 38.

[23] The federal government also controls six special-purpose local governments designated as 'development authorities'.

III. STATE AND FEDERAL POWERS

In this section we examine state government, and assess the degree of autonomy provided under the Malaysian federal system.

Each state has its own written constitution, and these constitutions are, like the Federal Constitution, based squarely on the Westminster model, with the Ruler (or Governor in the case of those states without a monarch[24]) as head of state. There is a unicameral state legislature, and the usual Westminster conventions apply, governing the appointment of the head of the executive (styled *Menteri Besar*, or Chief Minister[25]), acting on advice, assenting to passed bills, and so on. Having one's own constitution is usually of course a marker of autonomy in a federal system. It would however be an exaggeration to say that federalism enables the Malaysian states to operate their own preferred system of governance. To the contrary, the state constitutions are required to conform rigidly with the 'Westminster' principles by virtue of Schedule 8 of the Federal Constitution, which overrides the state constitutions. Thus their margin of variation in governance is somewhat limited, and is largely evident only in religion (Islam being a state matter under Schedule 9 of the Constitution), and symbolic aspects of their different monarchical traditions.[26] Local government, although a state matter, is in practice standardised, governed by federal legislation, and under state government direction, as is discussed below.

One major reason for federal structures is that they are a means of accommodating ethnic or religious differences, and this factor is often seen as both defining and justifying federalism.[27] This is often assumed to be the case in Malaysia due to its ethnic diversity, but in fact it is only a marginal factor, and does not explain why the federal system exists. Almost all ethnic groups, including the *orang asli* (peoples indigenous to Malaya), who mainly inhabit the jungle and mountainous areas, are spread across most or all of the states. Even strongly Malay populations, like those of Kelantan and Terengganu, have quite large Chinese minorities concentrated mainly in urban areas. On the other hand, some ethnicities are concentrated more in some states than others. Sabah and Sarawak with their Bornean indigenous groups,[28] such as the Iban and the Kadazan, who form a majority in these two states, exhibit a diversity quite different from Malaya and from each other. More obvious are considerable differences between states in culture, history, and economic development. This is especially the case for Sabah and Sarawak. Sarawak was carved out of the Brunei

[24] That is, Malacca, Penang, Sabah and Sarawak.

[25] Sarawak has a 'Premier', following amendment to the state constitution in 2022.

[26] Adib Vincent Tung Abdullah, *Titles and Ceremonial Traditions of the Royalty and Nobility of the State of Perak, Malaysia* (Ipoh, Perak Academy, 2019).

[27] F Palermo and K Kössler (eds), *Comparative Federalism: Constitutional Arrangements and Case Law* (Oxford, Hart Publishing, 2017) 97ff.

[28] The Constitution, at Article 161A(7), specifies 28 different groups, including Malays, as natives of these states.

Sultanate and ruled by the 'white rajahs' (the Brooke family) for a century before World War II. Sabah was controlled by the North Borneo Company before becoming, along with Sarawak, a British colony between 1945 and 1963. There are also geographical considerations. Sabah and Sarawak are large states with vast tracts of jungle, and abundant natural resources. Between them they have a much larger land area than the whole of Malaya with its eleven states, but only less than one sixth of the country's total population.

There is in short no single, special logic that explains the differences between the states; they are just different from each other along different axes. In this sense the states of Malaysia do not exhibit any greater or lesser diversity than the provinces of Indonesia, Philippines or Thailand, or the states/regions of Myanmar; but the diversity is, so to speak, more evenly spread than it generally is in those countries. The true reason for having a federal system lies, as we have seen, in the unique system of monarchy. Under this system the Rulers of the nine Malay states take turns on a five-yearly rotation in serving as the head of state (*Yang di-Pertuan Agong*, or supreme head) of the federation itself.[29] Whatever the reasons for having it, the federal structure provides a welcome if limited form of political ventilation in what still remains a highly centralised system of government.

The conferring of a measure of autonomy on the states in 1957 implies that the most important functions are given to the federal government rather than the state governments.[30] Schedule 9 of the Constitution contains five lists of legislative powers, respectively, federal; state; state (supplemental for Sabah and Sarawak); concurrent; and concurrent (supplemental for Sabah and Sarawak). Concurrent powers may be performed by either state or federal authorities, and any residual powers (that is, powers not mentioned in any of these lists) belong to the states.[31] These powers are exercisable by the relevant legislatures, and executive powers simply follow the legislative powers.[32] In the event of inconsistency between federal and state law, federal law prevails.[33] The result of Schedule 9 is that the federal government exercises powers over most significant functions, including not just the usual centrally exercised powers such as defence, external affairs, citizenship and immigration, judiciary and taxation, but also police, education, industry, transport, and health. What remains for the states is largely matters relating to development, land, agriculture, and natural resources, local government and religion. Sabah and Sarawak enjoy greater powers, and this differentiation is examined below. Concurrent powers, such as social welfare, planning and public health, are in general exercised by the states.

[29] Constitution, Article 32.

[30] JC Fong, *Constitutional Federalism in Malaysia* (Kuala Lumpur, Thompson/Sweet & Maxwell Asia, 2008).

[31] *See Ketua Pengarah Jabatan Alam Sekitar & Anor v Kajing Tubek & Ors* [1997] 3 MLJ 23, where the Federal Court was reluctant to recognise such residual powers.

[32] Constitution, Articles 74 and 80.

[33] ibid Article 75.

IV. INTERGOVERNMENTAL RELATIONS

The exclusive arbiter over the constitutional division of powers is the Federal Court. It is also the exclusive arbiter of disputes of any kind between the federation and a state and between states.[34] Although the Federal Court has on occasion decided disputes of this kind, it has not often struck down a statute as being unconstitutional.[35] In two recent cases[36] in which state enactments were struck down, it has affirmed the approach taken in an earlier case[37] in laying down definitively the applicable criteria, under which the court will look at the 'pith and substance' of the law rather than its outward appearance in determining whether it is unconstitutional. All three cases concerned the power of the states over religion, in its relationship to the federal power over criminal law. In the latest case of *Nik Elin Zurina binti Nik Abdul Rashid and Anor v Kerajaan Negeri Kelantan* in 2024,[38] the Federal Court applied the pith and substance doctrine in striking down 17 provisions in state *syariah* (shari'a) laws creating criminal offences. It distinguished general criminal law, which is under the federal power, from specific religious offences, which are under the state power over Islam. The court also emphasised that it is the federal and state lists that determine the respective legislative powers, not whether the relevant legislature has or has not in fact passed a law on the subject matter in question.[39]

Despite the lists set out extensively in Schedule 9, other provisions in the Constitution nonetheless create a high degree of flexibility in their practical operation. In particular, under Article 76, parliament has power to legislate on matters appearing on the state list in three situations.

First, it may legislate for the purpose of implementing international agreements. Here it cannot legislate with respect to Islamic law or Malay custom, which are quintessential state powers; and not in any case without consulting the state government.

Second, it may legislate to promote legal uniformity between two or more states; in this case as well as for the first situation, the law only takes effect when passed by the state legislature, when it becomes state law. Additionally, parliament is given a specific power to legislate for ensuring uniformity of law and policy in relation to land and local government; but in this instance the law does not have to be passed by the state legislature and remains federal law.

[34] ibid Article 128(1).

[35] Under Article 74. In *City Council of Georgetown v Government of Penang* [1967] 1 MLJ 169, two State laws were struck down as inconsistent with Federal law. In *Noordin Salleh v State Legislative Assembly of Kelantan* [1993] 3 MLJ 344, a state party-hopping law was struck down because it violated Article 10 of the Constitution which gave the power to regulate freedom of association to Parliament only.

[36] *Iki Putra bin Mubarrak v Kerajaan Negeri Selangor* [2021] 2 MLJ 323; *Nik Elin Zurina binti Nik Abdul Rashid and Anor v Kerajaan Negeri Kelantan*, BKA-2-05/2022(D), 21 February 2024.

[37] *Mamat bin Daud v Government of Malaysia* (1986) 2 MLJ 192.

[38] Above n 36.

[39] ibid para 58.

The Constitution also recognises the importance of creating uniformity in relation to these issues by creating a National Land Council and a National Local Government Council.[40]

Third, parliament can legislate where simply requested to do so by a state legislature.[41] The National Land Code 1966 and the Local Government Act 1976 are notable examples of the use of this power and these laws impact directly on territorial governance. They are federal laws dealing with state matters; they were passed at the request of all the states following agreement between the federation and the states in the respective national councils, rather than under the special powers mentioned above for land and local government. Again, they do not apply to Sabah or Sarawak, which, as on many other issues, have their own laws.

Although executive powers follow legislative powers, Article 80 of the Constitution provides similar flexibility to Article 76 by allowing federal law to confer executive authority on a state. A good example is the Immigration Act 1959, as amended in 1963, which gives the governments of Sabah and Sarawak control over immigration in their respective states.[42] It is also permissible for state and federal authorities to exercise executive powers on behalf of each other. State powers must be exercised so as to ensure compliance with federal laws, and not so as to impede the exercise of federal powers.[43]

These provisions, taken together, indicate that the notion of cooperative federalism,[44] or what in Indonesia we saw referred to as *tugas pembantuan*,[45] describes Malaysian federalism accurately. The Constitution channels the preponderance of power to the centre without reducing states to the position of mere agents of the federal power and without creating too much structural rigidity. This system has not required any significant adjustment since 1957, in spite of the 1963 constitutional changes pursuant to MA63. This indicates that the Reid Commission successfully reconciled the aspiration for a degree of state autonomy with the needs of national development. The only significant amendments to Schedule 9 relate to tourism, which was added to the federal

[40] Constitution, Articles 91, 95A. See also Articles 83 and 92 on land acquisition and development plans. These provisions concerning land and local government do not apply to Sabah or Sarawak: Article 95D.

[41] See also Article 76A, which gives States limited powers to pass laws on Federal matters; and Articles 83 and 85–88 which allow the Federation to acquire state land in the national interest and to declare an area a development area, which gives Parliament power to pass laws otherwise prohibited by Article 74. In practice development areas have often been simply absorbed into the Federal Territory (eg, Putrajaya), or declared as special economic zones, eg the Iskandar Development Region in Johor.

[42] MA63, Annex E.

[43] Constitution, Article 81.

[44] C Saunders, 'Co-Operative Arrangements in Comparative Perspective' in G Appleby, N Aroney and T John (eds), *The Future of Australian Federalism: Comparative and Interdisciplinary Perspectives*, (Cambridge, Cambridge University Press, 2012).

[45] See p 51.

list in 1994;[46] and water, which was transferred from the state to the concurrent list in 2006.[47] The former was slipped into a major constitutional amendment relating to other issues and without consultation with the state governments, which had their own tourism initiatives. However, states have not been prevented, in practice, from promoting tourism.

The strongly centripetal aspect of Malaysian federalism was, at least until a reversal of the trend commenced in 2008, reinforced by the dominant-coalition system. During the period 1957–2008, Sabah and Sarawak excepted, almost all states were controlled by the BN almost all of the time. This meant that the policy of state governments was kept very much in line with that of the federal government. For example, the BN leader at the federal level (that is, the Prime Minister) decided who would be the chief minister at the state level, even though constitutionally this decision should have been that of the majority in the state assembly.[48]

Cases of states controlled by opposition parties were both rare and strongly contested by the centre.[49] In Sarawak in 1966 and in Kelantan in 1978 the extreme measure of an emergency proclamation was invoked, purely in order to oust a chief minister whom the BN wished removed.[50] In the Sarawak case, Chief Minister Stephen Kalong Ningkan was dismissed by the Governor on the basis of a letter signed by half of the assembly members expressing lack of confidence in Ningkan. This dismissal was ruled unconstitutional by the High Court,[51] following which the federal government proclaimed an emergency in Sarawak and amended the state constitution so as to facilitate Ningkan's removal for a second time. Ningkan then alleged a fraud on the Constitution, and took his case to the Judicial Committee of the Privy Council in London, which, in an astonishing decision spelling disaster for states' rights in Malaysia, held that the constitutional chicanery employed by the federal government was within emergency powers as set out in Article 150 of the Constitution.[52] In the Kelantan case a similar method was employed to manipulate the operation of the state constitution to oust the chief minister, with the added feature of bringing the state under what was in effect martial law. It should be emphasised that in both of these cases there was no breakdown in public order, nor even any evidence that such breakdown might occur. Justification for using emergency powers, even in terms of the very broad interpretation of those powers adopted by the

[46] Constitution (Amendment) Act 1994.

[47] Constitution (Amendment) Act 2005.

[48] Wong Chin Huat and J Chin, 'Malaysia: Centralised federalism in an electoral one-party state' in R Saxena (ed), *Varieties of Federal Governance: Major Contemporary Models* (Cambridge, Cambridge University Press, 2011) 208.

[49] ibid 217ff.

[50] For full accounts of these episodes, see C Das, *Governments and Crisis Powers: A Legal Study on the Use of Emergency Powers* (Kuala Lumpur, Current Law Journal, 1996) 163ff.

[51] *Stephen Kalong Ningkan v Tun Haji Openg and Tawi Sli* [1966] 2 MLJ 187.

[52] *Stephen Kalong Ningkan v Tun Haji Openg and Tawi Sli (No 2)* [1967] 1 MLJ 46; *Stephen Kalong Ningkan v Government of Malaysia* [1968] 2 MLJ 238.

Privy Council, was entirely lacking, and in Ningkan's case his counsel was able to furnish the court with ample evidence of a conspiracy on the part of the federal government to remove Ningkan.[53] In 1981 Article 150 was amended to introduced a very broad ouster clause,[54] preventing the courts from reviewing any aspect of the exercise of emergency powers.

In addition to these striking interferences in the operation of the state constitutions, the federal government has also on occasion interfered politically behind the scenes to manipulate state government formation, and undermine or change governments by inducing the defection of assembly members.[55] This occurred in Perak in 2009, where a government opposed to the BN was removed by presenting to the Ruler evidence of loss of confidence in the chief minister without a no-confidence vote in the assembly. The Ruler declared the position of chief minister vacant, a mode of dismissal that was then upheld by the Federal Court.[56]

It may be that, after 2022, with the spread among the states as well as at the federal level of anti-hopping laws[57] – laws that prevent members changing parties without losing their seats in the legislature – such manipulations are now, in a political ecology of fragmentation, more difficult to achieve. But what is striking about the Malaysian federal system is that, apart from the issue of MA63, the measure of autonomy prescribed by the Reid Commission, albeit limited in its extent, has ultimately been preserved. This is despite a measure of authoritarian hyper-centralisation under the long rule of the BN.[58] The transition to a more fluid political system under which several states have, since 2008, been under opposition control, has ensured the survival, for now at least, of the original model of federalism. This political change appears not to have affected the general smooth running of state government and even intergovernmental relations.[59] State governments have the fiscal benefit of grants guaranteed by the Constitution,[60] and together with the states' own sources of revenue, they are sufficiently well endowed to carry on state government. But for major development projects they are still (unduly, it is suggested) dependent on the federal

[53] Y Ghai, 'The politics of the constitution: Another look at the *Ningkan* litigation' (1986) 7 *Singapore Law Review* 147.

[54] Article 150(8).

[55] Wong and Chin (n 47) 218ff.

[56] *Datuk Nizar Jamaluddin v Datuk Seri Zambry Abdul Kadir* [[2010] 1 MLJ 285; Harding (n 3) 120.

[57] Constitution (Amendment) (No3) Act 2022.

[58] FE Hutchinson, 'Malaysia's federal system: Overt and covert centralisation' (2014) 44(3) *Journal of Contemporary Asia* 442; Wong and Chin (n 47); K Ostwald, 'Federalism without decentralisation: Power consolidation in Malaysia' (2017) 34(3) *Journal of Southeast Asian Economies* 488; RO Tilman, *Quest for Unity: The Centralisation Theme in Malaysian Federal-state Relations, 1957–1975* (Singapore, ISEAS, 1976).

[59] Yeoh (n 10); T Yeoh, *Federal-State Relations under the Pakatan Harapan Government* (ISEAS Publishing, 2020).

[60] Constitution, Schedule 10; Harding (n 3) 138ff.

government. It is possible that a latent desire for more state autonomy will be more evident in the future as the federal design of 1957 comes increasingly into question.

V. LOCAL GOVERNMENT

In this book localism and subsidiarity are presented as the central concern in territorial governance. Examining Malaysian local government occurs in a different register from the other countries discussed, as we have seen, because of federalism and the absence of local elections. In the Malaysian case local government is not local *self*-government. Nonetheless local government is a site for considering territorial governance precisely because there is an ongoing debate about the possible restoration of local elections, at least in some areas such as cities. It is quite bizarre that the residents of a large modern city such as Kuala Lumpur, which is a federal territory, are not only unable to elect their councillors but have their mayor (the *Datuk Bandar*) and city council simply appointed directly by the federal government. Kuala Lumpur is thus the most disenfranchised major city mentioned in this book. Other Malaysian cities at least have their councillors chosen by the state government, offering a modicum of democratic accountability via state elections.[61]

A. Historical Development

During the pre-colonial period, the Malay states were divided territorially into districts that were headed by territorial chiefs. These chiefs still exist as part of official protocol at the state level, although their powers were long since taken away and given, first to district officers under colonial indirect rule, and later to district councils. Under traditional Malay governance, the chiefs held a great deal of power, so that the Ruler was in most cases restricted to presiding over important criminal matters and external affairs, but little else. His position was essentially, although prominent, formal and symbolic more than executive. Most practical government was done locally by the chiefs, and their consent was generally required for all major central decisions. This changed with British intervention and the residential system, in which the Ruler was given higher status and power.[62]

Malaysian local government along its present lines can be traced back to the British occupation of Penang, which later formed, with Malacca and Singapore,

[61] For the appointment system, see below.

[62] JM Gullick, *Indigenous Political Systems of Western Malaya* (London, Athlone Press, 1988); A Milner, *The Invention of Politics in Colonial Malaya* (Cambridge, Cambridge University Press, 2002).

the colony of the Straits Settlements. From 1801 local authorities and planning laws were established gradually in the colony, starting with Penang, and later in the Malay states, but only as and when it appeared necessary in a particular urban setting.[63] As independence loomed after 1945, experimentation with democracy was undertaken at the level of urban local government. By the time of the Federation of Malaya's independence in 1957 there were, however, no fewer than 289 local authorities, mainly district councils.

Two major changes have been made to local government since 1957.[64]

First, in 1965, local government elections were suspended as an emergency measure, and have not since then been reinstated.[65] At the same time a Royal Commission of Inquiry on Local Authorities was established, which recommended in 1968 (the Nahappan Report) the continuance of local elections and a reduction in the number of local authorities. Unfortunately, the proposed reforms were overtaken by an episode of inter-ethnic violence in May 1969. The tense environment that resulted from the riots resulted in the Development Administration Unit (DAU) of the Prime Minister's Department rejecting the Nahappan Report's recommendation for reinstating local elections. It was argued that elected local government, which facilitated the 'domination of the haves over the have-nots', and provided for 'over-democratised over-government at the local level', was no longer consonant with the objectives of a developmental state.[66] There is no enforceable right to local self-government in the Constitution, although it is clear that local government itself is a constitutional topic, and the Constitution provides for a National Local Government Council.

The passing of the Local Government Act 1976 was the second major reform, designed to implement the other main recommendation of the Nahappan Report. The 1976 Act, preceded in this by the Local Government (Temporary Provisions) Act 1973, regularised local authorities in Malaya, which by 1973 had grown in number from 289 to an unwieldy 373, in five different categories. With implementation of this legislation during 1973–88, and an equivalent exercise in Sabah and Sarawak, the total number of local authorities in the whole of Malaysia was eventually reduced to 138 and the categories to three: municipal councils, city councils, and district councils. As was explained earlier, the three types of local government authority are congruent, carrying out the same

[63] Lee Lik Meng, 'Town planning law in Malaysia: Politics, rights and jealousies' (1991) 15 *Habitat International* 105.

[64] For the reforms of the 1970s, see MW Norris, *Local Government in Peninsular Malaysia* (London, Gower, 1980); Phang Siew Noi, *Local Government System in Malaysia* (Kuala Lumpur, Dewan Bahasa dan Pustaka, 1996).

[65] Elections were suspended by the Emergency (Suspension of Local Government Elections) Regulations 1965. The Local Government (Temporary Provisions) Act 1973 abolished all elected local authorities and gave the power to appoint local authorities to the State Governments; see now Local Government Act 1976, s 15; P Tennant, 'The decline of elective local government in Malaysia' (1973) 13 *Asian Survey* 347.

[66] J Saravanamuttu, 'Act of betrayal: The snuffing out of local democracy in Malaysia' (*Aliran Monthly*, 2000), aliran.com/archives/monthly/2000/04h.html.

functions, and there are no intermediate authorities between the local and state governments. At present there are 156 local governments, of which 38 are municipal councils, 18 are city councils, which are led by a *Datuk Bandar* (Mayor), and 94 are district councils.

Local government is, as we have seen, designated under Schedule 9 as a state matter. The creation of a body to coordinate policy, the National Council on Local Government, which is discussed below, indicates that local government is a structure that is mandated by the Constitution and could not, for example, be simply absorbed into state government. Nonetheless, as mentioned above, local government in Malaya is governed by uniform legislation in the form of the 1976 Act, as well as other statutes,[67] so that its character varies little across the states.

It should be noted that this uniformity only applies to the eleven states of West Malaysia, and not to Sabah and Sarawak, which have different laws and legal systems, as well as different legal and administrative history.[68] Sarawak has 12 divisions which group between two and five districts, most of which have sub-districts, numbering 57 altogether. Each district is headed by a district officer, and sub-districts are headed by Sarawak Administrative Officers. Below sub-districts are villages led by a Penghulu or Tua Kampong (village head). In Sabah there are five divisions, 27 districts, and 12 sub-districts. District officers and village heads are all appointed by the state government. Sabah has five divisions grouping 28 districts, and eleven sub-districts which are not independent of the districts. There are however no villages in the administrative sense, unlike in all the other states.

B. Powers and Revenue

Local government is the lowest level of Malaysia's multi-layered system of government, employing only seven per cent of all public employees. Nonetheless, the powers of local governments are extensive, including development control; public housing; roads, other than highways; local transport, including bus routes and taxi licensing; parks and public places; public nuisances; garbage collection and disposal; and a wide range of other environmental functions.[69] All of these are important aspects of both urban and rural living. Some services are provided via public-private partnerships, many of which are policy-orchestrated by the

[67] For example the Street, Drainage and Building Act 1974 and the Town and Country Planning Act 1976.

[68] Local government in Sabah is governed by the Local Government Ordinance 1961, and the equivalent legislation in Sarawak is the Local Authority Ordinance 1948, the Kuching Municipal Ordinances 1988 and the City of Kuching North Ordinance 1988.

[69] This is a brief summation. For a full list, see the Local Government Act 1976, s 101, containing 34 extensive subsections setting out all of these powers.

federal government.[70] Housing and planning are closely interrelated and form the most significant area of government activity that local governments control. In a rapidly developing and rapidly urbanising country these functions are some of the most important that are carried out at *any level* of government. They are counter-balanced by the environmental powers of local authorities, which attempt to minimise the adverse effects of rapid development.[71]

Local councils consist of between eight and 24 persons who are appointed by the state governments from amongst prominent citizens resident in the locality for terms of three years.[72] Councillors have therefore tended to reflect the interests of the political party or parties in power at the state level; in Peninsular Malaysia at least, political parties operate at the national level and there are no purely local parties, although obviously some parties are perceived as being stronger in some specific areas or originated therefrom. With regard to Kuala Lumpur, since it is a Federal Territory, the *Datuk Bandar* ('Mayor') is appointed by the Federal Government for a period of five years, and the *Dewan Bandaraya Kuala Lumpur* (Kuala Lumpur City Council) is placed under the Prime Minister's Department.[73]

In general terms, Malaysian local authorities derive their revenue from three main sources:

(i) local taxation in the form of property assessments or the equivalent (about 51 per cent);
(ii) rents and fees for services, and licences (about 32 per cent); and
(iii) fiscal transfers from state and federal governments, for example for road maintenance or specific development projects (about 17 per cent).

However, due to the over-reliance of most councils on assessments, weaker local authorities, and especially rural ones, are often still struggling with financial resources when carrying out their operations.[74] As a result, these authorities rely heavily on grants from the federal government or the state.[75] In this regard, a good relationship between the local government and the federal and state government is necessary to obtain funding on a consistent basis. It is at this point that the political patronage system becomes very important for local government, and there are instances of deliberate political partisanship in funding allocations.[76]

[70] K Singaravelloo, 'Fostering public-private partnership in a win-win situation: The experience of a Malaysian local government' in L Montanheiro and M Spiering (eds), *Public and Private Sector Partnerships: The Enterprise Governance* (Sheffield, Sheffield Hallam University Press, 2013).

[71] Maizatun Mustafa, *Environmental Law in Malaysia*, 2nd edn (Alphen-aan-den-Rijn, The Netherlands, Kluwer Law International, 2013).

[72] Local Government Act 1976, ss 3 and 13.

[73] Federal Capital Act 1960, ss 4 and 7.

[74] Ahmad Yunus, 'United Cities and Local Governments (UCLG) Country Profile: Malaysia' (2016) 8–9 (Global Observatory on Democracy and Decentralisation).

[75] ibid; Phang Siew Noi, *Financing Local Government in Malaysia* (Kuala Lumpur, University of Malaya Press, 1998).

[76] Lim Mah Hui, *Local Democracy Denied? A Personal Journey into Local Government in Malaysia* (Petaling Jaya, SIRDC, 2020).

The result of a lack of adequate resourcing has been an understandable emphasis on maintaining services rather than on development and a response to changing needs. This affects rural areas more than urban areas. Little has been done, despite much rhetoric, to improve provision of services at a similar or lower cost by privatising local government services. There is consequently a deficit in effective enforcement of relevant laws, with authorities seemingly unable in many ways to fully utilise their powers. This is especially the case with collection of local rates.[77]

One particular problem that seems capable of being easily addressed is that, since local government employees do not form part of the public service as such but are employees of the local authority in question, they cannot be simply transferred by a local government. Thus, meritorious employees can get stuck at middle levels of promotion for years, there being few opportunities for promotion, and may leave the service for better prospects elsewhere; mediocre employees on the other hand tend to remain where they are.[78]

VI. LOCAL GOVERNMENT IN INTERGOVERNMENTAL RELATIONS

We have seen that the Malaysian Constitution provides a measure of autonomy for state governments from the federal government, and that centralisation has been a dominant theme of inter-governmental relations. The same is largely true for local government, which may also be said to enjoy, under the 1976 Act, a measure of autonomy from state and federal governments, albeit less than that enjoyed by state governments. However, the lack of electoral accountability means that very little autonomy exists in practice. As a result, the local government system is in practice far more centralised than those of Thailand, Indonesia and the Philippines.

Intergovernmental relations are rendered more complex than a mere statement of constitutional and administrative law might indicate, due to the operation (historically speaking) of the dominant-coalition system in the past. For almost all of the post-independence period and in almost all states, at least up until 2008, appointees at federal, state and local government levels were appointed from within the BN power structure. This meant that state chief ministers were in effect appointed by the Prime Minister; state executive councils (equivalent of the cabinet at federal level) were appointed by chief ministers; and local councillors were appointed by the state government almost exclusively from the ranks of party members.[79] In this system intergovernmental relations

[77] AT Hussain and M Brahim, 'Administrative modernisation in the Malaysian local government: A study in promoting efficiency, effectiveness and productivity' (2006) 14 *Pertanika Journal of Social Sciences and Humanities* 51.

[78] ibid.

[79] NGO representatives have sometimes been appointed.

were therefore in large part a matter of intra-party relations. The lean towards party interest has not substantially changed during the post-2018 period.[80]

A number of factors continue to contribute to a lack of autonomy on the part of Malaysian local governments.

First, as is mentioned above, local governments are not elected. Local government elections are not specifically required by the Constitution, and have been suspended since 1965. As a consequence of this, as we have seen, the appointment of local councillors by the state governments, is usually, although not always, made on the basis of allegiance to the party in power at the state level. Accordingly, local government is stitched into the patronage-based, clientelist system that characterises Malaysian politics generally, rendering it especially unlikely that local councillors will decide against the desires of the state government.[81] This factor is critical in terms of the autonomy of local governments. We will return to it in due course when considering possible reforms.

Second, state governments exercise a good deal of control over local governments. They have powers under the 1976 Act, section 103, to give directions of a general character to local governments; this power is in practice expanded even further on occasion to directions of a very specific character, not just general policy issues.[82] In addition, local council budgets must be submitted to the state government for approval not later than 20 November of each year;[83] and the raising of loans by local governments is subject to the consent of the state government.[84] Furthermore, all local government by-laws, rules, regulations, and even assessments, are subject to state government approval.[85] State governments also exert some control over local governments' exercise of planning powers. States are governed planning-wise by a system of structure plans under the Town and Country Planning Act 1976 (TCPA). Local plans are drawn up by local governments, but are still subject to approval by the state government. Oddly enough, though, the TCPA allows local governments to make rules regarding regulation of land development, classes of use, and regulation of height, design, appearance of buildings and density of developments; and these rules *prevail* over state government rules if they conflict. This is one of very few areas where local governments can go against the wishes of the state government.

Third, we have to consider the National Council for Local Government ('NCLG'), a body established under Article 95A of the Constitution in 1960.[86]

[80] Wong and Chin (n 48).

[81] Lim Mah Hui, *Local Democracy Denied? A Personal Journey into Local Government in Malaysia* (Petaling Jaya, SIRDC, 2020).

[82] For example, the study of the SPICE controversy in Penang, in A Harding, *A Baseline Study of Local Government in West Malaysia*, NUS Law Working Paper 2022/014, 25.

[83] Local Government Act 1976, s 55.

[84] ibid s 40.

[85] ibid s 103.

[86] See Article 95A, and also Article 76 of the Federal Constitution, which provides for the federal legislature to make laws for the purpose of uniformity between states.

The state governments must follow the policies made by the NCLG. For example, when the state governments of Selangor and Penang (then held by federal opposition parties) requested the Election Commission (EC) to conduct local government elections, the EC held (it is suggested, incorrectly) that the NCLG's agreement was necessary.[87]

The NCLG consists of a federal minister as chairman (normally the Prime Minister), and one representative from each of the states (normally the Chief Minister) appointed by the head of state on government advice; and generally no more than ten representatives of the federal government. Given this composition, the NCLG is highly influential, and the Prime Minister, normally chairing the meetings, determines its agenda and direction.[88] Ultimately, the NCLG's agenda and interests reflect those of the federal government.[89] For this reason, the NCLG is considered by some to be quite improper in a federal system, as it can be said to trespass on states' rights.

The setting up of the NCLG is considered to be part of the extensive local government reforms that took place between its establishment and 1988. It was established to coordinate policies and laws between the federal, state and local spheres of government, such that uniformity of local government laws and policies in Malaysia could be achieved. After consultation with state governments the NCLG can 'formulate policies for the promotion, development, control of local government throughout the federation and for the administration of any laws relating thereto'.[90]

Fourth, as is the case in most countries, it is universally acknowledged that local government finance faces considerable challenges in Malaysia, except in some wealthier areas such as Penang and Selangor.[91]

Taken together, these factors restrict the considerably the freedom of operation of local governments.

VII. LOCAL DEMOCRACY, ACCOUNTABILITY, AND PUBLIC PARTICIPATION

The abolition of local elections in Malaysia has sparked persistent debate ever since 1965 with regard to their possible reintroduction.[92] The argument for reintroduction is the argument for local self-government, that is, that democracy is fundamental, and that local government, reflecting the principle that local

[87] Chacko (n 11).

[88] T Yeoh, *Federal-State Relations under the Pakatan Harapan Government* (ISEAS Publishing, 2020).

[89] Ostwald (n 58).

[90] Constitution, Article 95A. See, further, Phang Siew Nooi, *Decentralisation or Recentralisation? Trends in Local Government in Malaysia* (University of Malaya, 2008).

[91] K Singaravelloo, 'Local government and intergovernmental relations', ch 11 in Noore Alam Siddiquee (ed), *Public Management and Governance in Malaysia: Trends and Transformations* (Abingdon, Routledge, 2013) 211.

[92] Chacko (n 11).

electors know their situation better than metropolitan decision-makers, will answer the needs of local people best if their local councillors are accountable to them. The argument against reintroduction is that Malaysia does not need three levels of elected government, that the cost of holding elections is better expended elsewhere, and that local politics leads to destabilising interethnic relations. The cost of holding elections across all local authorities has been estimated at RM308 million (about US$65 million).[93] While this is not a very large sum, many feel that with the shortfall in public finances due to the 1MDB scandal and the pandemic's impact on the economy, now is not the right time to reintroduce local elections, even if it were, in general terms, warranted.

It is also a point of disagreement whether the appointment system or holding elections leads to greater efficiency. One recent councillor argues that, during the period of democratic local government in the 1950s and 1960s Ipoh City Council was well known for its efficiency; this was noted as a fact by the Nahappan Report.[94] The appointment system can certainly ensure that decisions are made speedily, but this does not mean the right decisions are being made (or are being made in a cost-effective manner). There are, it is true, cases of councillors appointed for a three-year term because they are persons of experience or distinction, as envisaged by the 1976 Act,[95] and these councillors do act as a public voice of some kind in the council's deliberations. Nonetheless, the overwhelming majority of councillors are appointed purely because of party affiliation; they are dismissed by one commentator as 'yes-men and apple polishers'.[96] Moreover, even these 'independent' councillors, it should be noted, were appointed only after opposition wins in some states in 2008. The fact is that as a result of the appointment system, most Malaysians have no idea who their local councillors are, and tend to raise local government concerns with their MP or state assembly member, who are more familiar to them, but of course have no jurisdiction over local government matters.[97]

For all this, elections, if reintroduced, would by no means be the only avenue for public participation in local decision-making. Although there are relevant statutory provisions affording opportunities for public participation in specific statutory contexts,[98] the most important avenue for the expression of views on local government matters is simply exercise of the fundamental political liberties of freedom of speech, assembly, and association, guaranteed, although also

[93] A Annuar, 'Zuraida: Third vote in Malaysia would cost RM2m per local council, RM308m for all' *Malay Mail* (14 July 2020) www.malaymail.com/news/malaysia/2020/07/14/zuraida-third-vote-in-malaysiawould-cost-rm2m-per-local-council-rm308m-for/1884291. The estimate is based on a figure of RM2m per council, ie the estimate now would, one assumes, be RM312m for 156 councils.

[94] Lim (n 76) 23.

[95] Section 10(2).

[96] Goh Ban Lee, *Counselling the Councillors* (Kuala Lumpur, FOMCA, 2007) cited in Lim (n 76) 22.

[97] Lim, ibid.

[98] See below.

in some respects subject to statutory restrictions, by Article 10 of the Federal Constitution.[99]

This exercise of civil liberties has led to important recent developments in administrative law, in which the Federal Court in two planning cases[100] has given standing to residents' and civil-society associations to challenge successfully local government planning decisions. These cases illustrate the importance of the judiciary in securing good governance and public accountability of local governments.[101] The judgments embrace several important areas of judicial review: the rule of law and the ultra vires principle; the binding nature of local plans due to their being based on public participation, requiring what was referred to by the court as 'slavish compliance' by the authorities; the requirement for reasons to be given for certain kinds of decision affecting the public; the avoidance of conflicts of interest as an aspect of natural justice; the need to take account of relevant considerations which might include public opinion; the need for liberal rules of standing to challenge administrative actions; and the need for full and frank disclosure on the part of public authorities in litigation. These cases are striking for their forthrightness in asserting the power of judicial review and the comprehensiveness and practical impact of the principles they lay down. In a system with no local elections, the decisions offer a promising alternative in terms of democracy and accountability. They offer the possibility of extending their principles in such a way that public opinion may well prove to be always relevant to local government decision-making in matters affecting the public interest.

A major obstacle to accountability is the lack of transparency on the part of local governments, such that matters are often decided before the public is aware of them. There is no general freedom of information legislation (although a federal law on this is mooted and a state law already exists in Selangor and Penang) that would require divulging of local government papers. Meetings of a full council, normally held monthly, are required by the 1976 Act,[102] to be open to the public and the press 'unless the local authority by resolution otherwise decides', and in practice they do so decide. Even where meetings are public, the public is not allowed to speak. Thus there actually is no regular method for

[99] A Harding, 'Practical human rights, NGOs and the environment in Malaysia' ch 11 in M Anderson and A Boyle (eds), *Human Rights Approaches to Environmental Protection* (Oxford, Clarendon Press, 1998); A Harding and Azmi Sharom, 'Access to environmental justice in Malaysia (Kuala Lumpur)' ch 5 in A Harding (ed), *Access to Environmental Justice: A Comparative Study* (The Hague, Kluwer, 2007); A Jaria Mydin, 'Access to public participation in the land planning and environmental decision-making process in Malaysia' (2011) 1(3) *International Journal of Humanities and Social Science* 148.

[100] *Perbadanan Pengurusan Sunrise Garden Kondominium v Sunway City (Penang) Sdn Bhd & Ors* [2023] 2 CLJ 333; *Datuk Bandar Kuala Lumpur v Perbadanan Pengurusan Trellises & Ors* [2023] 5 CLJ 167.

[101] See also *Majlis Daerah Hulu Selangor v United Plantations Bhd* [2021] MLJU 1205.

[102] Section 23.

members of the public to ask questions. Without information, citizens' freedom of expression, even if not restricted, may well come too late to be effective.

VIII. TERRITORIAL GOVERNANCE REFORM

A Penang state assembly member, reflecting widely-held opinion, has argued that the state governments could become more effective if there were a decentralisation of power from the federal government: 'It will be better for Penang as we are in the best position to know what is needed for our state instead of bureaucrats stationed far away in Putrajaya'. An example he provided was that 'even when the state government wants to reinstate the Penang Voluntary Patrol Team (PPS), it cannot be done without federal approval'. In fact the PPS was held by the Court of Appeal to be constitutionally within state powers.[103] He also pointed out that federal funds were being distributed unfavourably to the states: 'Penang received only 3 per cent of the tax revenue collected from the state between 2001 and 2008'. He reported that the budgets of all 13 states in Malaysia combined were equivalent to only 6 per cent of the federal budget in 2013 and the was figure reduced by 0.2 per cent in 2018.[104]

The question arises what ends are served by a federal system in the country with the smallest population and land area of the five discussed in this book. Given the origins of federalism in Malaysia, it seems reasonable to conclude that the states represent elements of culture more than they represent an exemplary form of subsidiarity. Central to these elements are the nine monarchies. The Rulers exercise substantial influence, if not actual political power, at the state level, and collectively at the federal level.[105] They are also heads of Islam in their states, and the fact that religion and customary law are also state matters adds to the cultural diversity thesis. State powers are deeply connected with what one might call spatial localism, being mainly concerned, apart from cultural matters, with such matters as land tenure, Malay reservations, local government, forestry, and natural-resource exploitation.

Local government is also oriented towards spatial localism, governing issues such as development planning, housing, local roads and transport, and environmental issues. Although state and local government functions should not be underestimated, they do not extend to social issues such as education, health, and policing; and they have few independent sources of finance, other than land assessments. Local government policy is formulated by the NCLG in consultation with federal and state governments, and under the political system as outlined above the federal government gets its way. Local authorities are not

[103] *Government of the State of Penang v Minister for Home Affairs & others* [2017] 4 MLJ 770.
[104] 'Backbencher wants more autonomy for Penang' *Malay Mail* (11 December 2018), www.malaymail.com/news/malaysia/2018/11/12/backbencher-wants-more-autonomy-for-penang/1692628.
[105] Harding and Kumarasingham (n 14).

represented at all in a process designed to serve their needs, despite the existence of a Malaysian Association of Local Authorities,[106] which could easily represent them in such policy deliberations.

The argument is often heard that deficiencies in staffing, and especially in technical expertise, make decentralisation at the local government level a risky enterprise. This of course is an outcome of the system of public employment, not a necessary consequence of having local government or subsidiarity per se. Subject to democratic controls, and adequately funded, there is no reason to suppose that local authorities would not perform very well, as they did during the period 1954–65.

Reforms to the local government system, especially regarding elections in some urban areas, were promised by the Pakatan Harapan ('PH') government, which left office on 1 March 2020. Subsequent governments have not stated any intention in this regard.[107] Under the dominance of the BN government (1957–2018) demands for reintroducing local government elections were easily suppressed. Since 2018 political fragmentation, accompanied by the need to deal with the pandemic, has hampered deep attention to policy questions such as the future of local government. The system of local government has long been thought in need of reform, but any concerted reform process seems a remote possibility at the present time.

The question of utility also raises the inevitability of a downside to federalism, in particular when there is local government to consider as an additional layer. If federalism is an immovable fact, is it still the case that Malaysia with its population of 33 million needs *three* levels of government, let alone three levels of *elected* government? Inefficiencies and lack of coordination do arise when different governments are responsible for overlapping, inter-locking, gap-creating, or sometimes contradictory, functions. Obvious examples are provided by foreign investment and environmental management. Foreign investment approval is given by the Federal Government; but land has to be obtained from the State Government; and the local authority's permission is required to build a factory. Environmental regulation is another case where powers are spread across all three levels of government, leading to complexity in environmental policy and decision-making,[108] and confusion over water supply, water resources, and drainage.[109] The efficient secret that allows this system to work quite well, by and large, in practice is its flexibility and its reliance on institutionalised forms of cooperation. This feature was much in evidence during the pandemic of 2020–21, in which coordination required no emergency measures

[106] See the Association's website at www.mala.com.my.

[107] The most recent proposals in this regard, by the Pakatan Harapan government in July 2018, mentioned only reintroducing local elections in some densely-populated urban areas; in any event these were not acted upon. See, further, Chacko (n 11).

[108] *Ketua Pengarah Jabatan Alam Sekitar v Kajing Tubek* [1997] 3 MLJ 23; and Fong (n 30) 56–57.

[109] Rasyikah Md Khalid, Faridah Jalil and Mazlin bin Mokhtar, 'Fifty years of water resources management in Malaysian federalism' in Harding and Chin (n 8).

for a whole year before January 2021. In spite of some different approaches at the state level, some resistance to federal impositions, and a degree of political instability, the Malaysian governmental coordination against the COVID-19 pandemic, including that of local governments, was clearly competent.[110]

In conclusion, when we compare Malaysia with the other countries discussed in this book we find that, despite its diversity and despite having a federal system, it has probably the most centralised government structure. Consideration of special autonomy for Sabah and Sarawak, considered in chapter eleven, indicates that overreaching centralism is not beyond reform, and reconsidering federalism, it is suggested, should lead to reconsidering local government too. These two forms of territorial governance are, in a diverse society, inevitably tied together.

[110] Azmil Tayeb and Por Heong Hong, 'Malaysia: Improvised Pandemic Policies and Democratic Regression' in V Ramraj (ed), *Covid-19 in Asia: Law and Policy Contexts* (Oxford, Oxford University Press 2020) ch 22.

5

Myanmar

'There are five evils – fire, flood, thieves, enemies and government':
Burmese proverb

In traditional Southeast Asian 'galactic' states power emanated from the ruler at the centre and spread outwards as far and as strongly as it could be felt.[1] Burma[2] was no exception. Territorial governance took the form of provincial governors appointed by the King. Below the level of governors were hereditary local officials such as township heads and village heads, operating within a patronage-based political system. This system was put in place in the twelfth century, and hereditary village heads performed the functions of intermediary between the village and the centre, and of mediation and peace-making. This system was upended in the colonial period, in which these local heads were replaced by salaried agents, loyal to the British government and brought in from outside the area, mainly to collect taxes. Above these a system of 'village circles' (now called 'village tracts') was imposed. To use the terms adopted in chapters one and three, villages became 'administrative' rather than 'organic', in a bureaucratic, impersonal system described by Michael Aung-Thwin and Maitrii Aung-Thwin as 'order without meaning',[3] and by Thant Myint U as 'the final death blow to the old system of local government'.[4] Beyond the Bamar (Burman) heartland, at what was conceived as a great distance from the centre, lay the principalities ethnic states (*naingam*) now referred to as ethnic states (*pyi nay*), conquered but in an uneasy, shifting, tributary relationship with the centre.[5]

In modern times the problem of the states within a system of territorial governance defines the problem of Myanmar itself. The failure to achieve a resolution of this problem has resulted in protracted conflict since 1948, extreme centralisation, and a complete absence of democracy during the long period of

[1] SJ Tambiah, 'The galactic polity in Southeast Asia' (2013) 3(3) *Journal of Ethnographic Theory* 503.

[2] It is conventional to use the term 'Burma' for the country known since 1989 as 'Myanmar'.

[3] Michael Aung-Thwin and Maitrii Aung-Thwin, *A History of Myanmar Since Ancient Times: Traditionalism and Transformation* (London, Reaktion Books, 2012) 33.

[4] Thant Myint-U, *The Making of modern Burma* (Cambridge, Cambridge University Press, 2001) 215.

[5] Aung-Thwin and Aung-Thwin (n 3) 224.

military rule (1962–2010 and 2021 to date).[6] Myanmar is as a result of this troubled history currently in the throes of a tragic civil war that began in May 2021. The war is being fought between the State Administration Council (SAC, the military junta formed after the coup d'état of 1 February 2021, which controls the Tatmadaw or armed forces), and the National Unity Government (NUG, which controls the People's Defence Force) and their allies, who include various ethnic armed organisations (EAOs) which have been in persistent hostilities with the Tatmadaw since the 1940s.[7] Any discussion of a system of territorial governance must therefore be either historical, based on the position as at 31 January 2021, or hypothetical, as a future constitution is contemplated.[8] Any new constitutional design may seem a distant prospect, but it is not so distant as to render pointless any consideration of what territorial governance might look like in future. And in any such design, it is obviously highly relevant to consider how territorial governance has operated in the past, especially during the period of restricted democracy between 2011 and 2021.[9]

Accordingly, in this chapter it will be assumed that the Constitution of the Union of Myanmar 2008 is for now the authentic text for discussion of territorial governance.[10] The status of that constitution is however a moot question, as both sides in the civil war appear to have based their legitimacy as the country's government at least partly on it, while in essence rejecting it. The SAC claim that the emergency proclamation of 1 February 2021 (in essence however a coup d'état[11]), which has been persistently renewed every six months since then, is an exercise of constitutional powers lawfully assumed on that date by the Commander-in-Chief.[12] The NUG claim that their legitimacy depends on the general election held under the 2008 Constitution in November 2020, whose rejection led to the coup.[13] Yet in many respects both sides have distanced themselves from reliance on the that constitution. The forces opposed to the Tatmadaw have drawn up a 'Federal Democracy Charter' (FDC), which, as a road map to a future constitution, and rejecting the 2008 Constitution, acts, so

[6] J Saffin, 'Seeking constitutional settlement in Myanmar' ch 1 in A Harding and Khin Khin Oo (eds), *Constitutionalism and Legal Change in Myanmar* (Oxford, Hart Publishing, 2017).

[7] Moe Thuzar and Htet Myet Min Tun, 'Myanmar's National Unity Government: A radical arrangement to counteract the coup' (Perspective No 8, Singapore, ISEAS-Yusof Ishak Institute, 2022).

[8] E Bulmer, *A New Constitution for Myanmar: Towards Consensus on an Inclusive Federal Democracy* (IDEA, 2022).

[9] M Crouch, *The Constitution of Myanmar: A Contextual Analysis* (Oxford, Hart Publishing, 2019) ch 7; M Brand, 'Achieving genuine federalism? Myanmar's inexorable path towards constitutional devolution and decentralised governance' ch 7 in Harding and Khin Khin Oo (n 6).

[10] Thus the present tense is used in this chapter, as if matters stood as they were on 31 January 2021, except where otherwise stated.

[11] See eg S Choudhry and A Welikala, 'Myanmar's military coup d'état is unconstitutional: How should the international community respond?' (*IACL-AIDC Blog*, 18 February 2021).

[12] T Noel, *Unconstitutionality of the 2021 Military Coup in Myanmar* (IDEA, 2022).

[13] Bulmer (n 8) 44.

far as they are concerned, as the de facto current constitution of Myanmar.[14] The FDC and its signatories appear nonetheless to assume that territorial governance as it stands under the 2008 Constitution is the starting point for discussion about future arrangements.[15]

The assumption in this chapter is therefore not that the territorial governance system set out in the 2008 constitution actually governs Myanmar.[16] Rather, it is that we can learn a good deal from that system that would be relevant in future, given attempts to construct a new, federal constitutional order at some juncture.[17] What might be learned in this way could be both positive and negative. The ostensible embrace of decentralisation in the 2008 Constitution can be set against ways in which that decentralisation also failed to flower in practice or to gain popular trust. It seems indisputable that for a future constitution to consolidate democracy and the rule of law in Myanmar, it will have to say a great deal about territorial governance within a federal structure, and probably a structure that extensively entrenches and guarantees democracy at all levels, and the autonomy of the federation's subjects.[18] Its chances of success would depend on the way in which the subjects of the federation are defined, the extent of the autonomy given to them, and on the kind of democracy that would be entrenched, not just at state or regional level, but at the lower levels too.

A new constitution will have to engage with an extraordinary situation in that, of all the countries discussed in this book, Myanmar has had, albeit fleetingly, more levels and varieties of territorial governance than any other. At the highest level are seven states and seven regions, together with one Union territory (Naypyidaw), five Special Administrative Zones and one Special Administrative District. Below these are 74 districts and 330 townships; and below them are 3,470 urban wards, and 13,590 rural village tracts, with 63,214 villages forming the lowest level. The likelihood is that future territorial governance will have a similar extent and complexity, but with a greater degree of decentralisation than is accorded by the 2008 Constitution.

I. A FEDERAL OR UNITARY SYSTEM OF GOVERNMENT?

A future constitution for Myanmar, if and when it emerges, will in all probability be a loose federation with most powers given to the states/regions. The question we can begin with, therefore, is whether the previous constitutions, especially the 2008 Constitution, brought into effect in 2011, represented in

[14] IDEA, *Myanmar's Federal Democracy Charter: Analysis and Prospects* (Constitution Brief Interregnum Series, 2022).

[15] Bulmer (n 8) 32.

[16] For the current situation, see below, on territorial governance under civil war conditions.

[17] Saffin (n 6).

[18] Brand (n 9).

any respects a move towards or precedent for federalism, or else adopted quasi-federal features.[19]

The 1947 Constitution was adopted at independence and designed to give effect to the Panglong Agreement of 1947, in which Prime Minister General Aung San had made accommodation with various ethnic groups that were given special status in the Constitution.[20] That constitution provided for a unitary state with a Westminster-style framework,[21] but it had some quasi-federal features when it came to this special status. Notably, it provided a precedent for the *Amyotha Hluttaw* (the House of Nationalities, the upper house established under the 2008 Constitution) in creating a Chamber of Nationalities, a body having about half the number of members but similar legislative powers compared to the lower house, the House of Deputies. The Chamber of Nationalities had 125 members: 72 members representing the states (albeit, unlike the *Amothya Hluttaw*, in unequal numbers, according to population), and 53 representing the rest of Burma (that is, from what are now referred to as the 'regions' of the Bamar heartland).[22]

'Special councils' with broad legislative powers were provided for Shan, Kachin, Karen and Karenni (later called Kayah) States. These powers and the executive powers accompanying them included the state constitution; economic issues, land, and agricultural affairs; policing; communications; education; health; and local government.[23] There was also a Chin Special Division (later Chin state), and a Kaw-Thu-Lay Special Region (later Karen state).[24] These had a narrower range of powers. The arrangement was asymmetric in that devolved special council powers were not congruent with each other, and that the areas that did not enjoy this special autonomy (that is, the rest of Burma) were legislated for directly by the union parliament. State boundaries could not be altered except with the agreement of states affected.[25]

This arrangement did not present a federal system in another respect, namely that the members of the special councils were simply the elected members for the relevant state in each of the houses of parliament, and the states did not (unlike under the 2008 Constitution) have their own separately elected legislatures. A minister for each state was appointed at the union level by the President in consultation with the state council, and was designated as the executive head

[19] For discussion of the evolving constitutional position in the light of ethnic and political pluralism, see Ny Nyi Kyaw, 'Myanmar's pluralist constitution: Nation-building versus state-building' ch 6 in JL Neo and Ngoc Son Bui (eds), *Pluralist Constitutions in Southeast Asia* (Oxford, Hart Publishing, 2019) especially 161ff.

[20] D Williams, 'A second Panglong Agreement: Burmese federalism for the twenty-first century' ch 3 in Harding and Khin Khin Oo (n 6).

[21] Crouch (n 9) 18ff.

[22] Constitution of the Union of Burma (1947), Schedule 2.

[23] ibid Schedule 3, para 2, State Legislative List.

[24] ibid s 181.

[25] ibid ss 199–200.

of that state.[26] This minister was also a member of the union government, along with ministers for Karen and Chin affairs. This feature is considered a design fault that contradicts the logic of Westminster political constitutionalism and led to the demise of the 1947 Constitution in 1962, due to political differences within the government.[27]

One other feature of territorial governance under the 1947 Constitution is controversial and problematical. It provided for the possibility of states seceding after a period of ten years, following the support of two thirds of the special council and a plebiscite.[28] Opinion is divided as to whether this was a good idea. It offers a seemingly cast-iron guarantee of autonomy, in the 'spirit of Panglong'. But on the other hand, it offers the possibility that the very notion of secession would poison intergovernmental relations and weaken the government, which was the fatal problem of the 1947 Constitution.[29]

The 1974 Constitution, adopted at the height of the socialist period of the Burmese Path to Socialism, provided for a highly centralised form of government.[30] It did not afford any relevant precedent, except for its territorial division into seven states and seven 'divisions' (now 'regions').[31] This division is reflected in the 2008 Constitution. The states are named after the ethnic group that predominates in that part of Myanmar, and the regions are divisions of central Myanmar, in which the Bamar majority predominates. To a certain extent, however, inevitably, the various populations are mixed in many areas, or displaced beyond the boundary of the state bearing their name.[32]

However, Myanmar did not emerge as a federal state in 2011, as the clear intention and effect of the 2008 Constitution was to create a unitary state. However, some of its features and language lean towards federalism. The ethnic areas mainly inhabited by and named after the so-called 'national races' – the Rakhine (Arakanese), Chin, Kachin, Karen, Kayah, Mon, Shan – are referred to as 'states' (*pyi nai*).[33] There are also seven regions[34] with a Bamar majority, and these enjoy powers and status equal to those of the states.[35] In fact the entire structure of territorial governance, from states/regions down to villages,

[26] See eg for Shan state, under ss 160–61.

[27] Bulmer (n 8) 25.

[28] Constitution of the Union of Burma (1947), ss 201–206.

[29] Bulmer (n 8) 26. For more on this issue, see p 43.

[30] Crouch (n 9) 22.

[31] For a summary description of the differences between the states, see Crouch (n 9) 126–27.

[32] For this reason five Self-Administered Zones and one Self-Administered Division have been created, for which see below.

[33] Constitution of the Union of Myanmar 2008, ss 8 and 49. See further Ardeth Thawnghmung, 'National Races in Myanmar' in *Oxford Research Encyclopedia of Asian History* (Oxford, Oxford University Press, 2022).

[34] ibid. Formerly 'divisions'.

[35] This is a basic constitutional principle. See Constitution of the Union of Myanmar 2008, s 9, and s 13, which guarantees state/regional democracy.

is guaranteed by the Constitution.[36] There is also a complex process for redefining the boundaries of the states/regions, such that in essence redefinition cannot occur without the assent of the state/regions and townships affected.[37] The states/regions have their own legislatures (*hluttaw*), chief ministers, and ministries. The union legislature (the *Pyithu Hluttaw*) is made up of an elected lower house, the *Pyidaungsu Hluttaw*), and an upper house with almost equal legislative power, the House of Nationalities (*Amyotha Hluttaw*) consisting of 168 members, 12 of whom are elected from each state/ region. This body also includes 25 per cent military appointees (56 in all), as do the lower house and the state/regional assemblies.[38] The composition of the *Amyotha Hluttaw* is typical of upper houses in federal systems. At another level, the constitutionally entrenched devolution of extensive powers to state/regional assemblies and governments is also suggestive of federalism.[39] The Constitutional Tribunal has (inter alia) the function of acting as umpire as between union and state/regional powers, a typical function of an apex court in a federal system.[40] In a striking case in 2012 the Tribunal held that states/regions were empowered by Schedule 2 of the Constitution to pass municipal laws, despite the fact there was already a union law on this subject.[41]

On the other hand, these features are not necessarily unique to federal system, and several other features of territorial governance run decidedly *counter* to the model of federalism. Secession is specifically prohibited.[42] Amendment of the Constitution does not require the assent of states/regions.[43] The states and regions do not have their own constitutions,[44] and their internal governance systems are exactly similar to each other, being governed by the 2008 constitution.[45] Their assemblies are dissolved along with the parliament, and their chief ministers also cease to hold office at the same time as the President.[46] The chief ministers of the states/regions are appointed by the President from amongst a list of assembly representatives. The chief ministers are not, as one

[36] 2008 Constitution, s 51. Although it does not guarantee democracy at the sub-regional levels, democratic elements can be discerned. See below.

[37] ibid s 53. The names and boundaries of villages, village tracts, wards, districts and townships may not be changed except with a recommendation by the state/region chief minister to the President: s 54.

[38] This feature of legislatures at both levels is obviously a problem in terms of democracy and was heavily criticised by the NLD during 2014–21: A Harding and Nyi Nyi Kyaw, 'The long struggle for constitutional change in Myanmar' (2022) 50(2) *Federal Law Review* 192.

[39] Residual powers lie with the union: s 98.

[40] 2008 Constitution, s 46. This is of course true not only of federal systems, but of unitary states too. *cf* the role of the Constitutional Court and the Supreme Court in Indonesia, for which see ch 3.

[41] Municipal Law Case, 3/2012; see Crouch (n 9) 134.

[42] 2008 Constitution, s 10. Secession was however allowed under the 1947 Constitution, ch 10, although not under the 1974 Constitution.

[43] 2008 Constitution, ss 433–36.

[44] This is not conclusive. India and Malaysia both have a federal system, but Malaysian states have their own constitutions, while Indian states do not.

[45] 2008 Constitution, ss 161–95, 247–74.

[46] ibid ss 168, 262(m).

would expect in a federal system, elected by the assembly, and the President's choice cannot be rejected by it.[47] Moreover they report to the President, and may be dismissed by him.[48] The President may even specify the state/region ministries and their number.[49] The states and regions are obliged to render assistance to the union government in the preservation of the stability of the Union, community peace and tranquillity and prevalence of law and order; to report to the union government; and to discharge functions assigned to them by the union government.[50] Projects undertaken at state/regional level must also be consistent with union government policies.[51] State/region governments are obliged to coordinate with the union government in the appointment of ministers and public servants, and the central government's own General Administration Department acts as their administrative arm.[52] All of these factors are inconsistent with federalism.

Perhaps even more important than these factors limiting autonomy within the system of territorial governance is, as Melissa Crouch points out,[53] the fact the Myanmar people simply do not conceive of their constitution as federal, and the 2008 Constitution does not operate in practice in any way consistently with a federal spirit or a federal objective, as this chapter will reveal. Moving to a system of federalism would represent a big but necessary change, not so much in the extent of powers formally given to the federation's subjects as in the nature of political and legally-guaranteed autonomy and the system of intergovernmental relations. Yet this is what any successful equivalent of the Panglong peace conferences of 1947 and 2018–19[54] would have to debate and ultimately achieve.

II. POWERS OF THE STATES/REGIONS AND INTERGOVERNMENTAL RELATIONS

As we have seen, the breadth of powers given to the states/regions is tempered by intergovernmental relations that give a high degree of control to the union government. The chief minister operates in a parliamentary system, being a

[47] ibid s 261.

[48] ibid ss 262(l), 264(b).

[49] ibid s 248(c)(i).

[50] ibid ss 250, 258(b), 259. *cf* '*tugas pembantuan*' in Indonesia: see p 51.

[51] ibid s 251.

[52] ibid ss 257, 260, 262. This department is extremely powerful and acts as a significant check on the autonomy of the states/regions.

[53] Above n 9, 124.

[54] See Union Accord Part I, 37 Principles, 29 May 2017: www.peaceagreements.org/viewmasterdocument/2075; Union Accord Part II, 17 July 2018, www.peaceagreements.org/generateAgreementPDF/2383; Union Accord Part III, 21 August 2020: www.peaceagreements.org/viewmasterdocument/2369; M Crouch, 'Constitutional touchstones: Peace processes, federalism, and constitution-making in Myanmar' (2020) 18(4) *International Journal of Constitutional Law* 1350, 1368.

member of the assembly and head of government. He is compelled to assent to laws passed by the assembly, which failing such assent become law anyway after seven days.[55] The other members of his cabinet are also members of the assembly, except that the Advocate-General and the local head of the GAD also sit in the cabinet, the latter as its secretary.[56] The role of the GAD in advising the government, administering the public service, and executing laws makes it a very powerful force in state/regional government.[57] Although the chief minister selects his ministers, this is done with the approval of the President. In addition to being responsible to and dismissable by the President, he may be impeached in the assembly.[58]

The problem with this system is that, as was found by a project to examine the establishment of state/regional assemblies up to 2015,

> the constitution is deeply constraining ... with the appointment of chief minister and the allocation of ministerial portfolios all currently vested in the president, lines of accountability inevitably flow upward rather than downward. This places significant limitations on the assemblies' capacity for independent action, and turns them into little more than rubber-stamp institutions.[59]

This situation is due to a host of structural difficulties such as the considerable power of the chief minister to control the assembly, the presence of 25 per cent military members, and the reliance on the GAD.[60] An example from 2012 makes the point graphically. The speaker of the Ayeyarwady region assembly led a failed attempt to impeach the regional government for allegedly disdaining the assembly and infringing the rights of assembly members, thereby restricting debate in the assembly. The chief minister was nonetheless able to block accountability for this situation.[61]

Nonetheless it is worth exploring briefly the extent of state/regional powers as a precedent, and their powers, at least as they are constitutionally established, are indeed quite broad, offering scope potentially for dynamic government.[62] They include housing and development planning; agriculture, fisheries, mining, and forestry; energy, transport, and infrastructure; and social welfare and culture. It can be added here that it is assumed state/regions also have authority over local government, and they have indeed passed municipal laws.[63] The

[55] 2008 Constitution, s 195(a)(i).

[56] ibid s 248.

[57] Asia Foundation, *State and Region Governments in Myanmar* (New Edition, 2018) 10, 16. See further the Region or State Government Law 2010, and the Region or State Hluttaw Law 2013, which supplement the constitutional provisions.

[58] I Holliday, Maw Htun Aung and C Joelene, 'Institution building in Myanmar: The establishment of regional and state assemblies' (2015) 55(4) *Asian Survey* 641.

[59] ibid 663.

[60] Asia Foundation (n 57).

[61] Holliday et al (n 58) 655.

[62] See s 180, and Schedule 2.

[63] Schedule 2 mentions municipal taxation and town and housing as a power belonging to the states/regions. The Constitutional Tribunal has also endorsed the regional lower of passing municipal laws, see above.

2010–21 period saw gradually increasing decentralisation to states/regions, especially after the change in the union government in 2015, and that is an experience that can form a basis for more thorough decentralisation in future.[64]

UNDP reported in 2019 on the state/region *hluttaws* as follows:

> the practices of the Region and State Hluttaws have evolved and have differentiated rapidly from the common institutional foundation that was put in place … recently as five years ago. The Mon and Shan State Hluttaws have made parliamentary decision-making more inclusive than originally foreseen, the Mandalay Region Hluttaw has developed its own mechanism for inquiries and the Tanintharyi Region Hluttaw has put in place an effective mechanism for managing a problematic budget review process. The practices of the Hluttaws are evolving rapidly, and the legal and procedural framework underpinning their work needs to follow suit.[65]

III. NATIONAL RACES MINISTERS

The National Races Ministers are a unique feature of Myanmar's constitutional arrangements that was introduced in the 2008 Constitution, and have great relevance to territorial governance. The ethnic diversity of Myanmar, as we have seen, is expressed primarily through the designation of ethnic states. But of course, ethnicity is distributed in complex ways, so that minority communities often live in another minority's homeland state, or in a majority Bamar region, and Bamar majority communities too live in those minority homeland states.[66] Given that there is no specifically ethnic as opposed to regional representation in the union parliament, as we have seen, the need arises to ensure that minority communities are given voice in the state/regional assemblies, in order to protect their interests. Alternatively, there was the possibility for such communities, where concentrated in a particular sub-regional area, to apply for status as a self-adminstered zone or district (SAZ or SAD), but that possibility is no longer available, and the requirements were not easily satisfied.[67] Under the 2008 Constitution, the union is required to assist in developing the language, literature, fine arts and culture of the national races; to promote solidarity, mutual amity and respect and mutual assistance among the national races; to promote socio-economic development including education, health, economy, transport and communication, and so forth, of less-developed national races.[68] Accordingly, representatives of national races with a suitable population are

[64] Asia Foundation (n 57) 91.

[65] UNDP, *Situation Analysis of Myanmar's Region and State Hluttaws: Functioning, Practices, and Challenges* (2019) 53. A similar conclusion is reached in Enlightened Myanmar Research Foundation, *Performance Analysis: State and Region Hluttaws (Local Legislatures) of Myanmar (2010–2015)* (Yangon, 2017).

[66] See further, p 151ff.

[67] See the following section for discussion of these.

[68] 2008 Constitution, s 22. See also the rights set out in ss 354, 365.

entitled to participate in the legislature of regions or states and self-administered areas.[69]

State/regional assemblies are formed by the election of two representatives from each township,[70] and representatives of each national race determined by the authorities concerned as having a population which constitutes 0.1 per cent and above of the population of the union. The government appears to recognise 135 races as satisfying the 0.1 per cent benchmark, but of course the entitlement applies only to races that have not already in that region their own named state, region, or self-administered area, where by definition they would be in a majority.[71] For this purpose the vote is given to members of the national races to elect such representatives.[72] The representatives are given special status by being referred to as 'Ministers for National Races' (MNRs), and being allowed on request to participate in state/region cabinet meetings. In addition, a new Ministry for National Races Affairs was created at the union level in 2015, under the Rights of National Races Protection Law.

Resulting from these provisions 29 MNRs were elected, with the express task of highlighting national races affairs.[73] The number varies from none (Chin State) to seven (Shan State) according to the state/region, and the Bamar and Karen have the highest number of MNRs, with representation in five of seven states. Ambiguity surrounded these officials, in that their status appeared to lie somewhere between elected representatives and members of the executive. It took an early decision of the Constitutional Tribunal to clarify that they should be accorded the considerable status and privileges of full ministers in the state/regional government, despite the fact that they may attend cabinet meetings only by invitation.[74]

The MNRs represent an innovative attempt to include ethnic minority voices where the electoral process might prevent those voices being heard. Given greater clarity around their role, this idea could be developed further in future.

IV. SELF-ADMINISTERED AREAS

Under the 2008 Constitution ethnic minorities, in addition to being served by MNRs at the state/ regional level, had the possibility of self-identifying

[69] ibid s 15. See also s 17.

[70] ibid s 161(a).

[71] ibid s 161(b).

[72] ibid s 391. This does not include the Rohingya people of Rakhine state, who do not have citizenship. The decision is made by the Union election Commission: s 262(a)(iv).

[73] Ardeth Thawnghmung and Yadana, 'Citizenship and minority rights: The role of National Race Affairs Ministers in Myanmar 2008 Constitution', in A South and M Lall (ed), *Citizenship in Myanmar: Ways of Being in and from Burma* (Copenhagen, NIAS, 2018) 113.

[74] Constitutional Tribunal, Case 2/2011; see also Case 2/2012 on the right to appeal this decision, and Case 1/2014 on the definition of national races; and the discussion in Crouch (n 9) 135ff.

in geographical areas where they predominated, and thereby attain special powers as a SAZ or SAD.[75] This facility applied only individually to each of the 135 national races[76] that did not already have a state/region of their own. Applications were determined only as part of, not a result of, the constitution-making process, and decisions were taken as early as 1995, taking effect only in 2010. Certain conditions applied. Determinations were based on geographically contiguous townships in each of which (at least two) the ethnic group concerned could show a majority of the population based on census data. There are four SAZs in Shan State (the largest of Myanmar's states), one in Sagaing Region, grouping two or three townships;[77] and there is one SAD, also in Shan State, grouping six townships in two districts amalgamated to form the Wa SAD.[78]

SAZs and SADs are of equal status. The administrative arm of the SAZ/ SAD is the Leading Body, comprising 10 members, including state/regional assembly members elected to represent townships in the SAZ/ SAD area, elected MNRs from the area, and military personnel. There is also an executive committee comprising three to five members of the Leading Body.[79]

The legislative and executive powers of the SAZs/ SADs[80] are set out in the Third Schedule to the 2008 Constitution, and are in essence little greater than those of the townships that form them. They are: law and order; development matters, urban and rural projects; roads and bridges; public health and various environmental functions; markets; and water and electricity. The SAZ/SADs could be advanced to a status resembling states/regions in future, with the possibility of resolving the identity/diversity problem via this innovative approach of self-identification.

V. LOCAL GOVERNMENT

Local government in Burma/ Myanmar has a long history.[81] As was mentioned above, the colonial government upended the system of village administration. However, it left behind many laws covering all aspects of local government, and

[75] Law on Self-Administered Areas 2010. See, further, M Crouch, 'Ethnic rights and constitutional changes: The recognition of ethnic nationalities in Myanmar/Burma' ch 6 in A Harding and M Sidel (eds), *Central-Local Relations in Asian Constitutional Systems* (Oxford, Hart Publishing, 2015); Crouch (n 9) 140ff.

[76] The figure 135 does not appear in any official document so far as can be ascertained. However, it is very commonly assumed in the literature to reflect accurately the demography of Myanmar.

[77] They are the Danu, Kokang, Naga, Palaung, Pa-O SAZs.

[78] These are simply prescribed by the 2008 Constitution at s 51 and cannot be altered except via constitutional amendment. This is in contrast to the continuing right of Indonesian villages to apply for customary status: See p 62.

[79] Self-Administered Zone or Self-Administered Division Leading Body Law 2020, ss 4–6.

[80] See ss 9, 196 and 277.

[81] For a summary history, see *Municipal Governance in Myanmar: An Overview of Development Affairs Organisations* (Asia Foundation, 2015) 1–3.

extending to all types of local government, from Rangoon (Yangon) itself to towns, villages and village tracts.[82] In this section we examine in outline territorial governance at the local, that is sub-regional level, which entails consideration of townships, districts, and wards/village tracts.

A. Townships

Townships are the most important of the sub-regional governments, with substantial powers. They are assisted by Development Affairs Organisations (DAOs), which are overseen by Township Development Affairs Committees (TDACs, normally called 'municipal committees).[83] Despite their name townships cover all rural as well as urban areas in Myanmar. Their areas also act as the 330 constituencies for national and state/regional elections. Their average population is around 160,000.[84]

The first Municipal Act was enacted for Lower Burma in 1874. Local government law was extended to Upper Burma with the 1887 Municipal Act, and then in 1898 a Municipal Act was enacted, covering the entire country, including frontier areas. Town municipal committees, recently reintroduced, date from the 1898 Act. This law framed local government for almost a century until it was repealed in 1993, and its structures continued to inform the development of local government after the opening of Myanmar in 2010. After independence, a Democratic Local Government Act was passed in 1953, providing for local elections. This law was suspended in 1961, but pilot projects implementing it had been implemented across ten districts.[85] The Municipal Act was replaced with a Development Committees Law in 1993, replaced in turn by municipal laws passed at state/regional level from 2013. During the period of military rule (1962–2010) there was no local self-government, and local services were run by development affairs organisations under the direct authority of the military government.[86]

The National League for Democracy, led by Aung San Su Kyi, won the 2015 general election, which signalled state/region *hluttaws* to enact or amend the existing municipal laws (several had been enacted in 2013 under the USDP government) forming TDAC/municipal committees.[87] Most of these are formed with a majority of elected members, of whom one will be the chair.[88] The

[82] These are set out in The Burma Code, vol vi (Rangoon, Government of the Union of Burma, 1948). The Municipal Act 1898 and the City of Rangoon Municipal Act 1922 are the most extensive and impressive laws in this collection.

[83] M Arnold, Ye Thu Aung, S Kempel and Kyi Pyar Chit Saw, *Myanmar: Overview of Development Affairs Organisations* (Asia Foundation and MDRI, 2015).

[84] UNDP (n 65) 46.

[85] Asia Foundation (n 57) 61.

[86] Arnold et al (n 83) 7.

[87] Asia Foundation (n 57) 62ff.

[88] See eg Municipal Law 2013, s 12 (Chin State).

municipal committees hold office for a period of five years, which is coterminous with that of the state assembly.[89] As may be expected in a decentralised system, the position varies as to the extent of democracy at this level. Some townships are led by appointed committees, while some others are elected, not (except for Yangon) on a universal franchise, like the union and regional governments, but indirectly via a system of household representatives. The functions of municipal committees again vary, but they are major service providers, generally with functions relating to development planning; water, sewage, drains and garbage collection; roads, bridges, and street lighting; issuing business and market licences; collecting taxes and fees; and disaster management.[90] In short, their functions are those typical of local government across the region.

Apart from carrying out these functions, municipal committees are important in that they are the only decentralised bodies under the control of the state/regional governments, and the only local governments supervised by an elected committee. There is usually a citizen complaints mechanism with appeals. The committees have broad discretion as to the use of their revenues, although their budgets must be reported to, and their decisions are subject to overruling by the state/regional government. They form an important link between townships and state/regional governments.[91]

The most developed municipal committee is that of Yangon, Myanmar's largest city. Under the Yangon Municipal Law 2018 its committee has eleven members, six of whom are elected on a universal franchise. By contrast a ten-member council governing the capital city Naypyidaw is simply appointed by the President.[92] Its administration is extensive, with seven functional working groups and three general departments.[93] In the working groups, one committee member is chair and the group comprises also technical officers and a secretary. This law also abolishes districts in Yangon Region, so that all powers are vested in the region government and the municipal committees. Its structure allows for the management of no less than 33 townships. Yangon, like Mandalay and the union territory of Naypyidaw, has a Mayor appointed by the regional (or in the case of Naypyidaw, the union) government.[94]

B. Districts

Myanmar's 74 districts are amorphous institutions that are organised with departments and a district committee, but have few actual functions, being

[89] ibid ss 4–6.
[90] Asia Foundation (n 57) 52.
[91] ibid 61.
[92] ibid 16.
[93] Yangon Municipal Law 2018, s 26.
[94] ibid s 1.

concerned principally with oversight, monitoring, communications, coordination, budgetary matters, and dealing with abuses of power and dispute resolution with regard to lower levels of government. They are not subject to democratic oversight, and offer ways in which the GAD is able to supervise local government. As with median local institutions generally, it is not clear that their roles justify their occupying such a median position in the system of territorial governance, being above the townships, wards and village tracts, but below the state/regional governments. It is suggested that in a reformed system they should be converted into simply being district offices of the regional government, which largely already exist under departments of the regional governments, thereby simplifying the structure, increasing oversight, and empowering the higher and lower levels of government.[95]

C. Wards, Village Tracts and Villages

We now come to the lowest level of local government, the wards/village tracts. Townships are made up of both wards in urban areas and village tracts, which have powers equal to those of wards, in rural areas. The 2008 Constitution does not make provision for local government at this level. It merely states that 'administration of ward or village tract shall be assigned in accord with the law to a person whose integrity is respected by the community'.[96] The implications of this are, however, considerable. First, it entails reverting to the pre-colonial system of local leadership. Second, in 2012 a Ward and Village Tract Administration Law was passed, introducing a measure of democracy in the selection of Ward Administrators and Village Tract Administrators (W/VTAs). This was a measure aimed at controlling local corruption in land matters.[97] They are now elected, not in the same way as state/regional *hluttaws* or parliament, via universal franchise, but via a more traditional step process. Household heads elect 10-household heads; 10-household heads then elect 100-household heads; and 100-household heads elect the W/TVA. Elections were held for the first time in January 2016, and around 100,000 candidates across Myanmar contested for 16,785 seats as W/VTA.[98]

Research on state/regional and municipal governance lays great emphasis on the importance of W/TVAs in terms of two-way communication supporting the higher levels of government, especially the elected members, and acting as a crucial link in the chain of governance, between the people and regional/

[95] Asia Foundation (n 57) 58.

[96] 2008 Constitution, s 289.

[97] HM Kyed, AP Harrisson, and G McCarthy, *Local Democracy in Myanmar: Reflections on Ward and Village Tract Elections in 2016* (Danish Institute for International Studies, 2016) 3.

[98] ibid 2. For background on local democracy, see Aung Myat Kyaw, *Study on Myanma Democratic Local Organisations and Laws* (Yangon, Win Win Kyaw Press, 2013).

township government.[99] The formal functions of these officials are set out in the 2012 Law.[100] They act as regulators and resolve local disputes.

One study reports as follows:

> Ward and village tract administrators have diverse roles and functions. When citizens want to apply for a new job, get a household certificate, a national registration card or do a land transaction, they must first pass through their ward and village tract administrators for recommendation letters. Local administrators are also the main mediators in petty crimes and civil disputes, when these cannot be resolved within the family. With the advent of local development funds, they also play increasingly important roles in local development. Because the administrators are now chairs of the Land Management Committee at the local level, they are also key actors in handling land issues, which is not least significant at a time when land disputes are increasing.[101]

Yet the point of interest is that, in many respects local leadership has reverted to the roles it fulfilled historically, prior to colonial intervention.

VI. TERRITORIAL GOVERNANCE DURING THE CIVIL WAR

Carrying on any form of territorial governance during a civil war with shifting de facto control in many areas obviously presents enormous difficulties. During the long period of persistent if intermittent hostilities between the SAC and EAOs from the 1940s to date peripheral areas have been under hybrid control as regards local governance, with EAOs and customary leaders responsible in practice for service delivery.[102]

In areas under NUG control at the time of writing, territorial governance is being reconstructed irrespective of the 2008 Constitution, but in accordance with the Federal Democracy Charter. In March 2024 the NUG announced 'comprehensive interim implementation of local administration and social services' in the townships it controls. Local administration is seen by the NUG as providing post-coup stability, and is set to expand to districts, wards, village tracts and villages, according to the security situation. The intention is to provide a federal approach for the whole of Myanmar. Despite the extremely adverse conditions, local governments have been established in no less than 173 townships (that is, in 85 per cent of all those in the regions, the states being in general still under the control of EAOs), and 10 districts. As an indication of the extent of the actual

[99] ibid; and UNDP, *Situation Analysis of Myanmar's Region and State Hluttaws: Functioning, Practices, and Challenges* (2019).

[100] 32 of these are listed, but most are minor regulatory, law and order, data collection, or reporting functions.

[101] Kyed et al (n 97) 2.

[102] K Jolliffe, *Ethnic Armed Conflict and Territorial Administration in Myanmar* (Asia Foundation, 2015).

services provided, these local governments currently run nearly 6,000 schools with 61,000 teachers and 728,000 pupils; and 77 hospitals and 177 clinics, reaching more than 750,000 patients. Local governments also provide policing and revenue collection.[103]

VII. CONCLUSION

Territorial governance is the most critical factor for Myanmar's future in terms of peace-making and implementing both federalism and democracy.[104] The chances of these depend heavily on participatory governance at all levels, not just at the level of states/regions. Decentralisation is a critical stepping stone towards a lasting system of subnational governance. Crucially, local governments can contribute significantly to development and effective delivery of public services.

The increased centralisation of powers under military rule encountered to some extent a counter-balance under the NLD government of 2016–21, in decentralised powers subject to increasing democratic oversight. As we have seen, there were constraining factors inhibiting decentralisation, which involved all three aspects – political, administrative, and fiscal. However, research has revealed an increased level of independence and assertiveness amongst the state/regional assemblies during 2013–18. And elements of democratic oversight have emerged at township and ward/village tract levels too. It is hardly surprising that it would take time after half a century of aggressive centralisation of power for such a situation to begin to develop from a standing start and very little collective experience. As at 31 January 2021 there was every prospect that a system of this kind would continue to develop in such a way as to effect genuine decentralisation. The time will no doubt come when this experience can be built upon to construct a new system of territorial governance in Myanmar. This chapter has attempted to explore the issues that will arise and lay out the experience of territorial governance at all three levels during the decade of democracy.

[103] Republic of the Union of Myanmar, National Unity Government, Central Committee for Interim Implementation of Local Administration and Social Services, 20 March 2024.

[104] M Breen, *The Road to Federalism in Nepal, Myanmar and Sri Lanka: Finding the Middle Ground* (Abingdon, Routledge, 2018).

6

The Philippines

'He who does not love the national language is worse than a smelly fish': Filipino proverb.

THE PHILIPPINES PRESENTS the most advanced and sophisticated system of territorial governance in Southeast Asia. This may also be seen as a necessity in a highly diverse society where more than 100 million people sharing more than 7,000 islands are divided by ethnicity, religion, history, culture, and geography.[1] What accounts for this system is that centralisation was never a very concerted effort or successful project in Philippine history until the Marcos dictatorship, which occupied only 14 years, implementing an extreme form of militarised centralisation.[2] One reaction to the Marcos era was the enactment under the 1987 Constitution of a Local Government Code 1991 ('the Code') designed to ensure that centralised dictatorship would not be repeated.[3] Under the aegis of the Code, the Philippines has decentralised powers to an extent that some propose taking matters further – towards a federal structure, a matter discussed later in this chapter.

In chapter two we looked briefly at the history of territorial governance in the Philippines, its political culture of localism, and its post-independence efforts towards decentralisation. We saw also how Article X of the 1987 Constitution provides for the basic principles of territorial governance, making extensive provision for local autonomy, and requiring the enactment of a local government code.[4] This chapter looks at the structure and merits of the system of territorial governance as it is now, more than 30 years after the Code was enacted. The Code itself, described as 'by far the most radical piece

[1] BDG Tiojanco, 'The Philippine people power constitution: Social cohesion through integrated diversity' ch 10 in JL Neo and Bui Ngoc Son (ed), *Pluralist Constitutions in Southeast Asia* (Oxford, Hart Publishing, 2019).

[2] NG Owen (ed), *The Emergence of Southeast Asia: A New History* (Singapore, Singapore University Press, 2005) ch 33.

[3] S Shair-Rosenfeld, 'The Causes and Effects of the Local Government Code in the Philippines Locked in a Status Quo of Weakly Decentralised Authority?' (2016) 33(2) *Journal of Southeast Asian Economics* 157, 159.

[4] Article X, s 3.

of legislation in the nation's history',[5] implements Article X, in no fewer than 536 sections, with strikingly comprehensive forethought on every aspect of territorial governance

An important part of the structure that emerged after 1987 is the provision for special autonomy, which is considered in chapter ten, as part of a discussion, also in Part III, of the other cases of special autonomy in Indonesia and Malaysia, and is therefore not covered in this chapter.

I. HISTORY OF TERRITORIAL GOVERNANCE

Prior to Spanish colonial intervention the Philippines, an archipelago of more than 7,000 islands, was not a unitary state. In the country's original state, the *barangay* (villages), under the leadership of local *datu*, who were originally hereditary leaders, but converted into elective ones by a law of 1786, were largely independent, forming the basic political and societal unit.[6] They remain to this day a natural focus of localism, evidenced by the fact that the Code makes more extensive provision for *barangay*[7] than for any of the other local governments. In 1978 President Marcos introduced the *Katarungang Pambarangay* Law (law on village justice), which formally reestablished traditional dispute resolution at the village level, and this system is continued in the Code.[8] The *barangay* will be discussed later in this chapter.

The colonial period involved two phases: the Spanish period (1565–1898), and the American period (1898–1946). Although the latter period was shorter, it immediately preceded independence and impacted more heavily on territorial governance, in diluting the centralisation that was characteristic of the Spanish colony. In 1899, the short-lived revolutionary Malolos Constitution created municipal and provincial assemblies, and promised decentralisation. During the American period elements of local autonomy were placed within a structure that was sufficiently centralised to ensure a smooth transition to independence. President McKinley's Instructions to the Philippine Commission in 1900 actually prioritised the establishment of self-governing municipal governments, and the overall trend was towards provincial autonomy.

> [A]s a consequence of the struggle of US administrators to reconcile this tension between their commitment to Tocquevillian ideals of local self-rule and their perceived need for more direct bureaucratic enforcement in key policy areas, the

[5] A Brillantes, 'Issues and trends in local government in the Philippines' in *The Local Government Code: An Assessment* (Institute of Government and Law Reform, University of the Philippines Law Center, 1999).

[6] DGE Hall, *A History of South-East Asia*, 2nd edn (London, Macmillan, 1964) 231.

[7] 56 sections, compared to 8 for municipalities and 10 for cities.

[8] PD 1508/1978. See G Tabucanon, J Wall and Wan Yan, 'Philippine Community Mediation, *Katarungang Pambarangay*' (2008) *Journal of Dispute Resolution* 501.

> Philippine governance structure evolved into a dysfunctional mix of political decentralisation, a weak system of local oversight, and a selectively interventionist central bureaucracy.[9]

Post-independence, a Local Autonomy Act was passed in 1959 and a Decentralisation Act in 1967.[10] The 1973 Constitution too embraced local autonomy in principle, but martial law under Marcos prevented any further decentralisation. A Local Government Code was passed in 1983, but did not in practice confer greater autonomy on local governments.[11]

Following the 'EDSA' revolution of 1986, Article X of the 1987 Constitution listed provinces, cities, municipalities, and *barangay* as subdivisions of the Republic enjoying local autonomy.[12] It required the passing of a code to 'provide for a more responsive and local government structure instituted through a system of decentralisation with effective mechanisms of recall, initiative, and referendum, [and] allocate among the local government units their powers, responsibilities, and resources …'.[13] Local governments were empowered to create their own sources of revenue, and were to be accorded a just share of national taxes.[14] Importantly, they were to be 'entitled to an equitable share in the proceeds of the utilisation and development of the national wealth within their respective areas, in the manner provided by law, including sharing the same with the inhabitants by way of direct benefits.'[15] Local government units could not be created, divided, merged, abolished, or have their boundaries substantially altered except with the approval of a majority of votes in a plebiscite in the units directly affected.[16] It was these principles, entrenching local autonomy, that the Code was designed to implement.

Under the Code the number of provinces and cities has increased, and there are now 82 provinces; 149 cities, 38 of which are designated as independent cities, having the same powers as a province; 1,489 municipalities; and 42,029 *barangay*.[17]

[9] R Matsuzaki, *State-Building by Imposition: Resistance and Control in Colonial Taiwan and the Philippines* (Ithaca, Cornell University Press, 2019) 135.

[10] Republic Acts Nos 2264, 5185. See also the Barrio Charter Act 1960, Republic Act 2370. For a history of decentralisation legislation, see TSE Tadem and MEL Atienza (eds), *A Better Metro Manila? Towards Responsible Local Governance, Decentralisation, and Equitable Development* (Singapore, Palgrave Macmillan, 2023) 31ff.

[11] *Batas Pambansa Blg* 337.

[12] Article X, ss 1–2; also, Article II, s 25. The Local Government Code 1991, Republic Act No 7160, ss 2, 3 go further in requiring decentralisation of 'more powers, authority, responsibilities, and resources'.

[13] Article X, s 3.

[14] ibid ss 5, 6.

[15] ibid s 7.

[16] ibid s 10.

[17] In 1991, immediately prior to the Code, the relevant numbers were respectively 75; 60; 1,543; and 41,820: World Bank and Asian Development Bank, *Decentralisation in the Philippines:*

In 1991, fulfilling the remit set out in Article X, the Code was passed into law.[18] It governs all general aspects of local government structures, elections, procedures, and powers; officials, their discipline and accountability; intergovernmental relations; taxation and fiscal arrangements; and many other matters. Since it applies to all four kinds of subnational units,[19] it is in effect a comprehensive code for territorial governance. In fact, the Code is by far the most impressive and thoughtful piece of local government legislation amongst the five countries under discussion, requiring virtually no assistance from other legislation enacted in the Philippines either before or since, save for some purely sectoral legislation. This chapter therefore inevitably takes mainly the form of a discussion of the Code, highlighting those matters of comparative significance.

II. GENERAL PRINCIPLES AND THEIR JUDICIAL INTERPRETATION

Some general matters and binding principles are best indicated at the outset.

The principles set out in Article X are largely repeated in sections 2 and 3 of the Code, which stress local autonomy, and the decentralisation of powers; legality; and democratic accountability via consultation, recalls, initiatives, and referenda. They also demand administrative efficiency, dynamism, and ecological balance, as well as adequate resources for local governments.

The judiciary has played a very important part in shaping territorial governance, and extracting principles from a mass of detailed statutory provisions. There is no real equivalent to this in any of the other four jurisdictions under discussion, in which judicial decisions have been of certainly some, but not overriding, importance, and have not always had a positive effect.[20]

One aspect that is unusual and of comparative interest is the manner in which the Code deals with the interpretation of local government powers. In territorial governance generally, much depends on judicial interpretation of powers that are generally expressed briefly and vaguely in local-government legislation. After all, can one say definitively what is meant by such terms as 'public health', or 'development', let alone 'autonomy' or 'supervision'? Thus local governments often have to take legal advice as to whether a particular proposal is within their powers. The normal rule in common law jurisdictions is that local government powers have to be specifically granted by statute and are subject

Strengthening Local Government Financing and Resource Management in the Short Term (Manila, 2005) 7. The increase in the number of cities is remarkable. All 38 independent cities have been created under the Code's dispensation (see below) for creating 'highly urbanised cities'.

[18] For comprehensive legal analysis of the Code, see AQ Pimentel, *The Local Government Code Revisited* (Central Book Supply, 2011); D Gatmaytan, *Local Government Law and Jurisprudence*, 2 vols (Diliman, College of Law, University of the Philippines, 2018).

[19] The Code also applies in areas of special autonomy, absent any special alternative provision: s 526.

[20] See eg pp 58ff.

to the overriding principle that local authorities cannot act ultra vires, that is, beyond the powers they are given by statute. Nonetheless their powers are held to include any powers that are reasonably incidental to the statutory powers they are accorded.[21] In most jurisdictions statute law on local government is silent on the issue of interpretation, save for a few salient definitions, and interpretation is left to the judiciary without specific guidance. However, the Philippine Code makes useful provision supplementing the common law rule, in effect implicitly embracing the principles of subsidiarity and localism, whilst also empowering the judiciary to determine in a creative fashion the extent of local autonomy. Section 5 provides that in the interpretation of the provisions of the Code,

> [a]ny provision on a power of a local government unit shall be liberally interpreted in its favor, and in case of doubt, any question thereon shall be resolved in favor of devolution of powers and of the lower local government unit. Any fair and reasonable doubt as to the existence of the power shall be interpreted in favor of the local government unit concerned.

It goes on to give general welfare provisions in the Code an explicitly developmental purpose, in that they are to be 'liberally interpreted to give more powers to local government units in accelerating economic development and upgrading the quality of life for the people in the community'.[22] On this theme section 16 on general welfare broadens the potential scope of local government duties to an almost breath-taking extent:

> Every local government unit shall exercise the powers expressly granted, those necessarily implied therefrom, as well as powers necessary, appropriate, or incidental for its efficient and effective governance, and those which are essential to the promotion of the general welfare. Within their respective territorial jurisdictions, local government units shall ensure and support, among other things, the preservation and enrichment of culture, promote health and safety, enhance the right of the people to a balanced ecology, encourage and support the development of appropriate and self-reliant scientific and technological capabilities, improve public morals, enhance economic prosperity and social justice, promote full employment among their residents, maintain peace and order, and preserve the comfort and convenience of their inhabitants.[23]

These provisions take the matter a good distance beyond the strict common law ultra vires rule. And in pursuance of a flexible, practical approach the Code even adds, for good measure, that, 'in the resolution of controversies arising under

[21] In the Philippines the expression is, 'necessary, appropriate, or incidental to efficient and effective provision of the basic services and facilities …': Code, s 17(a).

[22] Code, s 5(c). These principles are not, however, and quite naturally, applicable to taxing powers, which are, as with national taxation powers, construed strictly against local governments in favour of the taxpayer: s 5(b).

[23] For a striking instance of judicial application of s 16, see *Tano v Socrates*, GR No 110247 (1997); and see *Rural Bank of Makati v Makati*, 433 SCRA 362 (2004) ('power to exercise just about any act that will benefit their constituencies').

this Code where no legal provision or jurisprudence applies, resort may be had to the customs and traditions in the place where the controversies take place'.[24] This way of iterating the subject creates a welcome flexibility and encouragement towards innovation and dynamic development that would be supported by judicial scrutiny rather than crushed by what is sometimes termed 'the austerity of tabulated legalism'.

The Supreme Court wasted no time in affirming subsidiarity and localism in its first major case on the Code, *San Juan v CSC*:

> The task of genuine regional democracy is blocked and put back if [a government official] jealously hoards all discretionary authority and lacks the ability of local councils to develop self-reliance and resoluteness in the management of their own funds ... Our national authorities must respect not only the fundamental guarantees of local sovereignty, but also the spirit of liberty that these laws are founded on.[25]

However, in their decisions on local government the Supreme Court has tended to take a nuanced and balanced view, recognising the ultra vires rule, which (it should be noted) places legal limits on presidential oversight as well as local autonomy. In a case in the same year the Supreme Court cautioned that 'the principle of local autonomy under the 1987 Constitution simply means "decentralisation" ... It does not make local governments sovereign within the state or an "imperium in imperio."'[26] And in another 1991 case the same court pointed out that '[a]utonomy ... does not plan to break the partnership and interdependence between the central government and local government units, nor does it intend to usher in a federalist system ... Local governments are governed by the Constitution, but only to a certain extent, and for no other reason than to improve self-government'.[27] In *San Juan* the court also distinguished supervision and oversight, so that supervision involves interference, not to overrule, but to deal with dereliction of duty.[28] In line with Article X the Supreme Court has even refused to allow the government to appoint a caretaker leader of a *barangay*.[29] *Pimentel v Aguirre* is even more striking, given courts' general reluctance to intervene in budgetary matters. A presidential order withholding 10 per cent of local governments' internal revenue allotment was struck down for encroaching on the fiscal autonomy of local governments.[30]

[24] Code, s 5(e).

[25] *San Juan v CSC*, GR No 9229 (1991); see also the strong statement of the court in *Disomangcorp v Secretary of the Department of Public Works and Highways*, GR No 149848 (2004).

[26] *Basco v Philippine Amusement and Gaming Corp*, GR No 91649, 14 May 1991.

[27] *Ganzon v Court of Appeals*, GR Nos 93252, 93746 & 95245 (1991). See also *City of Manila v Laguio*, GR No 118127 (2005) for a strict application of the ultra vires rule, notwithstanding the Code's provisions on interpretation.

[28] Above, n 24. See also *Joson v Executive Secretary*, 290 SCRA 279 (1998).

[29] *National Ligangmga Barangay v Paredes*, GR Nos 130775 & 131939 (2004).

[30] GR No 132988 (2000). See also *Province of Batangas v Romulo*, 429 SCRA 736 (2004); *Alternative Center for Organisational Reforms and Development Inc v Zamora*, 459 SCRA 578 (2005).

The Supreme Court has nonetheless also made it clear that local government powers must be squarely based on law, limiting the scope of the general welfare clause by holding that the Code 'does not grant a local government agency blanket power to legislate on any matter it deems appropriate in the name of promoting the public interest'.[31] In another case it held it could not 'give judicial permission to a municipal government agency exercising its delegated right of eminent domain in violation of the statute that gave it that power'.[32] And where individual rights are concerned the Supreme Court takes a less expansive view of the general welfare provision. A law must

> conform to the following substantive requirements: (1) must not contravene the Constitution or any statute; (2) must not be unfair or oppressive; (3) must not be partial or discriminatory; (4) must not prohibit but may regulate trade; (5) must be general and … consistent with public policy; and (6) must not be unreasonable … There is no question that not even the strongest moral conviction or the most urgent public need, subject only to a few notable exceptions, will excuse the bypassing of an individual's rights.[33]

This reasoning is well illustrated by the case of *Lucena Grand Central Terminal, Inc v JAC Liner, Inc*, a case in which a city council prohibited the operation of all bus and jeepney terminals in the city, including existing ones, allowing only one common terminal outside the city. Operators were compelled to close their existing terminals and use the city's facilities. The Supreme Court invalidated the ordinance, holding that it could only be justified on the basis that public interest, not the interest of a particular class of persons, required interference, and that the means employed were reasonably necessary for the attainment of the object, not discriminatory, and not unduly oppressive upon individuals.[34]

The overall impact of these cases is to refuse to either local governments or central government the full range of powers they would no doubt ideally wish to enjoy, maintaining a balance that speaks to good governance as equally important to the advancement of other developmental desirables.[35]

It is also relevant that, unlike elsewhere, administration, it is held, does not have to strictly follow decision-making powers. For example, the Supreme Court has held that provinces can, in terms of the President's power of supervision of local governments, be constitutionally grouped for administrative purposes because the power to make political decisions remains with the units as constitutionally defined.[36]

[31] *Mosqueda v Pilipino Banana Growers and Exporters Association Inc*, GR Nos 189185 & 189305 (2016).

[32] *Heirs of Suguitan v City of Mandaluyong*, GR No 135087 (2000).

[33] *Legaspi v City of Cebu*, GR No 159110 (2013).

[34] GR No 148339 (2005). See also *Magtajas v Pryce Properties Corporation Inc*, GR No 111097 (1994); *City of Manila v Laguio* GR No 118127 (2005).

[35] See further, Gatmaytan (n 18) 12ff; GNM Sartillo, 'Restricted decentralisation: A review of Supreme Court decisions on Philippine local autonomy', Conference Paper, Chennai, India (2021), at eudl.eu/pdf/10-4108/eai.7-6-2021.2308582.

[36] *Chiongbian v Orbos*, GR No 96754 (1995); Constitution, Article X, s 13.

III. DIFFERENT UNITS, COMMON STRUCTURES

The Code makes detailed provision for each type of local government, its powers and procedures, its elected officials, its *sanggunian* (elected local council), and its entire range of administrative officers. And of course, fiscal matters also receive very detailed attention.[37]

The provisions relating to the different units of local government follow closely a set pattern irrespective of the type of local government in question. The *barangay* are in some respects an exception, and are dealt with separately.

A. Creation

First, the existential question. The Code makes extensive provision for the creation, conversion, merger, division, and abolition of local governments, which may only be done by Congress with the consent of the electorate in a plebiscite.[38] In this way the system allows for demographic change, and, as we have seen, the number of local government units, especially cities, has increased over the last three decades.

A *barangay* may be created out of a contiguous territory which has a population of at least 2,000 inhabitants (or in urban areas 5,000), provided this does not reduce the population of the original *barangay(s)* to less than this minimum requirement.[39] A municipality may be created if it meets an average annual income requirement,[40] has a population of at least 25,000 inhabitants, and a contiguous territory of at least 50 sq km. Similar requirements apply to a province, which must have a population exceeding 250,000, and contiguous territory exceeding 2,000 sq km.[41]

There is one exception in the case of *barangay*. The Code, in a nod towards pluralism, makes special provision 'to enhance the delivery of basic services in the indigenous cultural communities', which may be a minority in their local government area. In this instance *barangay* may be created in such communities simply by an Act of Congress.[42]

The case of cities is more complex. The Code recognises them as being either components of provinces, equivalent to municipalities, or fully independent of, and having similar status to, provinces.[43] The latter variety are referred to as

[37] Code, Book II.

[38] 1987 Constitution, Article X(10), and Code, ss 6–10. Further provision, including not just process but substantive requirements, is made for *barangay* by ss 385–86, for municipalities by ss 441–42, and for cities by ss 449–50. Sections 451–52 recognise cities as being either components of provinces or fully independent of provinces.

[39] Code, s 386.

[40] ie, for the last two years, based on 1991 prices.

[41] Code, s 461.

[42] ibid s 385.

[43] ibid ss 451–52.

'highly urbanised cities', and are required to have more than 200,000 inhabitants and comply with a city income requirement.[44] This provision is very helpful in terms of Ran Hirschl's proposal that cities deserve constitutional recognition as such, and as a device for dealing with the rapidity of development, which tends to outstrip legal definitions and boundaries, drawn up on the basis of a different set of facts.[45] So far no less than 38 cities have achieved this highly urbanised status since 1991.

B. Officials, their Powers and Duties

Each local government has a chief executive (the governor, mayor or, for *barangay*, the captain), and a deputy who also (mirror-imaging the functions of the Vice-President of the Republic itself) acts as chair of the local *sanggunian*.[46] The Code sets out at length the powers and duties of these elected officials.[47] The term of office of all elective local officials is three years, and no official may serve more than three consecutive terms.[48]

Legislative power is exercised by the *sangguniang panlalawigan* (provincial council), the *sangguniang panlungsod* (city council), *sangguniang bayan* (municipal council), or *sangguniang barangay* (village council), as the case may be. The Code makes extensive provision for democracy and good governance in the legislative process, even prescribing legislative committees, standing orders, rules about disclosure of interests, and so on.[49]

In terms of the subject matters over which local governments have jurisdiction, the approach is somewhat different from that of the other countries under discussion, where distinct functions are allocated to different levels of government, with provision for some concurrent powers. The Philippine Code was intended to devolve basic services such as education, health care, and the environment onto local governments. Powers are listed at considerable length in the all-important section 17, but usually in such a way that each level of government has a role or contribution to make in relation to each function, such as education, social welfare, and infrastructure. This makes it impossible to set out powers as clearly as we have done with the other countries. An example

[44] eg Cabanatuan's conversion into a highly urbanised city, considered in *Umali v Commission on Elections* GR No 203974 (2014). The plebiscite requirement was strongly enforced by the Supreme Court in *Miranda v Aguirre* GR No 133064 (1999).

[45] R Hirschl, *City, State: Constitutionalism and the Megacity* (Oxford, Oxford University Press, 2020) ch 5.

[46] Code, s 41.

[47] ibid, Book III, Title V.

[48] ibid s 43. *Barangay* officials also have a three-year term under Republic Act 9164, s 2. A bill placed before the Senate in April 2024 would extend the term of all *barangay* officials to six years with one extension.

[49] ibid ss 48–54.

amongst many that could be cited is health care as a 'basic service'.[50] *Barangay* have powers over health and social welfare services which include maintenance of *barangay* health centres and day-care centres. Municipalities have powers over health services, which include the implementation of programmes and projects on primary health care, maternal and child care, and communicable and non-communicable disease control services; access to secondary and tertiary health services; and so forth. Provinces too have powers over health services, which include hospitals and other tertiary health services; while cities have the powers of both municipalities and provinces. Such allocation obviously requires a good deal of coordination between the four types of local government. Some functions are nonetheless exclusive to one level. Local justice comes under *barangay*; forestry comes under municipalities; and fisheries come under provinces. And others, like the power of eminent domain, are simply common to all local governments.[51]

The difference of function between the types of local government unit is expressed by the Code in the following way. Despite being the lowest in the hierarchy,[52] the *barangay* is described as 'the basic political unit, [serving] as the primary planning and implementing unit of government policies, plans, programs, projects, and activities in the community, and as a forum wherein the collective views of the people may be expressed, crystallised and considered, and where disputes may be amicably settled'.[53] The municipality and the city, on the other hand, provide 'general purpose government for the coordination and delivery of basic, regular and direct services and effective governance of the inhabitants within [their] territorial jurisdiction'.[54] And the province is a 'political and corporate unit of government, [serving] as a dynamic mechanism for developmental processes and effective governance of local government units within its territorial jurisdiction'.

In this idealised structure, it is roughly correct to say that the *barangay* is in effect the people; the municipality/city acts upon the people; and the province acts upon the municipality/city.

C. Supervision and Intergovernmental Relations

As the Supreme Court has indicated in its characterisation of local autonomy, local government units are not sovereigns within the state, and are subject to checks and balances – these are stringent ones, as we shall see – to ensure constitutionality and good governance.

[50] Code, s 17.
[51] ibid s 19.
[52] See s 25, below.
[53] Code, s 384.
[54] ibid ss 440 and 448.

When it comes to supervision, section 25 of the Code establishes a clear hierarchy:

> Consistent with the basic policy on local autonomy, the President shall exercise general supervision over local government units to ensure that their acts are within the scope of their prescribed powers and functions. The President shall exercise supervisory authority directly over provinces, highly urbanised cities, and independent component cities; through the province with respect to component cities and municipalities; and through the city and municipality with respect to *barangay*.[55]

We have seen above the ultra vires limits placed upon the President's powers of supervision, and these limits naturally apply also, as public functions, to supervision by local governments of lower authorities.

Executive orders are subject to review by higher authorities. Governors review executive orders of component cities and municipalities; city and municipal mayors review executive orders of *barangay* Chief executives are required to forward such orders to the higher authority within three days from their issuance, and if not acted upon within 30 days, they are deemed valid. The basis of review is that the higher authority ensures that such executive orders are within the powers granted by law and are in conformity with local ordinances.[56]

Legislation and resolutions by the local *sanggunian* are subject to a veto power of the chief executive of the unit in question. In the event of such veto being exercised within 15 days of the measure being passed (or 10 days in the case of a city or municipality), the chief executive returns the ordinance, with his written objections, to the *sanggunian*, which may proceed to override the veto by a two-thirds vote of all its members, thereby validating the measure. The veto power does not, however, apply to *barangay*. It may be exercised on the ground that the measure is ultra vires or prejudicial to the public welfare.[57] Again, this mirrors the position at the national level, where the President has veto powers over legislation. The *sanggunian* may override the veto by a two-thirds' majority.[58]

Legislative measures are also subject to review by higher authorities in more or less the same way as executive orders, except that the higher authority may return the measure with comments or recommendations as to improvement. The *sangguniang panlalawigan* also has power to invalidate measures of cities and municipalities on the basis of the ultra vires principle.[59] Budgets are subject to review by the Ministry of Budget and Management.[60]

In this way, the propriety and constitutionality of local laws and executive measures is disciplined not just by the judiciary, but by higher authorities. As

[55] See also s 29.
[56] Code, ss 30, 32.
[57] ibid ss 54–55.
[58] ibid s 54(b). And see Constitution of the Philippines, Article VII, s 27.
[59] Code, ss 56–58.
[60] ibid ss 326–27.

we have seen in the case of Indonesia, the control of local legislation can be an intractable issue.[61]

Apart from controlling the propriety of individual measures, the Code provides for control of elective executive officials themselves, who may be disciplined, preventively suspended, or removed from office for cause.[62] The stated causes are, for example, culpable violation of the Constitution; dishonesty, oppression, misconduct in office, gross negligence, or dereliction of duty; commission of any offence that is serious or involves moral turpitude; or abuse of authority. Complaints are considered by the President or *sanggunian* of a higher authority, as the case may be, and action taken only after giving the official a full hearing. Removal from office, however, may only be effected by a court of law. Rights of appeal also apply.[63]

The Ombudsman also has powers over elective officials under the Ombudsman Act 1989,[64] which allows him to 'investigate and prosecute on its own or on complaint by any person, any act or omission of any public officer or employee, office or agency, when such act or omission appears to be illegal, unjust, improper, or inefficient'. The Ombudsman has prior jurisdiction over other investigatory agencies.[65]

By virtue of these extensive provisions, as we have seen elsewhere, local autonomy is balanced by the system of intergovernmental relations, which gives overall control to the central government. As we have seen, both centralised and decentralised powers are also in turn controlled by the judiciary.

D. Local Democracy

A number of the Code's provisions seek to provide for genuine local democracy.

The *sanggunian* are of course the primary democratic elements in territorial governance. We can take the *sangguniang bayan* (municipal council) as typical, as the other *sanggunian* follow the same pattern. It comprises the municipal vice-mayor as the presiding officer; the regular *sanggunian* members; the president of the municipal chapter of the association of *barangay*; the president of the federation of youth councils for the municipality; and three representatives of women, agricultural or industrial workers, and other sectors, including the urban poor, indigenous cultural communities, or disabled persons.[66]

In addition to the normal electoral process, elective officials are subject to the possibility of recall, which leads to an election. This may be initiated by

[61] See p 56ff.
[62] Code, ss 60–68.
[63] Gatmaytan (n 18) 452ff.
[64] Republic Act No 6770, s 15.
[65] Constitution of the Philippines, Article XI.
[66] Code, s 446.

a preparatory recall assembly, comprising the elected officials of the unit and component units, or a percentage of the relevant electorate, such percentage (between 10 and 25 per cent) depending on its size.[67] Recall is entirely a matter of confidence, not of any specific cause.[68]

Local democracy also includes the possibility of a local initiative or referendum, under which 'the registered voters of a local government unit may directly propose, enact, or amend any ordinance.'[69] The right of public initiative may be exercised by not less than 1,000 registered voters in the case of provinces and cities, 100 in the case of municipalities, and 50 in the case of *barangay*.[70] With an initiative the legislative body is given the opportunity to enact a proposal within 30 days, failing which the matter is put to the electorate to decide.[71] The difference between an initiative and a referendum lies mainly in the fact that an initiative is commenced by the voters, whereas a referendum is commenced by the legislative body. An initiative is a process that occurs against the wishes of the elected body,[72] whereas a referendum is a means by which that body can ask the electorate to approve or reject a proposal.

There is a more general duty on local governments to 'conduct periodic consultations with appropriate local government units, non-governmental and people's organisations, and other concerned sectors of the community before any project or program is implemented in their respective jurisdictions'.[73]

These innovative democratic provisions give much scope to local democracy and actual public participation in local decision-making.

The overall impact of these Code provisions is to grant wide powers over basic services to all of the levels of local government. But they also ensure that these powers are hedged about from both below, in terms of democratic accountability, and above, in terms of validation by higher authority. The judiciary has attempted to hold the ring between central authority and local autonomy, although not in a manner that gives full autonomy and uncontrolled discretion to local governments.

IV. THE BARANGAY: A FOUNDATIONAL POLITICAL UNIT

The Code makes special provision, unlike any of those applicable to the other types of local government, for *barangay* as the basic political unit of government.[74] It is surely significant that *barangay* are listed first in the

[67] ibid ss 69–75.
[68] *Evardone v Commission on Elections*, 204 SCRA 464 (1991).
[69] Code, s 120.
[70] ibid s 122. For referendum see s 126.
[71] The Initiative and Referendum Act 1989, Republic Act no 6735, s 13.
[72] Code, s 122 (a), (b).
[73] Code, s 2(c).
[74] ibid s 384.

Code, before the other types of unit, and are the subject of extensive provision, as we have noted, compared to the other local governments. 'Of the innovations that the Code introduced into our system of government', writes Pimentel, 'the most radical was the empowerment of the *barangay*.'[75]

The *barangay* is led by the *punong barangay* (captain),[76] and has a *sangguniang barangay* (local council), consisting of the *punong barangay* as chair, seven elected members, and the chair of the *sangguniang kabataan* (youth council).[77]

Each *barangay* also has a *barangay* assembly, which has no equivalent in the other local governments. It comprises all persons who are citizens and residents of the *barangay* for at least six months, being at least 15 years of age. The assembly meets at least twice a year to hear and discuss the semestral report of the *sangguniang barangay* concerning its activities and finances as well as problems affecting the *barangay*. Meetings are held upon call of the *punong barangay* or of at least four members of the *sangguniang*, or upon written petition of at least 5 per cent of the assembly members.[78] The assembly has the duty of initiating legislative processes by recommending to the *sanggunian* the adoption of measures for the welfare of the *barangay*. It may also adopt an initiative whereby the registered voters may directly propose, enact, or amend any ordinance. It may also hear the semestral report of the *sanggunian* concerning its activities and finances.[79]

The most unusual function, however, at the barangay level is *katarungang pambarangay* (village justice), which is exclusive to the *barangay* and administered by a *lupong tagapamayapa* ('the *lupon*', or judicial committee). The *lupon* comprises the *punong barangay* as chair and 10–20 members. It is constituted every three years, and its members are appointed by the *punong barangay* from amongst residents possessing integrity, impartiality, independence of mind, sense of fairness, and reputation for probity.[80] The function of the *lupon* is to provide a system of dispute resolution, supervising *pangkat ng tagapagkasundo* ('*pangkat*', or a conciliation panel called for a particular dispute). It meets regularly once a month to provide a forum for exchange of ideas among its members and the public on matters relevant to the amicable settlement of disputes, and to enable various conciliation panel members to share with one another their observations and experiences in effecting speedy resolution of disputes.[81] The *pangkat* consists of three members, and they are chosen by the parties to a dispute from the list of members of the *lupon*.[82] The *lupon* has the power to bring together the parties actually residing in the same city or municipality

[75] Pimentel (n 18) 4.
[76] His powers and duties are set out at length in the Code, s 389.
[77] ibid ss 390–91.
[78] Code, s 397.
[79] ibid s 398.
[80] ibid s 399.
[81] ibid s 402.
[82] ibid s 404.

for dispute settlement.[83] Civil courts may also refer a case to the *lupon*, even where the latter has no authority otherwise. And, with some exceptions, no matter within the authority of the *lupon* shall be filed or instituted directly in court or any other government office for adjudication, unless there has been a confrontation between the parties before the *lupon* chairman or the *pangkat*, and no conciliation or settlement has been reached. The Code provides for amicable settlement, conciliation, and arbitration of the dispute.[84] The customs and traditions of indigenous cultural communities are also applied in settling disputes between members of those communities.[85]

The *barangay* justice system, unique amongst Southeast Asian systems of territorial governance, is considered to have been highly effective in delivering justice in a harmonious manner at the village level.[86] It has been described as 'a highly structured grass-roots community mediation process instituted to enhance the quality of justice in the Philippine legal system by reducing congested court dockets. It also promotes justice by allowing people to amicably resolve their own disputes with the assistance of *barangay* neighbors'.[87] Its features are its use of three-person conciliation panels; that it excludes lawyers from the process; and is as we have seen in a general sense a compulsory process that reduces litigation in the courts. The process of conciliation is inexpensive, produces outcomes quickly, and gives the disputants agency in concluding agreements in an amicable setting, free of a winner-loser frame of reference.[88] There are even competitions among *barangay*, with awards given to those who resolve the most disputes.

In this way the territorial governance system hinges with the traditional dispute resolution process, thus legitimising the *barangay* as the basic political unit.

V. CRITIQUES

It is striking when reviewing the literature from various disciplines that calls for any significant amendment to the Code are virtually non-existent.[89] There are, as we shall see, those who advocate federalism, and for those advocates the Code would of course have to be done away with. But the premise even of such

[83] There are exceptions, including public functions, major criminal offences and offences with no offended private party, cases involving persons or real property outside the barangay,.

[84] Code, ss 410, 412 and 413.

[85] ibid ss 399(c), 412(c).

[86] A Tadiar, 'The impact of the barangay justice system on decongesting court dockets and broadening access to justice: Looking back and looking forward' (2008–2009) 83 *Philippine Law Journal* 498.

[87] Tabucanon et al (n 8) 512.

[88] ibid 513.

[89] There have amendments to the Code since 1991, but only on minor matters.

critiques of the unitary/decentralised form of territorial governance is not that decentralisation per se has failed, but that it needs to be taken a stage further, as the centre has too much control over local governments, and the defects are due to implementation.[90]

One assessment, echoed by several others, is as follows:

> Since the promulgation of the 1987 Constitution, local government units have attained greater local fiscal autonomy. Their incremental shares in the internal revenues and expenditure responsibilities of the national government have allowed them to respond more appropriately and faster to the needs of their constituents for basic public services. Indeed, [local government units] … have measured up to the task.[91]

Evidence is strong that in many provinces local leadership and vision as well as public participation in government has been facilitated in the structure the Code creates.[92] Lack of resources and capabilities of local governments to cope with the demands of a decentralisation have been blamed for poor performance in service-delivery.

Another study lists three main problems: '(1) the lack of sufficient fiscal resources and high level of unfunded mandates; (2) the weak accountability of local executives to their electorates; and (3) the persistence of patronage politics. Each of these factors limits incentives for local elites to be responsive and constituent-minded in service-provision and social expenditures'.[93]

The main problem that critics seem to advance is the third of these, that is, that decentralisation has been inhibited by local capture in form of what is variously described as 'clan politics', 'clientelism'[94] or a system of 'patrons, bosses and dynasties'.[95] 'In poor areas, the patronage or redistributive style of leadership – the so-called *kasal-binyag-libing* (wedding-baptism-burial) support that a mayor is expected to provide to his or her constituent – is the acceptable norm. Hence, without outside intervention, these poor areas will remain in the vicious circle of penury and misgovernance'.[96] Pimentel, however, opined that the 'political umbilical cord that attached … [local governments] to the central or national government through a system of patronage and dependence

[90] R Tusalem, 'Imperial Manila: How institutions and political geography disadvantage Philippine provinces' (2020) 5(3) *Asian Journal of Comparative Politics* 235; World Bank and Asian Development Bank (n 17).

[91] J Capuno, 'The quality of local governance and development under decentralisation in the Philippines', Department of Economics, University of the Philippines, Discussion Paper 0506 (2005); also World Bank and Asian Development Bank, ibid.

[92] M Teng-Calleja et al, 'Transformation in Philippine local government' (2017) 43(1) *Local Government Studies* 64.

[93] Shair-Rosenfeld (n 3) 168.

[94] M Kimura, 'Clientelism revisited' ch 1 in M Thompson and EV Batalla (eds), *The Routledge Handbook of the Contemporary Philippines* (Abingdon, Routledge, 2018).

[95] J Sidel, 'Patrons, bosses, dynasties and reformers in local politics', ibid ch 2.

[96] Capuno (n 91) 29.

has been cut, to some extent, so that they can now more or less chart the course of their own development.'[97]

The consensus is that more democracy, more accountability, and more effective rule of law is required. But the question remains whether improvement can be delivered under the Code or only by a move to a federal system.

VI. FEDERALISM

The Philippines has a long tradition of a unitary form of government since the Spanish period, and with this tradition, it seems that the people are stuck in a mode of thinking that unitarism is the appropriate form of government for the country.[98] Nonetheless, the issue of establishing a federal system in the Philippines was mooted in the late nineteenth century, and during the period of American rule.[99] It has also been discussed throughout the post-independence period. Proposals along such lines have been put forward on several occasions. The electorate, however, remains persistently disinclined to approve any amendment to the 1987 Constitution. Polling appears to show that Filipinos are undecided about the merits of moving to a federal system, and in the main are even unsure even what it would involve.[100] The issue has been complicated by the association of federalism with the establishment of a unicameral parliamentary system, implying also the lifting of term limits on the chief executive. There is in fact no necessary connection between these ideas, but they were, for example, linked in President Arroyo's appointment of a Consultative Commission on 'Cha-Cha' (charter change) in 2005.[101] The electorate's lack of enthusiasm is probably due more to distrust of the very notion of Cha-Cha than to any endorsement of centralisation as such. A People's Initiative to amend the constitution was struck down by the Supreme Court in 2006 for lack of facilitating legislation.[102] The debate was rekindled under President Duterte in 2019, with the creation of another Consultative Committee to review the 1987 Constitution. But again this has not been taken forward.[103]

[97] Pimental (n 18) 11.

[98] TSE Tadem and MEL Atienza, 'The evolving empowerment of local governments and promotion of local governance in the Philippines: An overview' in Tadem and Atienza (n 10).

[99] A Brillantes and JT Sonco, 'Decentralisation and local governance in the Philippines' ch 18 in EV Berman (ed), *Public Administration in Southeast Asia: Thailand, Philippines, Malaysia, Hong Kong, and Macao* (Abingdon, Routledge, 2011).

[100] S Rood, 'Finding federalism in the Philippines: Federalism – "the centerpiece of my campaign"' ch 2 in I Deinla and B Dressel (eds), *From Aquino II to Duterte (2010–18): Change, Continuity and Rupture* (Cambridge, Cambridge University Press, 2020) 70.

[101] JV Abueva et al (ed), *Towards a Federal Republic of the Philippines with a Parliamentary Government* (Manila, Kalayaan College, LOGODEF, Lihuk Pederal, and KAS Philippines, 2002).

[102] *Lambino et al v Commission on Elections*, GR No 174153 (2006).

[103] Rood (n 100).

Proposals have suggested grouping the current 82 provinces into eight to eleven states. Thus, a federation created in this manner would be an unusual 'staying apart' rather than 'coming together' type of federation. The arguments for federalism are the classic ones. They can be summarised in two major propositions.

First, the Philippines is a diverse country with acute differences in culture and identity, and federalism would allow expression of these differences. Significant here is the autonomy of Bangsamoro, which is discussed in detail in chapter nine. The argument is that all other areas too can benefit from this kind of autonomy,[104] and federalism in turn would cement the peace process in Bangsamoro.[105]

Second, it is considered that decentralisation under the Code has led to inequality between richer areas, especially Manila, and poorer areas of the country. Federalism would facilitate economic dynamism at the lower level of government by relieving the states of the strictures of a stifling centralised bureaucracy. It would spark dynamism and competition amongst the states, breaking dependency on the centre.[106] Federalism would bring government closer to the people's localised needs, of which local leaders would have first-hand knowledge.[107]

The arguments against federalism are also familiar.

Federalism would create duplicated or overlapping jurisdictions, as well as contradictory and inconsistent policies, which would not be in the interests of development. It also represents a threat to the integrity of a nation that has been painstakingly united. It would create more opportunities for corruption, and a system with too much government, rather than less. It would further empower local dynasties. Competition between states is likely to result in more inequality and rivalry, the states being unequally endowed with natural resources. The balance of central and local powers is already satisfactory under the Code.[108]

The success or otherwise of the Code, or at least perceptions of the same, is of course highly relevant in this debate. Some see the Code as ultimately failing to break down entrenched centralism.[109] Others see the Code as assurance that local autonomy, if not entirely fulfilled in the Code, has shown in its successes that decentralisation can be taken much further.[110] An intermediate view sees an

[104] It would of course, on this assumption, no longer be 'special' but universal.

[105] Some maintain that the autonomy accorded to Bangsamoro is in itself unconstitutional in a unitary system.

[106] M Yusingco, 'Rethinking federalism in the Philippines' (*50 Shades of Federalism*, 2020) at 50shadesoffederalism.com/case-studies/rethinking-federalism-in-the-philippines/.

[107] M Yusingco, '"Imperial Manila" is a constitutional design: Towards configuring executive authority in a federal system' (*Constitutionnet*, 20 March 2018).

[108] Abueva (n 101).

[109] Yusingco (n 106).

[110] A Brillantes (ed), *Innovations and Excellence in Local Governance: Understanding Local Governments in the Philippines* (Quezon City, University of the Philippines National College of Public Administration and Governance, 2003).

amended Code as having the potential to deliver 'maximum decentralisation', consistently with Article X, without resort to a federal structure.[111] This view is attractive, as it draws on the undoubted fact that the different possible structures are not clearly distinct from each other, federalism being simply a range of places on a spectrum between a centralised and a decentralised government structure.[112] However, it seems clear that the intention of the constitution-makers was to create local autonomy short of federalism, and reform taking the system of territorial governance further towards federalism might encounter the objection that such reforms are federalism by other means, and so unconstitutional. This leads us straight back to the charter-change problem. As we have seen, decisions of the Supreme Court on this issue, while reinforcing autonomy to a certain extent, also stress that this autonomy has limits under the present dispensation.

VII. CONCLUSION

The history of territorial governance in the Philippines presents a clear tension between centralising and decentralising forces. The desire to belong to a nation that is strong despite its diversity is not always consistent with the desire for autonomy at all subnational levels. Decentralisation has been seen as a success in the Philippines. In part this is due to the clear and intelligently designed structure that the Code has bequeathed, offering 'the most supportive statutory environment for local political participation in all of Southeast Asia'.[113] Justifying the Code, the late Senate Speaker and father of the Code, Aquilino Pimentel wrote:

> When I was mayor of Cagayan de Oro City, for instance, I felt terribly frustrated by the utter powerlessness of the office. I saw the local governments then as mere channels of the good graces of the central government. In several statements, I denounced the situation where we, local government officials, were expected merely to implement, give support an provide protection to whatever the central government had decided to do within our localities. We had no power to question why this or that project was being prosecuted in our localities.[114]

In part it is also due to the enthusiastic and dynamic leadership the system has encouraged, although not in all provinces. The main problem is how to correct the imbalances in resources and outcomes. Other problems are localised

[111] Yusingco (n 106).

[112] F Palermo and K Kössler, *Comparative Federalism: Constitutional Arrangements and Case Law* (Oxford, Hart Publishing, 2019) 17ff.

[113] T George, 'Local governance: People power in the provinces' in S Silliman and LG Noble (eds), *Organising for Democracy: NGOs, Civil Society, and the Philippine State* (Manila, Ateneo de Manila University Press, 1998) 225.

[114] Pimentel (n 18) 78.

corruption and local elite capture, or 'bossism'. It seems unlikely that federalism alone can solve these problems. Rather, it is suggested, the Code can be appropriately supplemented with administrative measures to monitor performance and provide assistance. A report by the World Bank and the Asian Development Bank in 2005 indicated that practical support measures rather than legislative changes were needed.[115]

For our purposes, however, what this chapter has shown is that radical reform and innovation in territorial governance (and we have seen several examples of the latter) can have dramatic effects. The issue is essentially whether effective territorial governance is to be enhanced by greater central control, or more autonomy. That issue remains to be resolved.

[115] Above n 17.

7

Thailand

'A small bird builds a nest big enough for itself': Thai proverb.

COMPARED TO THE other four countries considered in this book Thailand (known as Siam before 1939), is not on the face of it so high on the diversity index, considering that 97.5 per cent of its population of around 72 million is officially designated as being of Thai ethnicity.[1] It is nonetheless in fact quite diverse in terms of ethnicity, as many of those listed as Thai are actually, for example, of Chinese or Lao descent. The government lists (as anthropological rather than official fact) 69 ethnic groups, including several sub-groups of 'Thai', many of which are described as indigenous. Three southern border provinces (Pattani, Yala and Narathiwat) have a Malay/Muslim majority, and the northern hills are replete with minority populations, from Karen to Aha, Lisu and former Kuomintang Chinese. In Isaan in the East of the country the population is as much Lao as Thai. And although around 95 per cent are Buddhist, there is a good deal of religious diversity.[2] This is especially so in the Southern border provinces (considered below), which have been plagued with inter-religious conflict over the years. The area of the former Lanna Kingdom around the Northern city of Chiang Mai retains to a large extent its Lanna culture. This latter cultural difference impacts directly on territorial governance, as Chiang Mai 'represents the high-water mark of the desire to achieve true local autonomy'.[3]

From the adoption of the so-called 'people's constitution' in 1997 Thailand implemented decentralisation. This was an iterative process rather than a settled position, which was expressly required by the terms of the constitution. It was intended to 'transfer power from unelected civil servants and the local economic elites, who have tended to dominate the administration of policy at local government level, and to give additional powers to locally-elected representatives of the people'.[4] This development was, as in the cases of Indonesia and Philippines, part of a constitutional design attempting to prevent military

[1] Thailand Demographics Profile, www.indexmundi.com/thailand/demographics_profile.html.

[2] A Atipiboonsin, 'Volcanic constitution: How is plurality turning against constitutionalism in Thailand?' ch 9 in JL Neo and NS Bui (eds), *Pluralist Constitutions in Southeast Asia* (Oxford, Hart Publishing, 2019) 227–28.

[3] A Harding and R Leelapatana, 'Possibilities for decentralisation in Thailand: A view from Chiang Mai' (2021) 1 *Thai Legal Studies* 76, 79. Chiang Mai is considered later in this chapter.

[4] A Harding and P Leyland, *The Constitutional System of Thailand: A Contextual Analysis* (Oxford, Hart Publishing, 2011) 132.

dictatorship that had plagued Thailand ever since the overthrow of the absolute monarchy in 1932, but had overreached in 1992 with a violent crackdown on anti-military protests.[5] The principles of territorial governance set out in the 1997 Constitution were more or less repeated in the subsequent Constitution of 2007, and then watered down somewhat in the Constitution of 2017.[6] Nonetheless, two periods of military rule since 1997 (in 2006–07 and 2014–19), in conjunction with some other factors we will consider later in this chapter, have to a great extent limited the progress and impact of decentralisation.[7] One legacy of 1997 is local government elections; another is simply the idea of decentralisation, which seems to be gaining in its attractions even if not always in terms of actual legislated outcomes.[8] Since 2014, decentralisation, facilitating local influence of the pro-democracy red faction, has been regarded by the conservative or yellow faction as a threat to the governance system of Thailand, referred to as the 'democratic regime with the King as head of state' (DRKH).[9] The post-military government of 2019 reluctantly agreed to local elections in December 2020. This can be attributed to the fact that the demand for local self-governance seems now, despite DRKH, to be a permanent feature of territorial governance in Thailand.[10]

In the last three decades, there have been attempts to bring the delivery of local services closer to the citizen, to provide for local democracy, and to control localised corruption. These attempts are examined in this chapter. We shall also look at new proposals from Chiang Mai that seek a radical democratisation of territorial governance in that province, and by implication more generally. The long-running insurgency in Thailand's deep South is also examined, with an eye to the constitutional implications which might be involved in reaching a viable settlement through a version of special autonomy.

I. THE DEVELOPMENT OF TERRITORIAL GOVERNANCE[11]

The territory that now forms Thailand was settled over several hundred years by various ethnic groups, in particular Khmer (Cambodians), Mon, and

[5] G Lowatcharin and CD Crumpton, 'Local government and intergovernmental relations in Thailand' ch 14 in P Chachavalpongpun (ed), *The Routledge Handbook of Contemporary Thailand* (Abingdon, Routledge, 2020) 178–79.

[6] T Ginsburg, 'Constitutional afterlife: The continuing impact of Thailand's post-political constitution' (2009) 7 *International Journal of Constitutional Law* 83.

[7] A Harding and R Leelapatana 'Towards Recentralisation?: Thailand's 2014 Coup, Tutelage Democracy and their Effects on Local Government' (*50 Shades of Federalism*, 2020) 50shadesoffederalism.com/case-studies/towards-recentralisation-thailands-2014-coup-tutelage-democracy-and-their-effects-on-local-government/; and see below.

[8] Harding and Leelapatana (n 3).

[9] A Harding and R Leelapatana, 'Constitution-making in 21st-century Thailand: The continuing search for a perfect constitutional fit' (2019) 7(2) *Chinese Journal of Comparative Law* 266, 273.

[10] Lowatcharin and Crumpton (n 5).

[11] This section is largely based on Harding and Leelapatana (n 7), and Harding and Leyland (n 4).

Tai. By the thirteenth century, the Tai had become a dominant group within that territory.[12] Historians normally regard Sukhothai, Ayutthaya, Thonburi, and Bangkok as Thailand's four kingdoms. However, Thailand as a nation-state in its modern form had never existed before the reforms of King Chulalongkorn (1868–1910).[13] Before the mid-nineteenth century, the four kingdoms were in effect dominant city-states that ruled directly or indirectly over other semi-autonomous city-states. To the North around Chiang Mai and Chiang Rai another Tai group had already settled since the ninth century. Before the reign of King Chulalongkorn, the city-states they formed comprised a kingdom that was once dominant but later subjugated to Bangkok – the Kingdom of Lanna. It had an area covering a number of present-day northern provinces, with Chiang Mai serving as its capital. The Burmese conquered Lanna in the sixteenth century, but in the mid-eighteenth century, an extremely unpopular period of Burmese rule boiled over in a series of revolts. With Siamese assistance, Lanna chiefs successfully regained control over Chiang Mai in 1775. Yet, such assistance also turned Lanna and its successor – the Kingdom of Chiang Mai (1802–1899) – into a tributary state of Bangkok.[14] This meant that Chiang Mai was ruled by kings and princes who, as tributaries, held a degree of autonomy from Bangkok.

Thongchai Winichakul in his book *Siam Mapped* explains this system as follows:

> The King in Bangkok, to consolidate his power, had to fight to expand his umbrella of merit and righteousness, dharma. In effect this meant that as far as possible he needed to bring lesser kingdoms under the protection of his supreme merit. This relationship was not understood merely in terms of territory. Rather, these tributary provinces were bound to Bangkok by a ritual of submission, involving periodic payments to renew the allegiance, and with it the expectation of protection. Whenever the Thai royal capital was weak, local rulers often revolted by refusing to send tribute, and this in turn prompted military intervention from Bangkok.[15]

Regarding the reforms Winichakul observes further:

> the reform of provincial administration in Siam was first tested in the 1870s in Lanna and then developed and applied to the Lao region along the Mekhong, including Luang Phrabang and many other large and small tributaries. Finally, from 1893 onwards it was implemented in other regions including the inner provinces of Siam. It was a gradual process of displacing the traditional local autonomy … by the modern mechanisms of centralisation.[16]

[12] G Coedès, *The Indianized States of South-East Asia* (WF Vella (ed), S Brown Cowing (tr), Honolulu, University of Hawaii Press, 1968) 190–91, 195–96.

[13] C Baker and P Phongpaichit, *A History of Thailand*, 2nd edn (Cambridge, Cambridge University Press, 2009) ch 4; see also T Charoenmuang, *A Century of Thai Local Government (1897–1997)* (Bangkok, Khrongkan Chatphim Khopfai, 2007).

[14] Baker and Phongphaichit, ibid 7, 54.

[15] T Winichakul, *Siam Mapped: A History of the Geo-Body of a Nation* (Hawaii, University of Hawaii Press 1994) 85.

[16] ibid 102.

In 1939, the Lanna monarchy was abolished, its areas becoming provinces of Thailand, but its traditional sense of autonomy and its different culture from that of Bangkok were palpable then, and are still in some respects today.[17]

In the late nineteenth century, the ancient tributary system of central-local relations was significantly challenged by the advent of Western imperialism and consequent modernisation.[18] Bangkok, under the reigns of King Mongkut and King Chulalongkorn, faced imperialist threats from both the British and the French. The confrontation forced King Chulalongkorn to initiate fundamental legal and public administration reforms, beginning in the 1870s, by espousing the Western model of a 'nation-state'.[19] This reform, known as the 'Chakri Reformation', transformed Bangkok-Chiang Mai relations.[20] It coincided with the expansion of the kingdom as it also took over the Malay/Muslim Southern border provinces, stripping away tributary status and centralising power in the hands of civil servants and princes in Bangkok, as opposed to local dignitaries.[21] 'Although Thailand was never colonised', writes one commentator, 'its provincial administration is reminiscent of the colonial apparatus of administration established by the British in India and the French in Indochina.'[22]

Local government legislation followed with the establishment of Bangkok sanitary districts,[23] and a Local Government Act followed in 1914 – legislation that is in force to the present day. Provincial governors were appointed by the Ministry of the Interior (MoI) and even held office in local governments, thereby doubling down on central control. Under the modernised Siamese state all areas were brought under the direct control of Bangkok, and since then the country has been noted for having a highly centralised 'bureaucratic polity'.[24] As Lowatcharin and Crumpton point out, '[w]ith the establishment of a public administrative cadre organised according to historic Thai hierarchical principles,

[17] DM Engel and JS Engel, *Tort, Custom, and Karma: Globalisation and Legal Consciousness in Thailand* (Stanford, Stanford University Press, 2010); DM Engel, 'Blood curse and belonging in Thailand: Law, Buddhism, and legal consciousness' in A Harding and Munin Pongsapan (eds), *Thai Legal History: From Traditional to Modern Law* (Cambridge, Cambridge University Press, 2021); S Ongsakul, *History of Lanna* (Chitraporn Tanratanakul (tr), Chiang Mai, Silkworm Press, 2005) 195–213.

[18] C Baker and Pasuk Phongpaichit, *A History of Thailand*, 3rd edn (Cambridge, Cambridge University Press, 2014) 54–56.

[19] P Leyland, 'The origins of Thailand's bureaucratic state and the consolidation of administrative justice' ch 13 in Harding and Pongsapan (n 17); PA Jackson, 'The ambiguities of semicolonial power in Thailand' in RV Harrison and PA Jackson (eds), *The Ambiguous Allure of the West: Traces of the Colonial in Thailand* (Hong Kong, Hong Kong University Press, 2010) 45.

[20] C Kasetsiri, *Thailand: A Struggle for the Nation* (Singapore, ISEAS, 2022) 211.

[21] Winichakul (n 15) 88.

[22] D Arghiros, 'Political reform and civil society at the local level: Thailand's local government reforms' in D McCargo (ed), *Reforming Thai Politics* (Copenhagen, NIAS, 2002) 225.

[23] It seems to be almost universal that local government begins with public health concerns. The sanitary districts were only recently abolished.

[24] FW Riggs, *Thailand: The Modernisation of a Bureaucratic Polity* (Hawaii, East-West Center Press, 1966).

a bureaucratic elite emerged that has become a continuing powerful political, economic, and social influence in Thailand'.[25]

Despite the implementation of a highly centralised model of statehood, some foundations for the present-day decentralised system were established during the period of absolute monarchy pre-1932. Having heard claims by foreigners regarding Bangkok's sanitation, King Chulalongkorn, given his promise and effort to 'civilise' the new nation-state, passed a Royal Decree establishing Bangkok *Sukhaphiban* (sanitary district) in 1897 Chiang Mai *Sukhaphiban* was established in 1913.[26] In general, these bodies had typical local government responsibilities for waste management, provision of healthcare facilities, and prevention of diseases.[27] This system, although in no way designed to create political participation among local residents, at least provided a nascent idea of local public service, and was in existence until 1999, when local-government reforms began pursuant to the 1997 Constitution.

The liberal idea of local government autonomy was introduced to Thailand by Pridi Banomyong, the civilian leader of the People's Party, a group of bureaucrats and military officers who staged the revolution that formally abolished royal absolutism on 24 June 1932. Regarding local elections and local citizen participation in policy decision-making essential for cultivating a liberal democratic culture, Pridi succeeded in persuading the then legislature to pass the Municipality Act in 1933. This led to the creation of local municipalities (*thetsaban*) as decentralised local government units, at the levels of cities, towns, and villages, as distinct from the MoI-established units, namely provinces (*changwat*) and districts (*amphoe*) headed by appointed officials.[28]

Thailand's first city municipality was founded in Chiang Mai in 1935. In 1936, the first Local Assembly Election Act came into force, bestowing upon local citizens the right to elect members of the municipal assembly (19 members in Chiang Mai). Notwithstanding the recurrence of military coups precipitating the suspension of both electoral politics and decentralisation, other forms of decentralised agencies were gradually introduced across the kingdom to facilitate local development through local citizen participation and public service. These were created by the Provincial Administration ('PAO') Act 1955 and the Tambon[29] Council and Tambon Administration Organisation ('TAO') Act 1994. With their own legislative assembly and executive council directly elected by local citizens, *thetsaban*, PAO, and TAO provide the backbone of Thailand's general system of local government. Importantly, the endorsement of the right to local self-government as a constitutional right by the 1997

[25] Lowatcharin and Crumpton (n 5) 178.

[26] 'Declaration of the use of the Management of Provincial Sukhapiban Act in Chiang Mai' *Royal Gazette* (8 March 1913).

[27] Sukhaphiban Management Act 1908, s 13.

[28] Harding and Leelapatana (n 3) 86.

[29] Sub-districts.

Constitution further increased the significance of these organisations in the democratic process.[30]

This history has continually inhibited the decentralisation of power to provinces and the lower levels of local government, which 'under this system [became] little more than an outpost of the Ministry of the Interior'.[31] The model was therefore in essence deconcentration of central power, not decentralisation of power to local units. Royalist and military factions have continually espoused a Bangkok-centric form of tutelage democracy denoted in the DRKH slogan. This version of democracy indicates that the people's interest is protected, in the name of the King, by a military dictatorship. Using such a definition of democracy, these elites have laid claim to a legitimacy based on Thai traditions. Since the late 1950s DRKH hegemony has therefore tended to limit, rather than extend, decentralisation.[32]

Centralisation came under stress, however, in the 1990s, with disillusionment arising from military dictatorship leading to a strong push for decentralisation.[33] The TAO Act 1994 reinvented the TAOs, resulting in more than 6,000 of them being created by the end of the decade.[34] It was only in the 1997 Constitution, however, that decentralisation of power began to be taken seriously, and to be treated as a constitutionally-mandated objective. That constitution was drafted by representatives of Thailand's 76 provinces, and led to a more radical approach, given effect, as we saw in chapter two, by constitutional provisions and the Decentralisation Plan and Process Act 1999 (DPPA). Several pieces of local government legislation were passed in 1999, which year can be said to mark the 'big-bang' in Thailand's decentralisation movement.[35] The 1997 Constitution was 'a milestone in accelerating the movement towards decentralisation and enhancing the importance of local governments'.[36] The DPPA performed a similar function to the Philippines Local Government Code and the Indonesian Laws on Regional Autonomy in transferring 245 major functions and services[37] to local governments, and also provided that 35 per cent of total expenditure of the national government in every fiscal year had to be allocated to local government units by 2006.[38] More importantly, local self-government was accomplished with elections as a result, being required for more than 7,000 local governments at sub-provincial levels.

[30] Sections 78, 284.

[31] M Nelson, *Central Authority and Local Democratisation in Thailand* (Bangkok, White Lotus Press, 1998) 26.

[32] Harding and Leelapatana (n 3). See, further, R Leelapatana, 'The monarchy-led urban development: Lessons from Bangkok's planning regime' (2023) *Chinese Journal of Comparative Law* 1.

[33] Lowatcharin and Crumpton (n 5) 180.

[34] ibid.

[35] Harding and Leyland (n 4) 22, 122ff.

[36] Lowatcharin and Crumpton (n 5) 180.

[37] ibid.

[38] Section 30(4). See also, however, the Determining Plans and Process of Decentralisation to Local Government Organisations (No2) Act 2006, which relaxes the time-frame for compliance.

During the 2000s centralised government, which had hardly in practice begun, being diluted by the decentralisation reforms, was increasingly called into question in light of both the troubles in the Southern border provinces and the polarisation between the red and yellow factions.[39] The red-yellow conflict also had a strong regional element to it, with the main support for the red faction being concentrated in the North and Northeast, especially Chiang Mai, while support for the yellow faction tended to be concentrated in and around Bangkok and parts of the South.[40] In general decentralisation was supported by the red faction but opposed by the yellow.[41] The polarisation ultimately led to the military coup of 2014, and the local government system is still somewhat in recovery mode from five years of suppression of such autonomy as it had enjoyed.

During the period of military rule 2014–19, the military junta implemented a number of draconian measures that reversed the decentralisation process. In 2014 two junta Announcements suspended all local elections.[42] A problem then arose in that these measures prevented the election of local legislators and executive heads in place of those whose terms had expired. The solution was to establish appointment committees at provincial level to fill the vacancies, but the composition of these committees was problematical. It reflected an attempt to convert decentralised entities into deconcentrated ones. The deputy director of the provincial Internal Security Operations Command (ISOC) sat on the committee, which was chaired by the provincial governor, who was in turn appointed by the MoI. The measures also provided that two-thirds of the newly-appointed members of local legislatures had to be former senior civil servants. By the issuing of two further measures in 2014,[43] military officials, provincial governors, and district heads were given powers to review and veto local budgetary allocations. These attempts at limiting the powers of decentralised bodies undermined local democracy, which was already ultimately to be set back by five years during the period of military rule.[44]

Elections for different categories of local government were held, for the first time since the 2014 coup, in 2020–21.[45]

[39] See below.

[40] Harding and Leyland (n 4) 121.

[41] As we shall see, Chiang Mai, where the yellow faction is in favour of decentralisation, is an exception.

[42] NCPO Announcements Nos 85 and 86/2557.

[43] NCPO Announcement No 104 /2557; NCPO Order No 88/2557.

[44] D Unger and C Mahakanjana, 'Decentralisation in Thailand' (2016) 33 *Journal of Southeast Asian Economies* 172.

[45] Asian Network for Free Elections, '2021 Thai TAO elections: A long awaited return to local democracy' (30 November 2021) at 2021 Thai Tambon Administration Organisation Elections | Asian Network for Free Elections, see anfrel.org/tag/2021-thai-tambon-administration-organization-elections/. See also the Election of Local Assemblies or Local Administrators Act 2019.

II. THE CONTEMPORARY SYSTEM OF TERRITORIAL GOVERNANCE

The current 2017 Constitution, like its predecessors of 1997 and 2007, devotes a chapter (chapter XIV) to local government. Section 249 provides that 'local administration shall be organised in accordance with the principle of self-government according to the will of the people in the locality'. Other principles recognised in chapter XIV[46] are sustainable development, decentralisation, privatisation, budgetary support, local elections, public participation, and suppression of corruption. Section 254 reflects the right of public petition at the national level[47] by providing that '[p]ersons having the right to vote in a local administrative organisation have the right to sign a joint petition for introducing an ordinance or for removing a member of a local assembly or a local administrator'. Similar to other examples we have seen, local democracy also applies to the establishment of local governments. Section 249, paragraph 2 provides that '[i]n establishing a local administrative organisation in any form, due regard shall be had to the will of the people in the locality together with the capacity for self-government in respect of revenues, number and density of the population, as well as areas under its responsibility'. The Constitution does not, however, prescribe for the regularity of local elections;[48] and since the constitution is always abolished following a coup, there is no formal obligation to hold local elections during the period of military rule, as we have seen.

The constitutional provisions, although reflecting large changes in territorial governance since 1997, compare somewhat poorly with those of Indonesia and the Philippines, in that they use the phrase 'as provided [or prescribed] by law' eight times in six brief sections. This indicates that the constitution would not be a serious instrument for achieving further decentralisation, or even the entrenchment of the localism or subsidiarity apparently established under chapter XIV. The drafting of this chapter gives power to parliament to rapidly reverse decentralisation if it chose to do so, notwithstanding decentralisation being constitutionally mandated. Nor is there any specification in the Constitution as to the structure, functions or powers of local governments, all of which are left to the DPPA.

The DPPA, passed under this constitutional mandate,[49] is a statute of only 37 sections, and considerably limited in its scope compared to its Philippine (536) and Indonesian (411) equivalents. Fifteen of those sections are devoted to the process of implementing decentralisation rather than to powers and processes of the local governments themselves. The Determining Plans and Process of Decentralisation to Local Government Organisation Commission

[46] 2017 Constitution, ss 251–53.
[47] ibid s 254. See also, ss 41(2), 43(3), 133.
[48] Previously, a four-year cycle was prescribed: 2007 Constitution, s 284.
[49] 2017 Constitution, s 284.

(the 'Decentralisation Commission'), established under section 6 of the Act, was given very broad powers to generate and implement the plan for decentralisation of powers to local governments. The Commission consists of 12 representatives of central government; 12 elected representatives from organisations representing local government; and 12 experts from the fields of public administration, local development, economics, political science, and law. The DPPA required all functions marked by the Act for decentralisation to be transferred within four years, that is, by 2003.[50] However, a period of ten years was marked as the ultimate deadline for determination of local responsibilities, based on differences in the readiness of each local government organisation, having regard to revenue, personnel, population, implementing budget, and the quality of public services currently delivered.[51] The most striking feature of the Act is that it provides, as we have seen, for 35 per cent revenue transfer to local governments.

Despite the decentralising objective of these constitutional and statutory provisions, the system that emerged from the decentralisation planning process is actually a hybrid between deconcentration of central administration and local self-government. These two concepts we distinguished in chapter one.[52] As in most systems of territorial governance, intermediate local governments – the provinces in Thailand's case – are given general functions of development planning, oversight and support. But in contrast to other countries studied in this book, provincial governors (other than the Governor of Bangkok[53]), and district heads too, are centrally appointed rather than elected. Provincial administration organisations (PAOs) are accountable to an elected council, whose size depends on the population of the province. They are directed to formulate provincial development plans and provide support for and oversight of sub-provincial governments.[54] PAOs are also given functions that overlap considerably with those of sub-provincial governments, but extend also to law and order.[55] However, the provinces (numbering 76) and districts (numbering 878) have elected councils, and the governor is responsible to the council (numbering between 24 and 48, according to size of population) as well as answering to the MoI. Similarly, district heads are accountable to an elected council and report to the provincial governor. Districts may, depending on a population criterion, be designated as cities or towns, in which event the normal size of elected council (12) is increased to 18 (for towns), or 24 (for cities).[56]

[50] DPPA, s 30(1).
[51] ibid s 30(2).
[52] See p 26.
[53] The Governor of Bangkok is elected, as are 57 members of the BMA council. Bangkok also has 50 districts and 180 sub-districts as of 2024. See Harding and Leyland (n 4) 125.
[54] ibid 124ff.
[55] DPPA, s 7.
[56] Harding and Leyland (n 4) 124ff.

Below the districts, at the level of village groups, are the *tambon* or sub-districts (7,255 in number), which have an elected council comprising two members for each village within the *tambon*. Of the *tambon* 2,232 are classified as urban municipalities, the remainder being rural. Each is headed by a *kamnan* (sub-district chief), who serves a five-year term. Local residents elect the *kamnan* from amongst the village headmen. A *tambon* consists of several *mooban* (villages). Each village sends two representatives as council members, so that the number of TAO councillors depends on the number of villages.[57] The *kamnan* and the village heads have always been the prime link between the rural population and the state. As we have seen elsewhere in the region, they have a mixed role as civil servants representing the state and as elected representatives.[58]

The lower levels of territorial governance, namely those of districts and *tambon*, are accorded broad competence over the following main areas: drainage, sanitation, and water and waste management; management of local infrastructure and utilities; employment training, tourism and promotion of investment; education and social welfare; culture preservation; housing; health services; forestry and natural resources; roads and transport; local planning and building control.[59]

As might be expected, a considerable degree of flexibility is provided by the DPPA. The Decentralisation Commission has power, where the law stipulates that more than one local government organisation has the function of delivering the same or similar public services, to determine to which of them responsibility should be assigned.[60] Local governments are also empowered to act on behalf of the central government; to collaborate with each other in executing functions allocated by the DPPA; and to request the state or other local governments to act on their behalf, according to the situation.[61]

III. DECENTRALISATION IN PRACTICE

As we have seen, the potential of far-reaching decentralisation has been inherently limited by the failure of the law to confer administrative autonomy congruently with legal/ political autonomy. Other obstacles have prevented fulfilment of the objectives of the 1997 Constitution. Soon after the enactment of the DPPA the Thaksin Shinawatra government (2001–06) came into power, and rather than pursuing decentralisation planning with vigour, began implementing an approach based on strong central leadership and 'new public management'.[62] Under this concept, 'the culture and status of bureaucracy at the

[57] ibid.
[58] ibid 126.
[59] DPPA, ss 16 and 19.
[60] ibid s 20.
[61] ibid s 21.
[62] Harding and Leyland (n 4) 130ff.

local government level (as also for central government) was to be transformed by injecting techniques of managerialism and by exposing the CEOs at PAO level to the ideas of business, risk and profit'.[63] At local level this meant conferring increased powers on local governors as CEOs. The Thaksin government was thus leaning in the opposite direction from that envisaged by the framers of the 1997 Constitution. However, Thaksin's party (TRT) was not able to dominate local politics, which as Michael Nelson explains, are organised around traditional cliques:

> Local politics is a largely exclusive affair. Political parties are basically absent at the provincial level; they have hardly any branch offices at the local level that could support the political participation of citizens. Instead we find informal cliques (*phuak*) of people who are active as national and local politicians. These cliques are based on a variety of relationships, for example family ties, friendship, business interests, or patron client ties.[64]

This is of course a phenomenon we have encountered elsewhere in discussing the outcomes of decentralisation.[65]

On the other hand, decentralisation has also led to useful innovations in both new public management and in public participation beyond the electoral process. For example, some units have invested in e-government, while others have contracted out facilities with an improvement in cost-effectiveness.[66] Despite overall policy control by the central government, and a lack of real autonomy or progress with decentralisation, the DPPA has led to a considerable degree of delegation to local governments. A total of 245 central government responsibilities were transferred from central and provincial governments to local governments, involving 50 departments in 11 ministries.[67]

In the realm of public participation, some units have conducted town hall meetings, civic fora, and local development planning fora.[68] Experiments in participatory democracy have been realised in a number of contexts. For example, the city of Khon-Khan (population 130,000) has instituted informal focus-group meetings for discussions between members of the community and municipal administrators relating to the environmental and societal impact of infrastructural development.[69] Another well-known project is the Community Forest Network of the Upper Ping River in Chiang Mai Province, which has been developed to allow the local community to self-manage the local forest while also protecting and conserving it in the interests of the local

[63] ibid.

[64] See Nelson (n 31) 259.

[65] See eg, p 118.

[66] Harding and Leyland (n 4) 130–31.

[67] Above n 36.

[68] W Krueathep, 'Local government initiatives in Thailand: Cases and lessons learned' (2014) 26(2) *Asia Pacific Journal of Public Administration* 217, 5ff.

[69] ibid; Harding and Leyland (n 4) 136.

community. However, the success of such schemes depends on generous funding and intensive professional support from academics and civil society.[70] Public participation, while vaguely encouraged by the constitutional and legal superstructure and occasionally iterated in practice, does not necessarily reflect general experience.[71]

Under the 1997 Constitution, the Election Commission of Thailand is given responsibility for conducting or overseeing elections for local assemblies and local administrators under the Election of Local Assemblies and Local Administrators Act 2019.[72] Their task covers all aspects of the electoral process, from determining constituency boundaries and establishing eligibility to vote, to the organisation of the elections themselves and the counting of ballots. The Commission also has investigatory powers to deal with vote-buying and election expenses.[73] These powers appear to have largely failed to counter the prevalence of vote-buying at the provincial and sub-district levels, which in turn has enhanced the dominance of local political elites and business interests, which trend is mirrored in national politics. Corruption is evident especially at the provincial level, where infrastructural development budgets are settled. This has further inhibited decentralisation and reinforced the reluctance of the central government to move away from the system of appointed provincial leadership.[74]

For example, as Harding and Leyland point out

> self-dealing is a common form of conflict of interest which occurs when members of local councils or administrators, or their families, are involved, or become involved, in a construction company or other company which is awarded a contract by the local administration. There have been cases where payment has been received for a project without any work being carried out. Another abuse has involved the direct use of public funds for personal benefit, or for canvassing votes.[75]

Such abuses have continued despite impressive statute laws such as the Organic Law on the Prevention and Suppression of Corruption 1999, which prevents any such conflicts of interest, but does not apply to local government, allowing local office-holders to avoid having to declare their assets. Similarly, the Municipal Act 1953, as amended in 2019, forbids mayors, council members and administrators from having an interest, directly or indirectly, in any municipal contracts.[76] There is clearly a need for law reform and stronger implementation

[70] ibid 137.

[71] See, however, the discussion of Chiang Mai below.

[72] 2019 Act (n 45).

[73] Harding and Leyland (n 4) 139ff.

[74] ibid.

[75] ibid 140.

[76] 1953 Act, as amended, ss 72–73. The Tambon Council and Tambon Administrative Organisation Act 1994, the Provincial Administrative Organisation Act 1985, and the Bangkok Metropolis Administration Act 1985 enact similar provisions relating to their respective types of local government authority.

if decentralisation is to move forward effectively. The ombudsman could play an effective role in referring cases to the National Anti-Corruption Commission.[77]

IV. THE CHIANG MAI METROPOLITAN ADMINISTRATION BILL: A TEMPLATE FOR CHANGE?[78]

In Thailand, while the benefits of decentralisation are widely acknowledged, many also see dangers in pursuing it. These include, as we have seen in other countries, the uncertainty of transition; potential inconsistencies in policy; and the facilitation of local corruption or local capture.[79] Some even see decentralisation as dangerous to national security or national unity.[80] In Chiang Mai decentralisation is thought to facilitate the maintenance of local belief systems and the recognition of local identity.[81] Despite the limitations on local autonomy in Thailand, a long-held the desire for autonomy burns strongly in Chiang Mai.[82]

Bureaucratic centralisation, along with many other traditional assumptions about government, has been challenged by political movements, principally the Progressive Movement (PGM). The PGM supports the current pledges to advance the Chiang Mai Metropolitan Administration Bill ('CMMA Bill'), which seeks to 'challenge the constitutional contours of central-local relations in Thailand' implementing devolution of powers, such as has been seen in, for example, the United Kingdom.[83] This bill has been blocked in parliament since 2013, as a result of the coup of 2014, but if enacted, it would undoubtedly send a ripple effect across Thailand by setting a decentralisation template for other provinces and cities to follow. Chiang Mai is Thailand's second city, and second cities are often a gathering-place for opposition to centralised domination from

[77] Harding and Leyland (n 4) 141.

[78] This section is based on Harding and Leelapatana (n 3). This template for change is gone into here in some detail, as it represents one of the most important innovations in SE Asian territorial governance.

[79] See eg this critique of decentralisation in the Philippines: M Shair-Rosenfield, 'The causes and effects of the Local Government Code in the Philippines: Locked in a status-quo of weakly decentralised authority?' (2016) 33(2) *Journal of Southeast Asian Economies* 157.

[80] A Harding and R Leelapatana, 'Towards recentralisation?: Thailand's 2014 coup, tutelage democracy and their effects on local government' (*50 Shades of Federalism*, 2020) 50shadesoffederalism.com/case-studies/towards-recentralisation-thailands-2014-coup-tutelage-democracy-and-their-effects-on-local-government/.

[81] D Engel and L Chua, 'State and personhood in Southeast Asia: The promise and potential for law and society research' (2015) 2 *Asian Journal of Law and Society* 211.

[82] Above n 3, 78.

[83] As has occurred in Sarawak in relation to devolution of powers in Malaysia's federal system: A Harding, 'Devolution of powers in Sarawak: A dynamic process of redesigning territorial governance in a federal system' (2017) 13 *Asian Journal of Comparative Law* 257, 272. The CMMA Bill, s 18, uniquely in Thai legislation, uses the term 'devolution' (Khwām cngrạk phạkdī).

the capital or metropolis, thereby advancing the principle of local autonomy.[84] As we have seen, Chiang Mai has a distinctive Lanna culture and history that differs from that of Bangkok and Central and Southern Thailand.[85] For example, as David Engel shows, its culture maintains an inter-subjective concept of justice in which there would be harmonisation but no winners or losers.[86]

The political crisis of 2010[87] led to violent clashes between red and yellow supporters in Chiang Mai and consequential adverse impacts on the local economy, and further hastened a Chiang Mai-based attempt to find areas of compromise between the red and yellow factions.[88]

In 2011 the CMMA Bill was drafted based on a people's initiative that involved citizens of different political factions that have polarised Thailand, contesting for government power since 2005 and sparking, as we have seen, two military coups. The idea of local autonomy thus contains the possibility for containing the worst of national political polarisation in a pluralist system of local government. The Bill was debated amongst citizen groups and presented to Parliament in 2013, supported by 12,000 signatures, under the then 2007 Constitution.[89] The coup of 2014 in effect ensured that the CMMA Bill would remain in limbo until the present, although, since the return of a limited form at least of democracy in 2019, it remains a tantalising possibility. In December 2020 local elections were held for the first time since 2014, but even though considerable interest has been expressed in the Chiang Mai model, the elections did not indicate widespread popular (as opposed to politician) support outside of Chiang Mai province for the democratisation of Thailand's PAO system.[90]

The idea of the CMMA is that of a 'self-governing province', which, according to Prin Nithat-ek,

> entails local people in each province participating in decision-making and determining their own developmental strategy and distribution of resources in politics, economy, society, culture, natural resource and environment, physical and mental health. The essence of self-governing province is to transfer political power that is concentrated in the central administrative system to a provincial community unit.[91]

In general, the CMMA Bill seeks to empower local autonomy by abolishing the MoI-supervised system of deconcentration, replacing Chiang Mai province

[84] J Hodos, *Second Cities: Globalisation and Local Politics in Manchester and Philadelphia* (Philadelphia, Temple University Press, 2011) ch 7 ('Identity and governance in the second city').

[85] Engel (n 17).

[86] We may compare with this *barangay* justice in the Philippines: see p 117.

[87] Engel (n 17).

[88] Harding and Leelapatana (n 3) 90.

[89] 'The Chiang Mai Bill proposed' (*Thai PBS*, 26 October 2013) news.thaipbs.or.th/content/203740.

[90] S Strangio, 'In Thailand, local elections see stagnating progressive vote' (*The Diplomat*, 22 December 2020): thediplomat.com/2020/12/in-thailand-local-elections-see-stagnating-progressive-vote/.

[91] P Nithat-ek, 'The rise of antagonism: The Chiang Mai province people's network for self-governing administration and its reaction against the hegemonic centralising state' (2017) 13 *Journal of Social Sciences, Naresuan University* 187, 192–94.

with a devolved body called Chiang Mai Metropolitan Administration. The theory of local governance represented by the Bill involves a number of other elements that follow from the rejection of deconcentration and the embracing of decentralisation. First, it adopts from the example of Japan the idea of two-tiered local government, involving democratic participation by the lower level and cooperation between the two levels.[92] Second, it involves the notion of a citizen assembly at the provincial level, counterbalancing the granting of legislative power to the elected council and executive power to an elected governor.[93] Third, it involves transfer of 70 per cent of the province's revenue from the central government in Bangkok to the province, as opposed to the present allocation which reverses these percentages. This presents a dramatic shift in allocation of powers on the basis of subsidiarity – retaining only military, foreign relations, judiciary, and fiscal powers with the central government, with all other functions devolved to local authorities.[94] The citizen assembly is crucial to this enterprise in providing an element of direct democracy that can be compared to the creation of similar bodies in some Western states, such as those that led to abortion reform in the Republic of Ireland.[95] However, rather than being chosen on a random basis reflecting the composition of society, as with the Irish model, the Chiang Mai model involves a selection system that more resembles the notion of functional constituencies, if we understand these as including representation of lower-level local government bodies (in Chiang Mai there are 25 of these).[96] A major reason for yellow interests being in support of the CMMA Bill is that they are convinced that in elections votes are simply bought; the selection system for the citizen assembly (the details of this system are to be decided by local regulations) tends to empower the civil society, which is largely controlled by yellow interests.[97]

In 50 of Thailand's 76 provinces the CMMA Bill has been studied with a view to being applicable more widely, and it has found favour there, leading to consideration of a Provincial Self-Government (PSG) Bill in parliament. This Bill too is currently blocked.

The CMMA Bill is directed towards replacing the prevailing model of Thai nation-state as applied in Chiang Mai – that is, the scheme of 'deconcentration', by which the central government appoints the Chiang Mai provincial governor and other district chiefs – with the principles of devolution and delegation, set out in section 18. It therefore seeks to establish a two-tiered system of local government. The upper tier concerns the establishment of the Chiang Mai

[92] CMMA Bill 2013, s 7.

[93] ibid s 71.

[94] ibid ss 18(1), 118.

[95] M Palese, 'The Irish abortion referendum: How a citizens' assembly helped to break years of political deadlock' (Electoral Reform Society, 29 May 2018).

[96] See below.

[97] Harding and Leelapatana (n 3) 91.

Metropolitan Administration (CMMA), while the lower tier is organised in the form of 25 Chiang Mai Municipalities (CMMs).[98] Indeed, section 9 of the Bill imposes several currently provincial responsibilities on the CMMs, and is designed to support collaboration and improvement of technical expertise at the municipal level. However, the Bill mainly concerns the CMMA itself. To ensure a smooth and uninterrupted transfer of authority, functions, and obligations from the central government to decentralised agencies in Chiang Mai, the Bill further sets up a Chiang Mai Metropolitan Administration Committee, with the obligation to determine criteria, procedures, and plans for giving effect to the transfer of powers within two years of the Bill coming into effect. The members of this committee include the Prime Minister or a Deputy Prime Minister; five representatives of Chiang Mai local administrations; a group of three experts comprising a scholar, a representative of the NGOs, and a representative of local community organisations; and the Head of the Office of the Decentralisation Commission.[99]

Part IV of the Bill sets up the CMMA itself. This comprises three major elements. The CMMA Council ('the Council'); the Governor; and the Citizen Assembly.[100] The Council is the legislative branch of the CMMA, which consists of Councillors directly elected by Chiang Mai citizens for a term of four years, the number of Councillors depending on the population at the relevant time. The area governed by the CMMA is to be divided into constituencies with the approximate population of 30,000; each of these is to be represented by one Council member.[101] Its main function is to consider and approve Chiang Mai ordinances.[102] The Governor is also directly elected by Chiang Mai citizens for a term of four years.[103] The Governor holds authority not just to initiate policies and plans necessary for local administration, but also to dissolve the Council.[104] Unlike existing governors the Chiang Mai Governor may hold a referendum on significant matters affecting the CMMA.[105]

Whereas the Council and the Governor are generally based on the Bangkok model, the Citizen's Assembly is a striking innovation. Its status is 'equivalent to the Governor', although it is not clear what this implies in terms of the balance of power between them.[106] It can be explained in terms of the three Chiang Mai entities resembling the three sides of a triangle, but it should be noted that according to section 71 of the Bill, the Citizen's Assembly shall comprise 200 members, installed from a selection amongst four functional groups, namely civil

[98] CMMA Bill 2013, s 7.
[99] ibid s 14.
[100] ibid s 23.
[101] ibid ss 24–25.
[102] ibid Part VIII.
[103] ibid ss 56–58.
[104] ibid s 60(7).
[105] ibid s 141.
[106] ibid s 71(1).)

society organisations, *tambon* delegates; professional groups; and experts.[107] In order to understand the radical sweep of these provisions, we need to consider the duties of the Citizen's Assembly as enshrined in section 72, which are those of: (i) supervising and recommending policies and direction of development; (ii) tracking the performance of local Members of Parliament and civil servants, including by bringing lawsuits as an injured party, and by proposing a motion for impeaching members of the Council; (iii) promoting and supporting members of civil-society organisations to collaborate in sustainably managing the local environment and in conserving and reviving local traditions; (iv) organising public fora for Chiang Mai citizens and residents to exchange opinions; and (v) reporting problems in the CMMA or CMM administration. Deliberation in the Citizen Assembly, in line with local culture, is not based on voting or specific decision-making, but rather on consensus, the Assembly having no legal powers as such.[108]

Within its territory, the CMMA would have, according to section 72 of the Bill, authority in a very wide range of functions, from development planning, infrastructure and environmental and cultural conservation to policing, tourism, and education. Significantly, the Bill provides several mechanisms, in addition to the Citizen Assembly, aimed at encouraging local citizens to participate in administration. They have the rights to obtain information related to the CMMA and participate in the legislative process; express their political opinions with regard to CMA; be consulted; participate as members of a committee or sub-committee or a working group responsible for administering Chiang Mai; request a public hearing; and vote in a referendum. Furthering the democratic innovation inherent in the Bill, 5,000 residents of Chiang Mai may lodge a petition for the impeachment of a Councillor, or the Governor.[109]

The Bill is both extensive in scope and question-begging in detail. It represents a plan that requires much further discussion. More importantly, the Bill has also inspired the Law Reform Committee to propose two-tiered local governments by virtue of the PSG Bill, the abolition of the MoI-supervised system of deconcentration, the adoption of the 70/30 revenue share, a move to directly elected governors, and the introduction of the Citizen Assembly in all provinces.[110] Calls for PSG have fostered a sense of local identity within many local provinces, in particular, Pattani, a Muslim-majority province currently struggling with insurgency, as is detailed in the next section. Despite these promising provisions, enormous challenges still remain, especially regarding the reallocation of revenue, which appears too over-ambitious. As this model requires decentralisation at both city and district levels, the climate of reconciliation which has facilitated discussions among wide-ranging interests is crucial. In short, the

[107] ibid s 71.
[108] Harding and Leelapatana (n 3) 93.
[109] Section 147. But this device still requires the enactment of specific legislation.
[110] Harding and Leelapatana (n 3) 94.

CMMA Bill inspires the establishment of a radical reorientation in central-local relations that impacts not just on territorial governance but on Thai democracy itself. It conspicuously challenges the nation-state as it has been defined so far, after 90 years of constitutional government. However, while the Bill is radical in its implications, it was drafted from a non-partisan perspective in terms of 'colour-coded politics'. It is, in those terms, an orange rather than red or yellow proposal, and will reward discussion and refinement in the ongoing development of Thai democracy – if given the chance to do so.

V. INSURGENCY AND THE SOUTHERN BORDER PROVINCES[111]

Apart from decentralisation, Thailand's main issue in the field of territorial governance is the unrest in the Southern border provinces of Pattani, Yala and Narathiwat,[112] whose Malay/Muslim majority population constitutes about 80 per cent of a population of around two million.[113] Here we consider the circumstances leading to a prospective case for what would be a dramatic innovation in the Thai context – devolution of powers to a region of special autonomy. This instance can be compared to the actual cases of special autonomy considered in Part III. Internal conflict in the three provinces has cost more than 7,000 lives in the last 20 years.[114] Insurgency has become a major problem due to a combination of marginalisation and radicalisation of the Malay/Muslim population, resulting in a major insurgency seeking independence or at least autonomy, which has been pursued mainly by the National Revolutionary Front (BRN).[115] Various attempts have been made over the years since 2004, when serious violence erupted, to resolve this issue. The Thai state has not traditionally attempted to restrict the religious and cultural rights of the country's Muslim population, nor its right to its own law and education system. However, Prime Minister General Phibulsongkhram in the 1940s attempted to force assimilation of the Malay/Muslims by settling Buddhists in the three provinces, giving rise to minority-majority conflict, and by abolishing the *shari'a* courts.[116] As with other similar cases described in Part III there remain issues of identity, development,

[111] This section is largely based on Harding and Leyland (n 4) ch 4; and P Leyland, 'Thailand's troubled South: Examining the case for devolution from a comparative perspective' (2009) 11(1) *Australian Journal of Asian Law* 1.

[112] For a full account, see D McCargo, *Tearing Apart the Land: Islam and Legitimacy in Southern Thailand* (Singapore, NUS Press, 2009).

[113] J Liow, 'Thailand's Southern border provinces: Constructing narratives and imagining Patani Darussalam' ch3 in JCY Liow, *Religion and Nationalism in Southeast Asia* (Cambridge, Cambridge University Press, 2016).

[114] A Engvall and A Andersson, 'The Southern Conflict' ch 23 in P Chachavalpongpun (ed), *The Routledge Handbook of Contemporary Thailand* (Abingdon, Routledge, 2020) 296ff.

[115] ibid 295; McCargo (n 112) 142ff.

[116] S Imaizumi, 'Application of Islamic Law in Thailand', Institute of Developing Economies, Japan, Discussion Paper No 660 (2017) 12.

and discrimination in official appointments, and these have been exacerbated by the occasionally extreme responses of the government to mounting violence. The region is also amongst the poorest in Thailand, with a third lacking formal education and a 15 per cent unemployment rate. However, '[t]he insurgency has never just been about this economic marginalisation. There is a strong sense of internal colonialism and relative deprivation'.[117]

A. Origins of the Conflict

The origins of the present problems are to be found in Siam's imperialist expansion that formed part of its modernisation under King Chulalongkorn. This history has been outlined earlier in this chapter. Prior to their incorporation into the Siamese state in 1909, the three present provinces (formed in 1933) comprised local sultanates, which had been tributary states of Siam since the fifteenth century.[118] The Southern border of Siam had been in doubt for most of the nineteenth century, until settled by the Anglo-Siamese Treaty of 1909, that separated the Muslim sultanate from the Malay States of Kedah, Kelantan, Perlis and Terrenganu, which were transferred to British control.[119]

Despite concessions to the region's special circumstances and identity, the centralised power of Bangkok and the strong policy of unity and uniformity, resulting from the late nineteenth century reforms, pressed as heavily on the Southern border provinces as it did on Lanna, as discussed above. Dissatisfaction was expressed in tax and language rebellions in the region in 1922 and 1923. And as with Lanna, centrally appointed civil servants replaced local nobility as administrative heads.[120]

The seeds of the current conflict can also be found in the occupation of official positions and business opportunities by the Buddhist minority in the region, and the rejection of the Malay/Muslim population of the secular state education system in favour of their own *pondok* (Islamic schools).[121] The increasingly assertive conduct of the Muslim majority has also made the

[117] Z Abuza, *Conspiracy of Silence: The Insurgency in Southern Thailand* (Washington, United States Institute of Peace, 2009) 30.

[118] As Winichakul explains, '[a] powerful Bangkok king had to fight to expand his umbrella of merit and righteousness, dharma, as far as possible to bring lesser kingdoms under the protection of his supreme merit': T Winichakul, *Siam Mapped: A History of the Geo-Body of a Nation* (Honolulu, University of Hawai'i Press, 1994) 85. This relationship, in other words, was not understood merely in terms of territory. Rather, these tributary states were bound to Bangkok by a ritual of submission, involving periodic payments to renew the allegiance and, with it, the expectation of protection: T Loos, *Subject Siam: Family Law, and Colonial Modernity in Thailand* (Ithaca, Cornell University Press, 2006) 77.

[119] C Baker and P Phongpaichit, *A History of Thailand*, 2nd edn (Cambridge, Cambridge University Press, 2009) 53.

[120] Harding and Leelapatana (n 3) 83.

[121] Liow (n 113) 115.

Buddhist population feel increasingly under threat.[122] As a result there have emerged what have been called ethnic and religiously polarised 'communities of fear'.[123] The territorial governance system, which has not been varied in this region, has been directly impacted by the conflict in the sense that village headmen in rival Buddhist and Malay-speaking villages have undertaken responsibility for the protection of their respective communities, becoming in the process prime targets for extremist violence.[124]

The Thai government has nonetheless attempted to integrate the Muslim community by increasing the number of appointments to provincial positions such as district officer, and by enhancing educational opportunities.[125] A Southern Border Provinces Administrative Centre (SBPAC) was established in 1981 as a forum for the military, officials and community leaders, as an agency supporting local projects, and to act as an intermediary between the state and the Muslim community.[126]

Attempts to secure autonomy or a separate state have variously been pursued by the Pattani National Liberation Front (BNPP), the Pattani United Liberation Organisation (PULO), and the National Revolutionary Front (BRN), which is now the leader of the autonomy movement, but has proved an elusive adversary for the military both militarily and in the context of peace talks.[127] Their campaign, whether by violence or advocacy and negotiation, is for an independent homeland of Patani for citizens of Malay/Muslim origin.[128] Religion has become a prime focus for new jihadist groups with a radical Islamist agenda associated with fundamentalist organisations.[129] These build on the fact that violence 'reflects a disappointed, dissenting, and divided Malay-Muslim community, whose most capable leaders have been captured by Bangkok'.[130] This represents a 'shift from having recognisable organisations associated with prominent individuals to having multiple religious groups, often without clearly identified political, as opposed to religious, leaders [and] presents a problem for the authorities when seeking to have negotiations which engage all the relevant factions'.[131] The escalation of violence since 2004 has been attributed, in part at least, to the policies pursued by former Prime Minister Thaksin Shinawatra. In May 2002 the SBPAC was abolished by Thaksin because of its association with

[122] D McCargo, 'The politics of Buddhist identity in Thailand's seep South: The demise of civil religion' (2009) 40(1) *Journal of Southeast Asian Studies* 11, 14.

[123] M Askew, 'Landscapes of fear, horizons of trust: Villagers dealing with danger in Thailand's insurgent South' (2009) 40(1) *Journal of Southeast Asian Studies* 59, 85.

[124] McCargo (n 122) 14.

[125] D McCargo, 'Thaksin and the resurgence of violence in the Thai South: Network monarchy strikes back?' (2006) 38(1) *Critical Asian Studies* 39, 43.

[126] Leyland (n 111) 7; Harding and Leyland (n 3).

[127] McCargo (n 112) 168ff.

[128] Abuza (n 117) 16.

[129] ibid 128ff.

[130] McCargo (n 122) 20.

[131] Leyland (n 111) 8.

his opponents, the Democrat Party; but its replacement, the Southern Border Provinces Peace-Building Command (SBPPC), failed to gain the confidence of Muslim leaders.[132] Thaksin abolished the existing power structure in the region, replacing officials with his own appointees and strengthening the security forces, describing the insurgents as bandits and drug-traffickers.[133] However, as Phongpaichit and Baker have pointed out:

> [T]he far south's unique position as a cultural enclave under semi-colonial rule meant it was uniquely sensitive to the Thaksin government's centralisation of power [and this upsurge of Islamic consciousness] renewed stress on Thai culture, and rehabilitation of the military … as security forces became more concerned over possible links with militant Islam, the frequency of searches and seizures increased.[134]

The conflict has assumed a strong religious dimension in the Buddhist community too, with *wats* being increasingly employed as military bases, and this has affected the traditional status of Buddhism in the region, identifying it with the Thai state.[135] Rising Buddhist nationalism has demanded formation of militias such as Or Ror Bor (civil volunteers for village protection).[136]

B. Atrocities and National Reconciliation

As the situation deteriorated, atrocities were committed on both sides. In April 2004, 107 alleged assailants, mostly between 15 and 20 years of age, died in nine hours of clashes at the Kru-Ze mosque.[137] The 'Tak Bai Incident' was perhaps the most notorious example of an extreme response by the state. In October 2004 around 2,000 Muslim protestors encircled a police station. More than 1,000 arrests were made. Those detained were bound and then packed into trucks to be taken to a detention centre for interrogation. Of those subsequently transported in appalling conditions 78 died of suffocation.[138] A report by the government's independent commission directed blame on the military commanders. A series of revenge attacks by Muslim militants followed in the wake of this event.[139] It became known that the King was opposed to military force being used, and Thaksin changed direction, becoming more conciliatory.

[132] ibid.

[133] U Pathmanand, 'Thaksin's Achilles' heel: The failure of hawkish approaches in the Thai South' (2006) 38(1) *Critical Asian Studies* 73, 77.

[134] P Phongpaichit and C Baker, *Thaksin: The Business of Politics in Thailand* (Chiang Mai, Silkworm Books, 2004) 236.

[135] M Jerryson, 'Appropriating a space for violence: State Buddhism in Southern Thailand' (2009) 20(1) *Journal of Southeast Asian Studies* 33, 43.

[136] McCargo (n 112) 25.

[137] ibid 108ff.

[138] Abuza (n 117) 65.

[139] ibid 66.

A National Reconciliation Commission was set up under the chairmanship of former Prime Minister Anand Panyarachun, to look into the conflict and recommend solutions.[140]

The potential for the NRC to achieve results was undermined by the facts that representatives from the South were reluctant to become involved due to the danger of them being exposed to personal attacks, and that Muslims felt further alienated by Thaksin's emergency decree of July 2005.[141] This emergency, described in the press as a 'decree with a moustache', gave draconian powers to the Prime Minister.[142] When the NRC reported in March 2006, it recommended changes in territorial governance that were intended to form the basis for a settlement. It proposed decentralisation of political power and mechanisms for community participation in policy-making. These were coupled with proposals for a new regional administrative body, the Peaceful Strategic Administrate Centre for Southern Border Provinces (PSAC), which would assume responsibility for administration in the region. The report also put forward radical plans to address deficiencies in the judicial system by formally recognising Islamic law, and adopting Malay as a second 'working' language.[143] However, these recommendations were out of sync with the *zeitgeist* of a mainstreaming Buddhist nationalism, not to mention Thaksin's general policy of suppression.[144] After the coup of September 2006, the military junta substantially reinforced military efforts in the region, increasing the defence budget, but at the same time it courted the Islamic community by distancing itself from Thaksin's policy, apologising for the previous excesses and promising to recognise Islamic law.[145] A reconstituted Southern Border Provinces Administration Centre (SBAC) now included Justice Ministry officials, but was 'firmly subordinated to the security apparatus of the Internal Security Operations Command (ISOC) [perceived as] acting as a development organisation to support military security policy'.[146] Nonetheless the violence surged with a series of brutal beheadings and bombings directed mainly at Buddhists, as well as extra-judicial executions and disappearances.[147]

[140] McCargo (n 112) 10.

[141] ibid 64.

[142] A Harding. 'Emergency powers with a moustache: Special powers, military rule and evolving constitutionalism in Thailand' ch 11 in V Ramraj and A Thiruvengadam (eds), *Emergency Powers in Asia: Exploring the Limits of Legality* (Cambridge, Cambridge University Press, 2010); McCargo, ibid 64.

[143] Abuza (n 117) 193.

[144] McCargo observes that 'popular responses to violent incidents such as the March 2007 Yala minibus attack revealed the extent to which hardline nationalist discourse and anti-Muslim sentiments were becoming increasingly overt and mainstream elements of Thai Buddhist identity and thinking': above n 122, 32.

[145] Askew (n 123) 186ff.

[146] ibid 198.

[147] Engvall and Anderson (n 114) 296ff.

C. Not by Force Alone

As Peter Leyland maintains, '[i]t is not simply the fact borne out by wide experience that conflicts of this type cannot be resolved by force alone, but that a link can be demonstrated between the functioning of institutions under an agreed constitutional framework and a resumption of peaceful coexistence'.[148]

Various attempts have been made to bring the parties together to resolve the intractable issues in the region, notably in Langkawi in 2006, Bogor in 2008, then again in Geneva in 2011, and Kuala Lumpur in 2013.[149] Although these talks all failed to secure any forward movement, it was recognised that some form of innovation in territorial governance was needed. For example, the SBAC could be accorded devolved powers and separated from the military, placing it directly under the Prime Minister's Office, existing local government structures remaining in place.[150] Or, in another formulation, it could be run by a local Member of Parliament with an executive body comprising a permanent secretary and the governors of the three provinces. The main benefit of such a solution would be to ensure that the problems of the South were directly addressed by a powerful agency with a direct line to the prime minister and cabinet.[151] However, a major flaw would be the lack of local democracy, which we will find to be a major requirement in the cases of special autonomy in Bangsamoro and Aceh, and which is not supplied by any consultative mechanism.[152] Instead of democracy, proposals involved local input via a Chamber of the Southern Border Provinces, a consultative body composed of functional group representatives elected by the groups: religious leaders, teachers, health professionals, business representatives, administrators, and security officials. The fear was that the state would be weakened by new institutions falling under the control of Islamic militants with threats to security still present.[153]

The challenge is formidable, and not just due to the extreme polarisation. It is also problematical that the Islamic insurgency is no longer represented by separatist groups with identifiable agendas and leaders. Rather, it lacks clear political objectives, and has become increasingly fragmented.[154]

However, the challenge is not impossible to meet. In Part III we will encounter similarly intractable problems in Aceh and Bangsamoro, both of which have been dealt with via a ceasefire; an externally brokered political settlement involving a broad range of interests; and a law enshrining a form of special autonomy involving the conferring of substantial powers on the devolved unit,

[148] Leyland (n 111) 15.
[149] Engvall and Anderson (n 114) 301.
[150] Leyland (n 111) 12.
[151] ibid.
[152] See chs 9, 10.
[153] Leyland (n 111) 12.
[154] ibid 22.

and recognition of legal pluralism. In such a process ideological camels will doubtless have to be swallowed, and in particular it will need to be recognised that the highly valued centralism of the Thai state will require drastic modification, at least in this instance, if not more generally, by the interposition of a strong regional intermediate authority at the provincial level, with credible democratic checks and balances, and subject, as to constitutional validity, to the Constitutional Court. It would also likely require the conferring of wider jurisdiction on the *shari'a* court system, which was established in the three provinces and Satun in 1946.[155] Given the Muslim majority, there would also be a need for the protection of the rights of the Buddhist minority, perhaps in the form of a special human rights body for the region.[156]

Radical measures are needed to break the cycle of violence. Military rule from 2014 to 2019 effectively postponed any serious efforts to resolve the issues, given the national state of crisis, which continued after the restoration of civilian government in 2019, with numerous street protests. However, in February 2024, following a new round of peace talks facilitated by Malaysia, it was announced that both sides had agreed in principle to a peace plan.[157]

VI. CONCLUSION

Thailand's decentralisation presents several contradictory narratives: deconcentration v decentralisation; bureaucracy v democracy; red v yellow; Chiang Mai v Bangkok; Muslim v Buddhist. The state remains highly centralised despite a quarter of a century of ostensible decentralisation, most policy being implemented directly or indirectly from Bangkok. This approach offers the advantage of relatively uniform delivery of public services throughout the country. At the same time the narrative of decentralisation and citizen participation has been widely employed in recent years, signifying potentially a fundamental shift in approach. Constitution-making has offered the prospect at least of subsidiarity, power being exercised at the lowest possible level, and for the introduction of various types of citizen participation. In this chapter we have noted some positive experiments in this direction.

Lowatcharin and Crumpton, writing in 2020, are able to give a positive verdict on decentralisation:

> increases in development are evident throughout Thailand, especially in terms of infrastructure and the basic quality of life in rural jurisdictions. As the Thai people witnessed tangible changes in their local conditions, they have focused more attention

[155] Act on the Application of Islamic Law in the Area of Pattani, Naratiwat, Yala, and Satun Provinces 1946.

[156] Leyland (n 111) 22; A Harding, 'Buddhism, human rights and constitutional reform in Thailand' (2007) 2(1) *Asian Journal of Comparative Law* 1.

[157] 'Thailand, Muslim separatists agree on new plan to end violence' *Al Jazeera* (24 February 2024).

> on and have become more aware of the importance of local politics and local self-governance. Decentralisation has brought about a number of positive outcomes, including the increase of citizen participation, needs-based service delivery, accountability, and political education.[158]

However, a reluctance to embrace what has been called 'federalism all the way down'[159] is also understandable. Administrative capacity at the local level has been identified as requiring improvement, and progress is needed in transforming the nature of politics at the local government level, in particular to reduce the influence of local capture, and to facilitate the redistribution of revenue to local communities. A more serious but related objection concerns the potential for corruption if funding is channelled down to smaller units without effective oversight. However, the continuance of a highly centralised system of territorial governance has undoubtedly contributed to the conflict in the Southern border provinces, and a form of devolution here might form the constitutional basis for a possible solution. The prospect of devolution for the South is reinforced by a similar prospect for the North. A result of 'winner-takes-all' is one of the effects of a system where power is heavily concentrated at the centre. Little scope is given under this system of territorial governance for outlying regions, with different political loyalties and interests, to pursue divergent policies. The introduction of a more potent system of regional and local government could ensure that locally popular politicians have responsibility for forming and implementing policy at this level, and in turn this might assist in reducing the intensity of the underlying conflicts that represent Thailand's major problems.

[158] Above n 5, 180.

[159] H Gerken, 'Federalism all the way down' (2010) 124 *Harvard Law Review* 4.

Part III

Special Regional Autonomy

WE HAVE SEEN repeatedly in this book that territorial governance in Southeast Asia needs to recognise, at many levels, the diversity that is characteristic of the region. Moreover, this diversity is the leading reason for developing territorial governance along the lines we have set out in Part II.

The chapters in Part III look first at some experiments in conflict resolution by means of special (that is, asymmetric) regional autonomy, in first Aceh and Papua, Indonesia (chapter nine) and then Bangsamoro in the Philippines (chapter ten). In chapter eleven we look at Sabah and Sarawak in Malaysia, where there has been no insurgency, but there is historic regional autonomy. In considering these we can also take account of the discussions in chapter five (on special administrative areas in Myanmar), and chapter seven (on the troubled Southern border provinces, where special autonomy has not been adopted, but it remains a possibility). In this sense Part III is relevant to territorial governance in all five countries.

In these cases of special regional autonomy there are historic and still ongoing attempts to find a compromise between, on the one hand, the need for adherence of minority communities to the nation-state, and, on the other hand, recognition of deep differences in ethnicity, culture, language, or religion between national minority and majority communities. In some cases, there has been extreme violence, which has made the already awkward task of constitutional settlement more difficult, but, as we shall see, not entirely impossible. We will find that success in achieving resolution to conflict, or avoidance of conflict, along the lines of special regional autonomy, depends on two matters.

First, it is necessary to reach a broad political agreement regarding the principle of autonomy that involves the capacity and willingness to achieve a balanced form of regional autonomy.

Second, it is necessary to address many issues of detailed implementation that may (as we have repeatedly seen that territorial governance does) throw into question the principles upon which the overall governance system of the nation-state is based. We will also find that addressing these issues involves significant ongoing governance challenges, even after – sometimes long after – political agreement in outline has been achieved. In this Part we look at cases of regional autonomy, which have in common that a special form of autonomy has been granted to a region in order to resolve long-standing conflict or disaffection. This method of handling interethnic conflict is one of Southeast Asia's original contributions to territorial governance.

8

Autonomy and the Demand for a Homeland

I. GEOGRAPHY, DIVERSITY, AND GOVERNANCE

SOUTHEAST ASIAN STATES, as a result of colonialism and the partially-related deep history of migration both within and from outside the region, are complex in social composition and in human geography, as we have seen. This complexity continues to pose many challenges of geopolitics and national integration.[1]

Most Southeast Asian states were created in their present form well within living memory, but the communities they embrace find their geographical location and social and political relations with other communities deeply rooted in a history that by far predates the modern state.[2] This matter was outlined in chapter one. Very often, too, their law in the form of customary or religious law by far predates the positive law and the constitution of the nation state (or states in some cases) into which they have been, sometimes reluctantly, folded. This fact leads inevitably to legal pluralism, either as a matter of social practice or by specific recognition and incorporation by the state. For example, John Bowen's study[3] of a family land dispute in the Gayo highlands of Aceh (a province of Indonesia that is the subject of one of this Part's case studies) illustrates how resolution of the dispute involved a need to resort to *adat* (local custom), Islam, and state civil law, presenting three different legal conceptions of property in a small community. In Bowen's study the assumption of *adat*'s fundamental authority, virtually spiritual in nature, is unquestioned by the villagers as the basis of their legal consciousness. Yet the Gayo are also an ethnic minority within a strongly Islamic part of Indonesia that has, since the time of that study, intensively and controversially implemented Islamic law.[4]

[1] B Anderson, *Imagined Communities: Reflections on the Origin and Spread of Nationalism* (London, Verso, 2006).

[2] JC Scott, *The Art of not Being Governed: An Anarchist History of Upland Southeast Asia* (New Haven, Yale University Press, 2009).

[3] J Bowen, *Islam, Law and Equality in Indonesia: An anthropology of Public Reasoning*: (Cambridge, Cambridge University Press, 2003) 26–34.

[4] S Butt and T Lindsey, *Indonesian Law* (Oxford, Oxford University Press, 2018) 205ff.

In these modern Southeast Asian states, still struggling with issues of culture, identity and belonging, the apparatus of government is nonetheless based on Western-style constitutional or institutional frameworks.[5] These frameworks relate strongly to either the federal or the unitary idea of the state, neither of which in any event easily embraces the idea of asymmetric regional autonomy.[6] For most of the region's history, territorial governance has been the main mode of governance, at least before the advent of colonialism, and states have struggled to centralise power. The region is largely made up of territories that used to be kingdoms in their own right, many of these only relatively recently subdued by a metropolitan, centralising power, whether based on an expansionist kingdom, as in the case of Thailand, or colonial domination, as in Malaysia, the Philippines and Indonesia.[7]

An approach to conflict resolution based on special regional autonomy generally concedes, to one extent or another, the operation of different laws for different communities according to the territory that they occupy.[8] In the cases discussed here autonomy fully embraces legal pluralism based on geography rather than merely subject-matter.[9] The term 'legal pluralism' is used in this context to mean the same as Tamanaha's category of 'folk legal pluralism'.[10] Regional autonomy defines an area (a province or provinces, or parts thereof, or enclaves within them) as a minority 'homeland' that often also represents an important aspect of their identity. This constitutes the territory over which powers are devolved to the regional government *asymmetrically*, in order that the minority population may exercise a form of self-determination. In some instances, self-determination forms the basis, not just for self-rule, but for a

[5] Wen-Chen Chang, Li-ann Thio, Kevin YL Tan, and Jiunn-rong Yeh (2014), *Constitutionalism in Asia: Cases and Materials* (Oxford, Hart Publishing, 2014) ch 2 ('Constitutional Cultures in Asia'); A Welikala, 'Theorising constitutionalism in Buddhist dominated Asia polities', ch 3 in T Ginsburg and B Schonthal (eds), *Buddhism and Comparative Constitutional Law* (Cambridge, Cambridge University Press, 2022).

[6] In Europe, for example, as elsewhere, regional autonomy is a relatively recent experiment: M Weller and K Nobbs, (eds), *Asymmetric Autonomy and the Settlement of Ethnic Conflicts* (Philadelphia, University of Pennsylvania Press, 2010); Y Ghai and S Woodman, *Practising Self-Government: A Comparative Study of Autonomous Regions* (Cambridge, Cambridge University Press, 2013); TH Malloy and F Palermo (eds), *Minority Accommodation through Territorial and Non-territorial Autonomy* (Oxford, Oxford University Press, 2015); R Toniatti and J Woelk (eds), *Regional Autonomy, Cultural Diversity and Differentiated Territorial government: The Case of Tibet – Chinese and Comparative Perspectives* (Abingdon, Routledge, 2017).

[7] B Andaya, 'Political development between the sixteenth and eighteenth centuries' ch 2 in *The Cambridge History of Southeast Asia*, volume 1, part 2 (Cambridge, Cambridge University Press, 1992).

[8] Malloy and Palermo (n 6).

[9] Legal pluralism scholars tend to use phrases such as 'semi-autonomous social field' (Sally Falk Moore), or 'social arena' (Brian Tamanaha) to describe the entities to which legal pluralism attaches: B Tamanaha, *Legal Pluralism Explained: History, Theory, Consequences* (Oxford, Oxford University Press, 2021).

[10] Tamanaha, ibid 176 ff. As Tamanaha explains, this form of legal pluralism covers both social and territorial fields.

claim to sovereignty or secession.[11] This self-determination encompasses at least several important, and in some cases most, areas of decision-making short of those that can only lie with the national government, such as defence and international relations. As part of this self-determination, legal pluralism is often also invoked in support of the claim to self-determination. This is especially the case with areas of personal law based on custom or religion, which tends more than other areas of law to express the identity and social values of a minority group.[12] In fact, it is difficult to see why regional autonomy would be even needed, in Southeast Asia at least, if legal pluralism in some form or other were not to be invoked as part of the case for autonomy. This assertion will be strongly supported by the case studies. It follows from this aspect of legal pluralism that regional autonomy will impact heavily on the justice system as well as on the political and administrative systems.

Human geography is of enormous importance in mediating and finding the most useful mode of conflict resolution under territorial governance, because a great deal depends on the distribution of the population. In some cases, it is possible to define an area or areas that are more or less exclusively inhabited by a minority community that seeks an officially-recognised homeland, and such area may form a basis for the granting of concessions. This possibility is realised in all of the case studies. These concessions may be powers over religion or custom (the right to recognise religion or custom for certain legal or official purposes, or to regulate religious or customary observance); the ability to make special rules about language and education; or rights of access to public goods such as civil service positions for an under-privileged minority. All of these aspects of self-determination are relevant to the case studies that follow in this and the following chapter. Alternatively, self-determination may simply consist of powers over policy areas that have no specific relevance for a minority, but afford a general opportunity to legislate or make policy choices in the interest of the region's population, whether or not in a culturally-specific manner. But this is more an argument for general decentralisation than for the special regional autonomy discussed here.

Of course, a minority community may not be identified with a specific territory, but may be evenly spread geographically, or else compacted into small areas the size of a village or an enclave too small to form a basis for special regional autonomy, and which may not therefore present a viable solution for the minority claims of such groups. The more compacted a minority community is, the easier it is, obviously, to find territorial solutions. But this compactness needs to be found over a large enough area for autonomy to be meaningful and viable, and for its advocates to be heard and to be credible. This latter position is not

[11] Toniatti and Woelk (n 6) 107ff.

[12] See eg I Deinla, 'Legal hybridity, trust, and the legitimacy of the Shari'ah in the Bangsamoro' (2019) 41 *Law and Policy* 198.

generally the case for most minorities in Southeast Asia, which perhaps explains why regional autonomy has not been adopted more generally across the region, but only in specific and sometimes violently contested, and also reasonably large, areas. The problem with the large area such as a province forming the territorial basis for a claim of regional autonomy is that the larger such area is, the more likely it is to include other groups, especially other national minorities than the one that claims the area as its homeland. Difficult issues may arise where there are majority communities, or other minority communities, living in enclaves *within* the minority homeland, such as Christians and indigenous peoples living in Muslim-majority Bangsamoro, as discussed in chapter ten. This is a major policy problem that is not easy to cater for, but it will generally involve guarantees being afforded to all groups in the region, not just those claiming self-determination. For this reason, human rights will be of great importance as an aspect of the governance system that is adopted for the autonomous region.

A minority may well of course be spread across the territory of the nation-state *in addition* to being concentrated in a particular area or areas, as is the case with Thai Muslims, for example. In such cases a range of strategies may be required, such as legal pluralism in addition to regional autonomy.

It should be noted that, despite this chapter's focus on regional autonomy, only a few millions out of Southeast Asia's half a billion people actually live under a system of territorial autonomy.[13] Thus diversity in itself is not generally or necessarily associated with the demand of minorities for a homeland, for the cases considered here are in fact exceptions, albeit important ones in the light of the ever-present need for nation-building. What is important is that serious attempts have been made to resolve the most pressing problems that territorial governance both presents and might plausibly resolve.

II. ADVANTAGES AND DISADVANTAGES OF REGIONAL AUTONOMY

What, then, precisely, are the advantages and disadvantages of asymmetric regional autonomy in the context of Southeast Asia?

The first point is that these advantages are over and above the general advantages of subsidiarity at the territorial level; or else, they are similar but have greater intensity or cogency. These general advantages are discussed elsewhere in this book, but can be summarised as efficiency and effectiveness due to local knowledge; the ability to engage in policy experimentation; and the satisfaction of community preferences. It is often also said that subsidiarity gives voters the chance to select an area on the basis of their preferences, and territorial units

[13] Aceh has 4.7 million people, Papua 3.5 million, Bangsamoro around 4 million, Sarawak about 2.5 million, and Sabah about 2.3 million.

the chance to compete with others for skilled citizens and inward investment.[14] However, in the case of regional autonomy these two factors are not relevant, as the assumption is that the minority in question chooses the homeland in which to live, and is not therefore inclined to relocate in any significant numbers.

Second, these advantages apart, regional autonomy offers the security of control and self-determination, legally guaranteed, over a minority's own, traditional homeland. It reduces the cogency of demands for secession. As we shall see, this in turn also offers the prospect of a lasting peace in a disturbed region without the sovereignty of the state being fractured.[15]

On the other hand, regional autonomy also involves granting asymmetric powers that are not given to other regions, possibly creating political tensions elsewhere in the political system, not just in the specific region. Asymmetry points up differences in stark constitutional terms, which from one aspect is a significant guarantee, but from another is a provocation to units not granted such autonomy to make far-reaching demands for their own self-determination. Asymmetry, in other words, can lead to more widespread claims for a new form of symmetry that takes much power away from the centre.[16] In addition, regional autonomy emphasises difference by giving it specific official and legal recognition. If so, it may drive into reverse the project of nation-building, or even heighten the existing claim for recognition of separate identity. For example, as discussed in chapter nine, Islamic jurisdiction did not feature strongly in secession/autonomy claims in Aceh until it became part of the 2006 settlement; yet it is now the main marker of the difference between that province and the rest of Indonesia.[17] There is a tendency, once the flag of autonomy is raised, for markers of difference to be emphasised, rather than to be erased or abraded in the interests of equal citizenship.

If we examine the issue of autonomy historically, we find that, in the centralisation of power during the 1960s–80s, Southeast Asian pluralism tended to be eclipsed in favour of an all-encompassing nationalism, expressed as nation building and developmentalism.[18] This was often expressed in priorising a national language, for example in education. In fact, the centralising tendency of Southeast Asian states goes back much further than modern state-building. Repeatedly over several centuries, a powerful centre asserted dominance over other centres of power, only to concede power to them as their own influence waned. This centralising tendency was not just political, but also supported by cultural or religious dominance. Centralisation was often therefore achieved at

[14] D Halberstam, 'Federalism: Theory, policy, law' ch 27 in M Rosenfeld, and A Sajo (eds), *The Oxford Handbook of Comparative Constitutional Law* (Oxford, Oxford University Press, 2013) 586ff.

[15] S Woolf, 'Complex power-sharing and the centrality of territorial self-government in contemporary conflict settlements' (2009) 8 *Ethnopolitics* 27.

[16] This is evident, eg in the Philippines: see p 180.

[17] See p 164ff.

[18] M Woo-Cummings (ed), *The Developmental State* (New York, Cornell University Press, 1999).

the expense of cultural autonomy for minority groups and sometimes by violent suppression, as was seen in Burma/Myanmar's chronic border wars. Naturally there had to be a reaction against this loss (sometimes a complete loss) of autonomy, so that general decentralisation, undertaken in the Philippines since 1987, Thailand since 1997, and Indonesia since 1999, is one fruit of that reaction, as we saw in Part II.

In the Indonesian case, as was discussed in chapter three, the end of the new-order period in 1998 ushered in a dangerous interlude of inter-ethnic violence and potential secession in some areas. Secession was in the event forestalled by decentralisation to the lowest governmental levels – cities and regencies – as opposed to provinces, where increased powers might simply fuel secession.[19]

Decentralisation in the Philippines, as was discussed in chapter six, finds its origin in the 1987 Constitution, which has defined democratic governance in the post-Marcos era. The entrenchment of local decentralisation in the Constitution at Article X[20] is the most definitive and structured of any in the region, and was fulfilled, as demanded by Article X, in the impressive Local Government Code 1991.[21] These instances of decentralisation also of course implicitly raised questions about asymmetric regional autonomy, and the settlement of long-standing claims for self-determination, revived during the twentieth century, and into the twenty-first, often by violent means.

III. STRUCTURE OF THE CASE STUDIES

Each of the case studies that follow is directed to the need for the creation of regional autonomy in an attempt to resolve endemic violent conflict or disaffection. The response of the nation-state in terms of territorial governance is considered under four general areas of inquiry that determine the extent, nature, and purposes of the autonomy granted. These are:

(i) the *claim for regional autonomy* and its recognition, in light of the nature and trajectory of the demand for self-determination;
(ii) the *executive and legislative powers* that have been conferred on the region, including consideration of central-local relations, special powers, and cooperative structures;

[19] S Butt and T Lindsey, *The Constitution of Indonesia: A Contextual Analysis* (Oxford, Hart Publishing, 2012); D Horowitz, *Constitutional Change and Democracy in Indonesia* (Cambridge, Cambridge University Press, 2013).

[20] One may compare here Indonesia's Article 18.

[21] M Teng-Calleja, et al, 'Transformation in Philippine local government' (2017) 43(1) *Local Government Studies* 67.

(iii) the region's *internal governance system*, including provision for local (that is, subregional) government, democratic participation, and recognition of distinct or traditional political structures; and
(iv) *legal pluralism and rights*, or the guaranteeing of rights, including the rights of communities (both majority and minority) to be dealt with according to their own law or customs in distinct judicial structures, according to the notion of legal pluralism.

9

Regional Autonomy I – Aceh and Papua

I. THE CLAIM FOR REGIONAL AUTONOMY IN ACEH

FOR A LONG time the province of Aceh has asserted its unique identity as having a more Islamic culture compared to the rest of Indonesia.[1] While resistance to colonial rule has long historical roots, intermittent warfare broke out during several periods over the last 150 years in attempts to sever the province from the central rule of both the Dutch colonial government before 1945 and the Indonesian republic after its establishment. Separatists have argued that Aceh never really agreed to be part of the Indonesian republic in the first place, and, despite the implementation of regional autonomy since 1999, there are still those who advocate secession. They have also argued that Aceh is disadvantaged in terms of development and natural-resource exploitation. A rebel group, Gerakan Aceh Merdeka (GAM) has been the main advocate of this position in recent decades, both in mounting a damaging insurgency against Indonesian forces, between 1989 and 1999, resulting in extensive violence on both sides, and in forming the leading political party, Parti Aceh, implementing regional autonomy since it was realised from 2006.[2]

The process of dealing with the Aceh insurgency was Indonesia's first item on the decentralisation agenda, which began, with the end of Suharto's new order period, in 1999, and is properly seen, as we shall see, in that context.[3] Moves towards establishing peace resulted in laws on Aceh autonomy being passed in 1999[4] and 2001,[5] even as large protests demanded a referendum on independence, and again in 2006.[6] The attempts in 1999 and 2001 failed to

[1] This is specifically recognised in the Preamble to the Law on Governing Aceh 2006, for which see below.

[2] E Aspinall, 'Special autonomy, predatory peace and the resolution of the Aceh conflict' ch 19 in H Hill (ed), *Regional Dynamics in a Decentralised Indonesia* (Singapore, ISEAS-Yusof Ishak Institute, 2014).

[3] D Horowitz, *Constitutional Change and Democracy in Indonesia* (Cambridge, Cambridge University Press, 2013) 136ff.

[4] Law 44/ 1999.

[5] Law 18/ 2001.

[6] Law 11/ 2006.

resolve the conflict, as they did not go far enough in achieving autonomy to satisfy GAM demands. Continuing disturbance in the province also made implementation virtually impossible. Indeed, these early autonomy laws of 1999 and 2001 did little more than embrace the decentralisation that was in any event taking place across all of Indonesia during that period,[7] with imposed concessions rather than concerted, negotiated outcomes. Nonetheless lessons were learned from these laws, and much of Aceh regional autonomy as we now see it is based (albeit expanded) on the two precedents of 1999 and 2001, for example in granting *syari'at* (*shari'a*) jurisdiction and in economic concessions.[8]

The GAM leadership continued to demand independence, while central government forces occupied the province during 2003 and vowed to end the insurgency by military victory. What eventually broke the impasse was not so much new concessions by either side as the devastating tsunami that hit Aceh in December 2004, killing more than 120,000 people in the province's coastal areas. A sudden switch by GAM from demanding independence to demanding autonomy opened a path to agreement as to the province's future. Focusing minds on the terrible plight of the people, the disaster resulted in talks between GAM and the Indonesian government, beginning in Helsinki from early 2005, which resulted in permanent peace accords later in that year,[9] which in turn were given effect in the Law on the Government of Aceh 2006 ('LGA').[10]

II. EXECUTIVE AND LEGISLATIVE POWERS

The LGA is a comprehensive piece of legislation that acts, like the Bangsamoro Organic Law, considered in chapter ten, as a special constitution for Aceh, embracing both internal provincial government and central-local relations. It grants asymmetric powers to the provincial and local governments; that is, power 'in all public sectors except for governmental affairs which become the authorities of the [national] Government', which in turn cover 'governmental affairs having the characteristics of national affairs, foreign affair politics, defence, security, judicial, monetary, national fiscal, and certain affairs in religious sector'.[11] Thus residual powers, as is typically the case in a federal system, lie with the provincial government. Even with national government matters,

[7] See ch 3.

[8] Aspinall (n 2).

[9] E Aspinall, *Islam and Nation: Separatist Rebellion in Aceh, Indonesia* (Stanford, Stanford University Press, 2009) ch 8; H Heintze, 'The Autonomy of Aceh' ch 10 in R Toniatti and J Woelk (eds), *Regional Autonomy, Cultural Diversity and Differentiated Territorial Government: The Case of Tibet – Chinese and Comparative Perspectives* (Abingdon, Routledge, 2019).

[10] Law 11/ 2006.

[11] Article 7(1), (2); Arskal Salim, 'The special status of Islamic Aceh' ch 19 in RW Hefner (ed), *The Routledge Handbook of Contemporary Indonesia* (Abingdon, Routledge, 2018).

however, the national government may transfer or delegate some of its powers to the Aceh government, and district, city or *gampong* (village) governments, based on the duty of assistance (*tugas pembantuan*) principle. *Tugas pembantuan* is a uniquely Indonesian principle, evident in several provisions of the LGA, that entails a duty on the part of local authorities to assist the national government in the execution of its functions. In a system that confers much power on provincial and local authorities, this principle is a useful binding element in the government system. The duty is not, however, reciprocal.[12]

One critical issue in Aceh legislative autonomy is the right to veto central laws as applied to Aceh. GAM succeeded in inserting into the Helsinki agreement a provision that laws, executive orders and regulations affecting the province would have to be 'taken in consultation with and with the consent of the legislature of Aceh' and 'implemented in consultation with and with the consent of the head of the Aceh administration'.[13] Accordingly, Aceh would have had a veto over national laws and regulations affecting the province. However, in the event, the LGA at Article 8 waters down this agreement, requiring merely the 'consultation and advice' of the Aceh legislature in respect of laws, and the Governor of the province in respect of administrative measures. As in many other areas, details regarding such matters are to be established by presidential regulations.[14] The central government can also cancel any *qanun* (local regulation) simply on the ground that it contravenes the public interest, other *qanun*, or higher laws.[15] Qanun are also subject to judicial review in the Supreme Court of Indonesia.[16] Legislative power, while very broad in scope, is therefore subject to substantial procedural limitations.

While Aceh autonomy is to some extent a matter of symbolism, despite the limitations indicated above, it does go further than general decentralisation in some important respects. For example, of Indonesia's provinces only Aceh has powers over religion.[17] Although Islamic jurisdiction was not a major claim made by GAM in the peace process, it was offered by the Indonesian government in an attempt to undercut GAM's appeal. However, this concession is now embraced with enthusiasm by the former GAM leaders who govern Aceh. The LGA in its Preamble acknowledges the special characteristics of Aceh justifying special autonomy, consisting in the 'high tenacity and struggling power … deriving from the viewpoint of life based on Islamic *syari'at* which generates strong Islamic culture'.

Matters transferred to the provincial government are to be supplemented by funding as well as facilities and infrastructures, in accordance with the

[12] See, further, p 39.

[13] *Memorandum of Understanding between the Government of the Republic of Indonesia and the Free Aceh Movement*, Helsinki, 15 August 2005, Article 1.1.2.

[14] LGA, Article 8(4).

[15] Article 235(2).

[16] Article 235(4).

[17] Article 13.

principle of decentralisation, and again in accordance with the principle of *tugas pembantuan*.[18] Despite the general transfer of most functions to the province, there is a considerable element of subsidiarity that results in reserving a large number of important matters to the local governments, as opposed to provincial government. These include development planning and infrastructure; land and environment; population affairs and civil register; public order; health care; education; social issues; employment; small and medium-scale businesses; and, crucially, the implementation of Islamic law and inter-religious issues.[19]

Article 20 lays down some useful governance principles that can form a basis for judicial review as well as political accountability. These are compliance with Islam; legal certainty; public interest; order in government administration; disclosure; proportionality; professionalism; accountability; efficiency; effectiveness; and quality.

III. INTERNAL GOVERNANCE SYSTEM

The Government of Aceh is led by an elected Governor and Deputy Governor and is under an elected legislative assembly (DPRA).[20] This pattern is repeated at the local government level, as local authorities also have elected assemblies (DPRK). The DPRA plays a supervisory role in relation to government policy and implementation of *qanun*, and also has power to recommend to the President of the Republic the appointment or dismissal of the Governor.[21] The Governor is accountable to the President of Indonesia.[22] Similarly, district and city governments are led by a Regent or Mayor, assisted by a deputy.[23] These are supervised by the Governor,[24] who has the specific tasks also of coordinating the fostering and supervision of the governing of district/city government; administration of governmental affairs in Aceh and its districts/cities, including its *tugas pembantuan*; fostering in the administration of Aceh its special and specific characteristics; and safeguarding development equilibrium among the districts/cities.[25] The obligations of the Governor and local government heads are clearly based on good governance, on upholding the national ideology of Pancasila, as well as Islam; maintaining the unitary nature of the Republic; and liaising with the national government.[26] *Qanun Aceh* are, subject to the restrictions already mentioned above, enacted by the Governor with approval from the DPRA. District and city *qanun* are enacted by the

[18] Article 15.
[19] Article 17.
[20] Articles 21, 39.
[21] Article 23.
[22] Article 40.
[23] Article 41.
[24] Article 43.
[25] Article 43.
[26] Article 46.

regent/mayor with approval from the DPRK.[27] Draft *qanun* are subject to public input, verbal and written.[28]

The Governor and Deputy Governor, and the local government heads and deputy heads, as pairs, are directly elected by the people once every five years through a democratic, free, confidential election, conducted in a fair and just manner. They may be re-elected for one other five-year term only. Candidates for these offices may be nominated by a political party or an individual. In addition to various qualifications and disqualifications the candidate must obtain the votes of at least 3 per cent of the total number of residents in at least 50 per cent of the total number of districts /cities (or 50 per cent of residents in the case of local officials).[29]

One area of the LGA that is controversial is the internal organisation of the political process in Aceh. A ban on independent candidates in elections[30] was struck down by the Constitutional Court.[31] Article 82 of the LGA, on regulation of local political parties, also includes a provision prohibiting local parties from endangering the integrity of the (unitary) Republic of Indonesia, and a government regulation (No 20/ 2007) on local parties gives the provincial office of the (central) Ministry of Law and Human Rights, but not the provincial government, the power to approve their registration. This impacted on GAM itself, which had to change its name to Partai Aceh to satisfy the Ministry's requirements.[32]

Dismissal of elected officials is, however, a rather complex business, as we saw in chapter three in relation to provincial governors generally. Dismissal may only be initiated by a plenary meeting of the relevant assembly at which at least three quarters of members are present and the resolution is supported by at least two thirds of the members present. The Supreme Court then within 30 days of receipt of a request from the assembly has to examine and decide that the official has violated his oath of office or is incapable of performing his obligations; and its decision is final. If the Supreme Court so decides, the assembly must then meet and decide, under the same conditions as before, that the official be dismissed. The President must then process the dismissal within 30 days of the submission of the proposal by the assembly. However, the official may be suspended by the President without going through this procedure in the event he is declared by a court to have committed criminal offences sanctioned with imprisonment of a minimum of five years' imprisonment or more, or if he is accused of corruption, terrorism, coup d'état, and/or criminal offences against the security of the state.[33]

[27] Articles 232–33.
[28] Article 238.
[29] Article 67.
[30] Contained in LGA, Article 256.
[31] Constitutional court Decision 35/PUU-VIII/2010. See, further, S Butt, *The Constitutional Court and Democracy in Indonesia* (Leiden, EJ Brill, 2015) 166–68.
[32] Aspinall (n 2) 468.
[33] LGA, Articles 49–50.

As we have seen generally in this book, an important aspect of regional autonomy in terms of internal governance is the maintenance of traditional or indigenous modes of governance. The LGA provides for indigenous leadership in the form of a state guardian, the *Wali Nanggroe*, a supposedly non-political 'community unifier which is independent, respected and authorised to foster and supervise the administration of the life of indigenous institutions, traditional customs, and the granting of title/degree and other indigenous ceremonies'.[34] The *Wali* is envisaged as a resolver of conflicts, but (not surprisingly, in view of the array of legislative, executive and judicial powers available) his role has been largely, to use Bagehot's famous terminology, 'dignified' rather than 'efficient'.[35] He also has a role in fostering Aceh customs and traditional life based on the *syari'at*.[36] Apart from this, another indigenous institution, the *Majelis Adat Aceh* (Aceh Traditional Assembly) plays a role in public participation with a view to harmony and public order.[37] There is also extensive provision for governance under elected leadership in village units at the sub-district level (in order of size: *kecamatan*, *mukim*, and *gampong*), and for the clustering of sub-districts.[38]

Development planning is often an indicator of powers in territorial governance units, and in this regard the LGA makes relevant provision, to the effect that planning at the provincial and local levels is arranged comprehensively as part of the national planning system, and to ensure consistency between planning, budgeting, implementation, and supervision. It is also to be conducted with regard to Islamic values; social culture; sustainability of the environment; justice and fair distribution; and necessity. Public participation both verbally and in writing is also provided as a right. Local planning is to pay regard to local indigenous culture; providing of land for social and public facilities, road infrastructure network, irrigation and utilities; the needs of poor communities and disaster-prone and affected areas; providing of conservation zones and green open spaces as well as for the preservation of national parks; communications; and natural resources.[39]

A critical issue in view of past grievances is the management of oil and natural gas resources. Here the national and provincial governments are to manage together, via an implementing agency formed by agreement, the resources both inland and in the Aceh territorial sea. This agency is the Aceh Oil and Gas Management Body, formed in 2015 under central government regulation.[40] Similar provisions apply to the fisheries, trade and investment, social economic zones, development planning, ports, and land allocation.[41]

[34] Article 96.

[35] W Bagehot, *The English Constitution* (ed P Smith, Cambridge, Cambridge University Press, 2001) 5.

[36] LGA, Article 99.

[37] Article 98.

[38] Articles 112–15.

[39] Article 141.

[40] Regulation No 23 of 2015 Concerning Management of Oil and Natural Gas Resources in Aceh.

[41] LGA, Article 160.

Fiscal provision is made on the basis of ordinary regional revenue, fiscal balance funding, special autonomy funding, and other legitimate revenues.[42] District and city revenue comes from regional revenues. The special autonomy funding is funding transferred to the Aceh Government aimed towards financing development, especially the development and maintenance of infrastructure; empowerment of the people; eradicating poverty; education, social welfare, and health. This funding applies for 20 years (as from 2006). For years 1–15 the amount is 2 per cent of the ceiling of the National General Allocation Fund; and for years 16–20 it is 1 per cent thereof.[43]

IV. LEGAL PLURALISM AND RIGHTS

The implementation of Islamic law is a key outcome of autonomy as well as a major aspect of indigenous governance, and requires further explanation in terms of the legal pluralism it implies. The province has power to implement Islamic law via *qanun*, distinguishing the province from the whole of the rest of Indonesia.[44] This power includes not just Islamic jurisdiction over family law, civil law, criminal law and the judiciary, but also over religious services, Islamic teaching and proselytisation, and defence of Islam. The implementation of the *syari'at* is given to the provincial and local governments. Muslims resident in Aceh are obliged to comply with and practice the *syari'at*, and non-Muslims resident in Aceh are required to respect it. Other religious communities are, however, also protected.[45] Aceh residents are all persons residing permanently in Aceh, and all such persons, 17 years old or married, are provided with an Aceh residence identity card.[46] This jurisdiction has notably been exercised through *qanun* outlawing, for example, gambling, consumption of alcohol, and sexual immorality.[47]

The *syari'at* judiciary is part of the national judicial system,[48] and enjoys powers over all Muslims in Aceh. Aceh's *syari'at* court jurisdiction itself goes beyond what is seen in the rest of Indonesia and other parts of Southeast Asia, in embracing both criminal and civil law as well as the more obvious subjects of family law and succession that tend to define Islamic jurisdiction elsewhere.

Courts of first instance and appeal are provided. There is the possibility too of a final appeal, as well as judicial review in divorce cases, in the Indonesian

[42] Article 179.
[43] Article 183.
[44] Articles 13, 16.
[45] Articles 125–27.
[46] Article 212. As with other cases of special autonomy, and as an aspect of rights and legal pluralism, the issue arises, who is Acehnese for the purposes of Aceh governance? An Acehnese is every individual born or having Aceh blood line both present in Aceh or outside of Aceh and acknowledges themselves as an Aceh person.
[47] S Butt and T Lindsey, *Indonesian Law* (Oxford, Oxford University Press, 2018) 206.
[48] LGA, Article 128.

Supreme Court. The procedure in the *syari'at* courts is according to religious jurisdiction or criminal law jurisdiction, as the case may be, until provided for by *qanun*.[49] *Syari'at* judges are appointed by the President of Indonesia on the proposal of the Chairman of the Supreme Court. Any jurisdictional conflicts are resolved by the Indonesian Supreme Court.[50]

Most significant amongst the *qanun* is the *qanun jinayat* or Islamic criminal code,[51] which has been controversial.[52] This law involves severe *hudud* and *ta'zir* punishments, and applies to Muslims resident in Aceh as well as non-Muslims who commit offences together with Muslims, or who violate the *qanun* in terms of offences not provided in the Indonesian Criminal Code, which code is of course of general application. For Muslims the *qanun jinayat* takes precedence, according to its own terms.[53] At the same, any Aceh citizen committing a *jinayah* deed *outside* Aceh has the Criminal Code applied to them.[54] There are many objections to this *qanun*, and its validity has been challenged, albeit unsuccessfully, in the Supreme Court, on the grounds that it violates the hierarchy of laws and the Law on Law-making.[55] As is mentioned above, the Supreme Court has power, not yet exercised, to rule on the validity of *qanun*.[56]

There is of course a cost to such arrangements. The *qanun jinayat* is a legal irritant[57] in a number of respects. Such laws may not be in conformity with human rights as expressed in the Indonesian Constitution, in terms of being oppressive to women or minorities, or involving cruel or unusual punishments; and their applicability to non-Muslims, which as we have seen applies in some circumstances, is unprecedented in the region. The tension with national criminal law is also an obvious aspect of the legal irritant. However, the point is, as Butt and Lindsey have stated, that '[t]he result is the most ambitious attempt to formally apply Islamic law in modern Southeast Asia'.[58]

The internal Islamic governance system is further complicated by the Ulama Consultative Assembly, which is composed of ulama and Muslim intellectuals, paying regard to the need for female representation. The function of this assembly is to decide on legal guidance, requested or otherwise, relevant to regional administrative policies in the sectors of administration, development,

[49] Articles 130–32.
[50] Article 135.
[51] Qanun Aceh No 6/ 2014.
[52] Butt and Lindsey (n 47).
[53] LGA, Article 72.
[54] Article 129.
[55] Supreme Court Decision 60/P/HUM/2015.
[56] LGA, Article 235. The Supreme Court, not the Constitutional Court, exercises judicial review of subsidiary legislation such as *qanun* Aceh.
[57] G Teubner, 'Legal Irritants: Good Faith in British Law or How Unifying Law Ends Up in New Differences' (1998) 61 *Modern Law Review* 11.
[58] S Butt and T Lindsey, *The Constitution of Indonesia: A Contextual Analysis* (Oxford, Hart Publishing, 2012) 183.

the economy and community relations; and to resolve differences of opinion in the community. It may also make use of experts in relevant fields.[59]

The provincial and local governments are to respect ethnic diversity and the right of every ethnic group to be treated equally.[60] There are also obligations on these governments to protect the cultural heritage, art, and languages of the various ethnic groups, including the use of their languages in schools.[61] Specific further provision is also made for human rights.[62]

V. ACEH: CONCLUSIONS

A real fear of GAM in the process of negotiating autonomy was that it could be undermined over the long term by slow-slicing or manipulation of powers. This fear was not unrealistic, because many guarantees under the LGA are made subject, as is mentioned above, to the enactment of law and regulations. One commentator counted 49 such provisions; and quite apart from this many important matters required to be implemented by regulations (the same commentator counted 99 of those).[63] Thus political agreement in principle tends to involve the deliberate postponement, rather than resolution, of difficult questions.

Crucial to the entrenchment of autonomy in practice has been the positioning of former GAM leaders in the provincial polity. Partai Aceh has proved to be a dominant party in gubernatorial, provincial and local elections. The new economic dispensation, which is partly due to increased local shares of natural-resource exploitation, and partly due to additional funding from the centre, has enabled the provincial and local governments as well as individual leaders to become prosperous. Opportunities exist for corrupt practices, patronage, and rent-seeking. This factor has been seen as crucial in adhering these leaders to the new autonomy system. As Aspinall puts it, 'most former rebels are too busy pursuing their political and economic advancement to seriously consider a return to armed conflict'.[64]

The settlement based on territorial autonomy remains somewhat fragile, the danger being that of increased control from Jakarta, making use of ambiguous provisions in the LGA. On the plus side, Aceh autonomy has ensured peace in the province since 2004, representing a period of peace rarely experienced in the province; and Aceh remains part of the republic, which few during 1999–2003 had predicted it would.

[59] LGA, Articles 138–40.
[60] Article 211.
[61] Articles 213, 221.
[62] Articles 227–31.
[63] Aspinall (n 2) 467, 470.
[64] ibid 479.

This story of Aceh autonomy suggests, as with Bangsamoro, that regional autonomy has to be genuinely a simulacrum of real independence if it is to gain acceptance. This in turn raises in a unitary state the issue of sovereignty. The answer, I suggest, is that properly conceived autonomy does not necessarily offer such a challenge. It represents a compromise in which the pluralism of the modern nation state may both satisfy and rise above community aspirations. In short, the modern nation state can absorb identity claims without a disturbance of its equilibrium.

VI. THE CLAIM FOR REGIONAL AUTONOMY IN PAPUA

The province now known as Papua forms most of the Western part of the island of Papua (of which the Eastern part forms Papua New Guinea). Its population is mainly indigenous Melanesian. It contains some of Indonesia's remotest areas.

A secessionist group, Organisasi Papua Merdeka (OPM), has the agenda of complete independence from Indonesia and claims that Papua, not part of the Republic in 1945, was coerced into joining it without its real assent in 1969, following a controversial UN-sponsored referendum. OPM has staged low-level resistance to Indonesian rule since the 1960s. There are several groups variously pursuing armed resistance, international diplomacy, and territorial autonomy as means to achieving '*merdeka*' (independence).[65] As with Aceh, there are issues of local culture and natural-resource exploitation, allied with the province's under-development. Papuan autonomy was part of the decentralisation plan, and is provided by the Law on Special Autonomy for Papua Province 2001 (LSAPP) (Law 21/2001). The idea was to undercut the OPM with devolution of powers, but several mistakes followed.

What had been a single province in 1999 was divided into three, then into two provinces, and in 2022 into four (South Papua, Central Papua, Mountains Papua and South-West Papua).[66] This confusing and damaging process, largely resisted by local representatives as reducing Papuan identity, has been accompanied by an almost bewildering and persistent form of administrative fragmentation – an aspect of implementation of autonomy that is not present in the other case studies in this Part. In this process, referred to as '*pemekaran*' (blossoming), large numbers of regencies and districts have been created, which allows the province to be flooded with new government funding. There seems to be little in the way of real strategy or thought devoted to why or how this process should be undertaken, but the effect has been to reinforce the political

[65] C Webb-Gannon, 'Merdeka in West Papua: Peace, justice and political independence' (2014) 56(2) *Anthropologica* 353, 362. See, further, MS Widjojo (ed), *Papua Road Map: Negotiating the Past, Improving the Present and Securing the Future* (Singapore, ISEAS, 2010).

[66] See UN Group of Experts on Geographical Names, at unstats.un.org/unsd/ungegn/sessions/3rd_session_2023/documents/GEGN.2_2023_50_CRP.50_revised.pdf.

importance of *suku* (clans and sub-clans). Corruption has increased, violence has occurred around elections in some new areas where existing social fault lines were exacerbated, and poor governance conditions have become distressingly prevalent. An official central government administrative-performance review in 2011 showed Papua to be the worst-performing province of Indonesia and to contain the worst-performing districts. Three out of four Indonesian districts threatened with 'cancellation' in 2013 were in Papua.[67]

The powers of the province cover all sectors of administration, except in the field of foreign politics, safety and defence, monetary and fiscal, religion and judicature. This, apart from religion, confers almost plenary powers, similarly to the position in Aceh.[68]

The most significant features of the LSAPP are, first, its provision for return of 70 per cent of oil and gas revenues to the province for 25 years (the proportion then reduces to 50 per cent); and second, the creation of a Papuan People's Assembly (*Majelis Rakyat Papua*, MRP). The MRP's main purpose is to advise the Papuan government on the protection of the rights of the Indigenous people. Under the LSAPP, Article 19(1), the MRP is to comprise equal numbers of representatives of traditional *adat* communities, women, and religious figures, selected by their respective constituencies. The provincial government is under a duty, further, to protect customary law and Indigenous land rights.[69]

The main problem with the LSAPP is its provision for MRP membership, which involves appointment of 25 per cent of its members. This provision has been challenged in the Constitutional Court on grounds of lack of equality of access to opportunity and benefit (a right provided by Article 28H(2) of the Constitution), and breach of provincial powers under Article 18(2) to regulate and administer matters of government. The decision recognises the legitimacy of making appointments to the MRP as part of affirmative action to enable *adat*-community representatives to participate in decision-making and protect the environment and Papuan customs.[70]

In another decision, the Constitutional Court allowed a cultural exception to ordinary voting rules in a case involving the customary *noken* system, which is used in parts of Papua.[71] Under this system the village chief determines the distribution of votes by implicit consent of the villagers, described by the Court as 'community agreement' or 'acclamation'. This was justified by reference to the obligation under Article 18B(2) of the Constitution to respect *adat* communities and their traditional rights, and the need to maintain harmony in traditional communities with their own norms concerning elections.[72] It has,

[67] C Nolan, S Jones and Solahudin, 'The political impact of carving up Papua' ch 17 in Hill (n 2).
[68] LSAPP, Article 4.
[69] LSAPP, Article 11.
[70] Constitutional Court Decision 130/PUU-VII/2009.
[71] Constitutional Court Decision 4/PHPU.D-XI/2013.
[72] Butt (n 31) 169–71.

however, been criticised for treating Papuan rights as less important than those of Indonesians generally.[73]

Developmentally, Papua presents the paradox that, while it is the most abundant province in terms of natural resources it is also one of Indonesia's poorest, with five out of the country's ten poorest districts in 2011 being Papuan.[74] Papua also has one of the slowest rates of increase in standards of living. The developmental challenge, which has hardly yet begun to be met, is to reduce poverty and uneven development across the province as a whole. 'There can be no doubt', concludes one careful analysis, 'that this region is Indonesia's most serious development challenge'; indeed, it attains very low scores for human development.[75]

Governance indicators remain generally poor, although Papuanisation of local government has been one positive outcome of administrative changes. Little progress has been made over the last two decades in devolving powers much beyond those granted generally in decentralisation. On the positive side, *pemekaran* has furthered the 'Papuanisation' of local government, and empowered some previously unemancipated groups.

It is too early to say whether territorial autonomy in Papua will bring with it the dividend of a cessation of violence. Militarisation and violent displacement of more than 40,000 Indigenous people was reported as recently as 2020.[76]

[73] Nolan et al (n 67) 424.

[74] H Hill and Y Vidyattama, 'Hares and tortoises: Regional development dynamics in Indonesia' ch 4 in Hill (n 2) 75.

[75] ibid 79.

[76] Human Rights for Peace in Papua, 'New Release: The Humanitarian Crisis in West Papua, Internal Conflict, the Displacement of People and the Coronavirus Pandemic' (20 July 2020), www.humanrightspapua.org/news/32-2020/619-new-release-the-humanitarian-crisis-in-west-papua-internal-conflict-the-displacement-of-people-and-the-coronavirus-pandemic.

10

Regional Autonomy II: Bangsamoro Autonomous Region, Muslim Mindanao

I. THE CLAIM FOR REGIONAL AUTONOMY

MUSLIM FILIPINO IDENTITY has been the basis for claiming recognition of separate identity in the region now called Bangsamoro Autonomous Region, Muslim Mindanao (BARMM)[1] since at least 1921, when the first such claim was made against the United States' administration. The claim came to be backed by violence after the Jabidah massacre of 1968, which involved the slaughter of Muslim members of the armed forces in disputed circumstances.[2] The vindication of the Bangsamoro claim is a complex story, as it has been pursued and represented by a shifting cast of rival groups. Peace talks continued over several years between the national government and groups advocating autonomy, but these were punctuated by episodes of violence.[3] The Comprehensive Agreement on the Bangsamoro (CAB), was signed in 2014, between the Philippines government and the Moro Islamic Liberation Front (MILF), bringing an end to their prolonged violent confrontation.[4] But the region has not remained peaceful, as other violent groups have been operating. In the disputed Mamasapano incident in 2015 70 people died in a clash between government forces and MILF forces.[5] And in 2017 the Lanao del Sur provincial capital Marawi was occupied by the Islamic extremist group Abu Sayyaf, and was under siege for five months. This siege led to extensive military action, and widespread

[1] 'Bangsamoro' is made up of '*bangsa*' (nation), and 'Moro' (Moors, or Muslims, as designated in Spanish); R Buendia, *The Politics of the Bangsamoro Basic Law* (Yuchengco Centre, De La Salle University, Manila, 2015).

[2] ibid 16.

[3] F Adriano and T Parks, *The Contested Corners of Asia: Subnational Conflict and International Development Assistance, the Case of Mindanao, Philippines* (San Francisco, The Asia Foundation, 2013) 12 ff; I Deinla, '(In)Security and Hybrid Justice Systems in Mindanao, Philippines' ch 13 in J Wallis, L Kent, M Forsyth, S Dinnen and S Bose (eds), *Hybridity on the Ground in Peacebuilding and Development: Critical Conversations* (Canberra, ANU Press, 2018).

[4] Buendia (n 1) 28.

[5] Philippine National Police, *Board of Inquiry: The Mamapasano Report* (March 2015).

destruction of the city. More than 1,100 people died, around 1,780 hostages were freed, and 300,000 citizens were displaced.[6] Currently 72 out of the 77 private armed groups in the Philippines operate in Bangsamoro, hence the prevailing relatively peaceful situation since 2017 is potentially extremely fragile.[7] Splits have occurred regularly within the Bangsamoro movement, represented mainly by the MILF, the Moro National Liberation Front (MNLF) and the Bangsamoro Islamic Freedom Fighters (BIFF).[8] These splits have related to, first, dealing with the central government with a view to regional autonomy versus insisting on secession under an independent state; second, Muslim versus ethnic Bangsamoro identity (there are 13 distinct ethno-linguistic groups amongst Filipino Muslims as well as non-Muslim people with Bangsamoro identity);[9] and third, the precise territorial extent of the claim for recognition. The last of these represents a debate between embracing six provinces of Mindanao as a core homeland (favoured by MILF), or embracing autonomy for 13 Mindanao provinces having a Muslim majority (favoured by MNLF).[10]

The events of 2017 had the effect of intensifying the peace process, and the negotiation of regional autonomy appeared to dampen the desire to proceed by violent means. Discontent focuses for now on the difficulties in implementing autonomy rather than the question whether it should proceed.[11]

Like other Southeast Asian states, the Philippines presents a very diverse society, with more than 175 ethnic groups, 120 languages, and 7,600 islands. In recognition of this diversity, and as a means of diluting the dictatorial power of the centre during the Marcos era, general decentralisation was constitutionally mandated under the 1987 Constitution. This was done by Article X, whose decentralisation mandate was amply fulfilled, as we saw in chapter six, by the enactment of the Local Government Code 1991.[12] Sections 15–21 of Article X, in addition to decentralisation, require the enactment of regional autonomy laws in Muslim Mindanao and the Cordilleras.[13] This requirement is based on areas sharing what section 15 calls 'common and distinctive historical and

[6] Amnesty International, 'Philippines: "Battle of Marawi" leaves trail of death and destruction' (Amnesty International, 17 November 2017); R Gunaratna, 'The Siege of Marawi: A Game Changer in Terrorism in Asia' (2017) 9(7) *Counter Terrorist Trends and Analyses*, at www.jstor.org/stable/26351533.

[7] I Deinla and G Engelbrecht, 'A new dawn for Bangsamoro democracy? Political autonomy and inclusive participation in post-conflict Mindanao' (Asia Centre, 2019) 9.

[8] Buendia (n 1) claims there has been a major split once every six or seven years in recent decades.

[9] About 91.5% of people in Mindanao are Muslim; the remainder being Christian or indigenous: Deinla (n 3) 203.

[10] R Buendia, 'Prospects and Challenges of the Bangsamoro Basic Law under Duterte's Presidency: Resolution through Inclusive Governance' (Yuchengco Centre, De La Salle University, Manila, 2017) 19.

[11] Deinla and Engelbrecht (n 7) 9.

[12] Republic Act 7160.

[13] The purport of these sections has been clarified by the Supreme court of the Philippines in *Cordillera Broad Coalition v Commission of Audit and Lilia Yaranon and Others v Commission of Audit*, GR Nos 79956, 82217 (1990) as requiring legislative provision for political, not just administrative, autonomy.

cultural heritage, economic and social structures, and other relevant characteristics'. Thus regional autonomy is not only constitutionally required but goes far beyond the general decentralisation envisaged in Article X, in the interests of recognising the special characteristics listed in section 15.

It is not only post-2017 that attempts have been made, since the bringing into effect of the 1987 constitution, to find a solution to the Bangsamoro problem. Pursuant to Article X, an Organic Act for the Autonomous Region in Muslim Mindanao[14] was passed in 1989. However, successive attempts to make autonomy work proved unsuccessful, being rejected by some groups as creating too little autonomy for the region. The underlying issue is that over several decades the state has failed to address grievances in the Bangsamoro region, based on the linked phenomena of discrimination and underdevelopment. As one Filipino commentator puts it, the causes of the conflict are

> insubstantial political autonomy; socio-economic grievances and deprivation; and perceived injustice, discrimination, and alienation of the people from the mainstream of Philippine political and economic development. The issue boils down to political and economic equity and social justice, the crux of the state's responsibility and kernel of [the] nation's spirit.[15]

In March 2019, as a result of the peace negotiations commenced in 2017, a new political order was established in the BARMM, following the approval, in two referenda held in January and February 2019, of the Bangsamoro Organic Law of 2018 (BOL).[16] The first referendum was held to ascertain which districts agreed to become part of the new region; and the second was held to approve the BOL itself as the governing instrument of the BARMM. As a result of the referenda and the demographics of the region, the BARMM is geographically somewhat odd (for example, Isabela City is not part of it but the rest of Basilan, the province of which Isabela is part, is included).[17] However, the region is a large one, comprising five provinces, three major cities, 116 municipalities and 2,590 *barangay*.[18] Under this new political order, the former separatist group MILF took power. This change represented a promising new start for the region. Currently the region is being governed by the Bangsamoro Transitional Authority (BTA) under transitional arrangements set out in the BOL. Under this law, which provides the territorial governance framework for the region, there are ten political parties operating. Two are national parties, three are local ethnic parties, and five are Muslim parties, although these latter parties too have ethnic demographics.[19]

[14] Republic Act No 6734.
[15] Buendia (n 1) 25.
[16] Republic Act No 11054.
[17] For an indicative map, see Deinla and Engelbrecht (n 7) fig 1.
[18] The *barangay* include 63 in Cotabato province that decided to join the BARMM.
[19] H Juliano, 'Opportunities and pitfalls for political communication for the 2022 BARMM polls' (*Access Bangsamoro*, 10 December 2020) at www.access-bangsamoro.ph/posts/think-pieces/opportunities-and-pitfalls-for-political-communication-for-the-2022-barmm-polls.

The transitional provisions require the BTA to organise the handing over of power to new institutions set up under that law. This is set to occur after the first set of BARMM elections scheduled originally for 2022, and now for 2025.[20]

The BOL is in essence a mini-constitution that reflects a negotiated solution to long-running conflict in the region, and frames powers, governance, and even broad areas of policy and ordinary law within the constitutional order of the Philippines.[21] It not only defines the region as such, but also provides for its internal governance, and its political and financial power-sharing in terms of central-local relations.

The BOL will be examined here in light of the major issues outlined in chapter eight as salient in assessing the extent, nature and purposes of regional autonomy.

II. EXECUTIVE AND LEGISLATIVE POWERS

The BOL is remarkable in that, by conferring extensive powers on the BARMM, it leaves very little to the national government, whose powers over the BARMM are virtually those of the classic 'nightwatchman' state – defence, security, police and tax collection.[22] Yet even in these areas powers are essentially exercised jointly under numerous new bodies set up to facilitate cooperation between the region and the national government.[23] And even in the case of taxes, little of the revenue generated from the region is allowed to go to the national government.[24]

The BOL attempts to reconcile regional autonomy, democracy, social justice and the territorial integrity of the Philippines.[25] It does so by providing for parliamentary democracy for the region, and detailed provisions allocating powers and responsibilities to the BARMM government, in such a way that it allows the region in essence to take charge of its own destiny.

The rationale for this was cogently expressed by the Supreme Court of the Philippines (with special reference to Muslim Mindanao) in 2004 in *Disomangcop v Datumanong*:[26]

> The idea behind the Constitutional provisions for autonomous regions is to allow the separate development of peoples with distinctive cultures and traditions. These cultures, as a matter of right, must be allowed to flourish. Autonomy, as a national policy, recognizes the wholeness of the Philippine society in its ethnolinguistic,

[20] 'Duterte resets BARMM elections to 2025' (*Philippines News Agency*, 29 October 2021) at www.pna.gov.ph/articles/1158190.
[21] BOL, Article I (3).
[22] Article V.
[23] Article VI.
[24] Article XII.
[25] Article IV.
[26] GR No 149848, 25 November 2004.

> cultural, and even religious diversities. It strives to free Philippine society of the strain and wastage caused by the assimilationist approach. Policies emanating from the legislature are invariably assimilationist in character despite channels being open for minority representation. As a result, democracy becomes an irony to the minority group … However, the creation of autonomous regions does not signify the establishment of a sovereignty distinct from that of the Republic, as it can be installed only 'within the framework of this Constitution and the national sovereignty as well as territorial integrity of the Republic of the Philippines. … In the Philippine setting, regional autonomy implies the cultivation of more positive means for national integration. It would remove the wariness among the Muslims, increase their trust in the government and pave the way for the unhampered implementation of the development programs in the region.

Under regional autonomy as provided by the BOL, functions not dealt with by the BOL itself are vested in the national government, but BARMM functions include those that are 'necessary for, or incidental to, the region's proper governance and development'.[27] Article V in fact bestows no less than 55 items of jurisdiction on the BARMM. These items represent virtually plenary powers. They include notably government administration and the administration of justice; agriculture and food; waterways and water supply; energy and natural resources; waste disposal and the environment; land matters; trade, business, and industry, including special economic zones; internal boundaries; minorities, culture, customary law, and language; education, science and technology; disasters; housing; health, welfare and humanitarian services; *hajj* and Islamic finance; public utilities and power; planning, development, and infrastructure.

With regard to intergovernmental relations, under Article VI, the President of the Philippines exercises supervisory control over the BARMM, and can suspend the Chief Minister for a period not exceeding six months for violation of the law, the constitution, or the BOL itself. The also BOL establishes a National Government – Bangsamoro Government Intergovernmental Relations Body (IGRB), comprising regional and national representatives.[28] Its role is to coordinate and resolve intergovernmental issues in a non-adversarial manner. Unresolved issues are elevated to the President. The role of the IGRB moving forward will be critical for effective implementation and policy development, given post-conflict tensions and the extent of mutual distrust and a historic lack of coordination and cooperation. Improvements in education, security, and social welfare will be needed as well as development and natural-resource-conservation policies. BARMM is less developed and less urbanised than its adjoining regions. In fact, it is one of the poorest regions of the Philippines. Amongst several other intergovernmental bodies, an Intergovernmental Fiscal Policy Body is established to deal with the crucial issue of fiscal balancing.[29]

[27] BOL, Article VII (2).
[28] Article VI (2).
[29] Article VI (4).

III. INTERNAL GOVERNANCE SYSTEM[30]

An important aspect of regional autonomy is the right to be governed internally by a system that does not necessarily reflect the preferences or traditions of the nation-state itself. It is considered in the BARMM that parliamentarism offers more executive accountability than presidentialism, or 'strong-man rule'. As Michael Yusingco puts it:

> The establishment of a parliamentary form of government in the BARMM is by design. Bangsamoro reformists have long understood that the previous regional structure was a 'failed experiment' partly due to its parallelism to the national government framework. It was hoped that instituting a ministerial or parliamentary system would facilitate a more collective approach to regional governance and would steer the Bangsamoro away from the strongman-style mentality pervading in the previous regime.[31]

However, there is no experience of operating a democratic parliamentary system that depends very much on the development of understanding of constitutional conventions and parliamentary practices and procedures, a matter that currently engages a number of international governance agencies.[32]

The head of state is the *Wali*, described as a ceremonial head of state,[33] 'consistent with the parliamentary form of government'. Under Article VIII, the *Wali* holds office for six years, and is chosen by parliament from persons nominated by the Council of Leaders (for which, see below), which nominations may be made from amongst eminent persons who have been residents of the BARMM for at least 15 years and who are least 40 years of age. The *Wali* can be removed by parliament for cause.[34] He must not countermand any advice given by the Chief Minister. As a purely ceremonial head of state, he does not even enjoy the prerogative or reserve powers typical of heads of state in Westminster-type parliamentary systems. He does not appoint the Chief Minister on the

[30] Internal governance is provided for both by the BOL and the Bangsamoro Administrative Code, BAA 13/2020 (BAC). This analysis makes use of the BOL, which is a Republic Act, and has precedence over the BAC. The BAC fills out the BOL provisions on internal governance and other matters, but for ease of reading the text is not overburdened with parallel references. Any detailed analysis of internal governance needs, however, to take account of the extensive provisions of the BAC as well as those of the BOL.

[31] M Yusingco, 'Deliberative Democracy and the Bangsamoro Parliament, Ateneo School of Government Working Paper 21–008 (2021) 4, at papers.ssrn.com/sol3/papers.cfm?abstract_id=3791001.

[32] NG Prieto and F Kayltare, 'Strategic planning on forming political parties in Bangsamoro', International Institute for Democracy and Electoral Assistance, at www.idea.int/news-media/news/strategic-planning-forming-political-parties-bangsamoro; Yusingco, ibid 7, stresses the need for mutual respect and consultation, as evidenced 'in the passage of the Bangsamoro Administrative Code. Under the leadership of the Deputy Majority Floor Leader … a thorough and extensive consultation and deliberative process was undertaken prior to the bill's endorsement to the plenary. It was very clear that expert analysis and stakeholders' concerns were duly heard and considered in the drafting of the bill.'

[33] BOL, Article VIII, s 1.

[34] Article VIII (6).

basis of the confidence of a majority of members of parliament. Instead, the Chief Minister is simply elected by parliament.[35] Nor is he empowered to refuse the Chief Minister's request for a dissolution of parliament following the passing of a no-confidence motion in the Chief Minister,[36] which is usually a prerogative power in parliamentary systems. Even at the level of pure formality, laws are signed by the Chief Minister rather than the *Wali*.[37]

In an odd deviation from parliamentary norms, a no-confidence motion to be effective has to be passed by two-thirds of members of parliament.[38] In the event of a successful no-confidence motion the Chief Minister is obliged to advise a dissolution, which, as we have seen, must be granted. The special-majority requirement creates a potentially difficult situation if a motion fails to achieve the benchmark of 54 votes out of 80. A Chief Minister opposed by 53 members and supported by just 27 would remain in office despite failing to enjoy the confidence of two thirds of the members, unless they choose to advise a dissolution. Presumably a Chief Minister in this position, probably unable to get measures passed or budgets approved, would soon resign, facilitating a new Chief Minister election, or else a dissolution.

The executive power is exercised by the cabinet, headed by the Chief Minister. The Cabinet is appointed by the Chief Minister, and a majority of its members must be Members of Parliament. Two Deputy Chief Ministers are nominated by the Chief Minister and elected by Parliament; as BARMM consists of three subregions, they must each come from one of the subregions other than that of the Chief Minister.[39]

In this and other ways, the BOL gives a great deal of power to the Chief Minister as head of the executive in a cabinet system. They control all appointments in the government, issue all executive orders, and have power to proclaim a state of calamity in the event of a natural disaster.[40]

Given all of these provisions, and the absence of any reserve powers vested in the head of state, which would be characteristic of a parliamentary system of government, the governance system of the BARMM, despite the billing as 'parliamentary', begins to look more like a presidential system, contradicting the express intention of creating a more accountable executive.

One governance innovation of interest is the establishment of a Council of Leaders to advise the Chief Minister on governance matters.[41] It is chaired by the Chief Minister and comprises Members of Congress of the Philippines from the BARMM; provincial governors and mayors of chartered cities in the BARMM; and representatives of traditional leaders of indigenous people, women, and

[35] Article VII (31).
[36] Article VII (36).
[37] Article VII (25(c)).
[38] Article VII (36).
[39] Article VII (35).
[40] Article VII (32(g)).
[41] Article VI (9).

minorities and other sectors. The Council also nominates eminent residents of the BARMM suitable for appointment as *Wali*, although the decision to appoint the *Wali* is taken by Parliament.

Districting is within Parliament's powers, but as initially constituted under Article VII, Parliament is to consist of 80 members in three categories:

(i) 40 members chosen via proportional representation – parties submit a list of nominees to the Election Commission and are allocated seats based on the proportion of votes obtained for the whole region;
(ii) not more than 32 members chosen via election on a direct plurality system in single-member districts; and
(iii) at least eight seats allocated to non-Moro indigenous and settler communities, women, youth, traditional leaders, and *ulama*.

One issue that arises here is the difference between national and regional electoral processes and the expectations of indigenous communities that may have a different political culture from the majority community. In the case of parliamentary seats reserved for indigenous representatives, the electoral process is required to adhere to customary laws, based on consensus-building, inclusivity, and the strengthening of indigenous political structures.[42]

Members of Parliament hold office for three years and may not have more than three terms in office.[43] The Chief Minister is elected by Parliament at its first sitting following an election. In the event of no candidate obtaining a majority there is a run-off between the candidates with the most votes.[44]

One problematical issue to be dealt with in scenarios such as the BARMM is local government within the autonomous region. Is it to conform with the national local government law, or with the law of the autonomous region? The BOL provides that local government is a function within the jurisdiction of the BARMM, expressed as 'authority to regulate the affairs of its constituent local government units in accordance with this Organic Law and a Bangsamoro local government code to be enacted by the Parliament'; but the existing legal privileges of those units may not be diminished.[45] This means that local government must be as independent of the BARMM government as are Philippine local authorities in general under the Local Government Code 1991. For example, their boundaries cannot be altered without the consent of the majority of voters in a plebiscite.[46]

The BTA's jurisdiction will terminate following the first BARMM elections in 2025, and to that end a Bangsamoro Electoral Code was passed by Parliament in March 2023.[47] The BTA itself is composed of 80 members (like the parliament

[42] Article VII (9). For an Indonesian equivalent, see p 168.
[43] Article VII (11).
[44] Article VII (31).
[45] Article VI (10).
[46] Article VII (10).
[47] Bangsamoro Autonomy Act No 35/ 2023.

to be elected), 41 of whom are nominees of the MILF.[48] Under the transitional political arrangement, a MILF-led BTA is therefore mandated to govern through democratic processes and re-build democratic institutions in the BARMM, in line with the BOL. So far, the BTA has done an impressive job legislatively in preparing the way for the first government under the BOL's provisions. Under Article XVII (4), it is required to pass seven major laws to underpin the internal governance structure of the BARMM. These are an administrative code, an electoral code, an education code, a civil service code, a local government code (all of which have been passed), and a revenue code, and an indigenous people's code currently before parliament. The BTA has at the time of writing passed no less than 58 laws,[49] including a highly impressive and compendious Local Government Code, and an equally compendious Administrative Code which fulfils most of what is required by Article XVII. This latter Code goes well beyond administration to provide for much internal constitutional detail and for the justice system, as well as establishing several independent commissions, including a Human Rights Commission, and making extensive provision in policy areas such as education, health and transport. The first elected BARMM government will have a very clear and extensive legal basis for all areas of operation, as well as a developed administrative structure, when it takes over the government from the BTA in 2025.

The internal governance system is thus designed to differ from that of the nation-state, and to cater for local preferences regarding political structures, in which democracy and public participation are emphasised.[50] The BOL, in providing for a Westminster-type parliamentary system of government, sits somewhat uneasily as a 'legal irritant'[51] within the Philippines' presidential system, and is therefore considered by some to be unconstitutional.[52] There is certainly a lack of experience and knowledge in operating such a system, given the presidential and civil law traditions of the Philippines. Whether this system will continue to be operated in a democratic manner, especially given the powers allotted to the Chief Minister, remains to be seen. But the signs so far are promising in that democracy is being practised in this transitional phase.

[48] BOL, Article XVI (2) provides for MILF to have control over the BTA. Thus 41 MILF members were appointed, and 39 others as determined by the national government: 'New BTA unites former warring MILF, MNLF rebels' (*Philippine News Agency*, 14 August 2022) at www.pna.gov.ph/articles/1181310.

[49] A complete list may be found at Bangsamoro Autonomy Acts | Bangsamoro Parliament at parliament.bangsamoro.gov.ph/baa-new/.

[50] For example, 12 public consultations were held in various districts concerning the draft bill for the electoral code.

[51] G Teubner, 'Legal irritants: Good faith in British law or how unifying law ends up in new divergences' (1998) 61(1) *Modern Law Review* 11.

[52] 'SC to decide on BOL constitutionality: Palace' (*Philippine News Agency*, 7 January 2019) at www.pna.gov.ph/articles/1058164.

IV. LEGAL PLURALISM AND RIGHTS

Imelda Deinla writes with special reference to Bangsamoro that

> [t]o forge peace and strengthen the viability of the state system in a post-conflict environment, it is necessary to grapple with the enormous challenge of restoring trust and confidence among local stakeholders in the state. In this setting, the state and its institutions are historically regarded by local stakeholders for their predatory, oppressive, and unaccountable nature.[53]

Renewed trust in government at both levels depends heavily therefore on assurances that henceforth human rights will be strictly observed and past injustices rectified. Human rights are therefore fully provided for in the BOL to protect the rights of BARMM residents generally, that is, not just the Muslim population, but indigenous and settler communities too.[54] Their rights are protected by the Human Rights Commission, established under the BOL and further provisions of the Bangsamoro Administrative Code (BAC).[55] Given the history of human rights abuses in the region, following a report by the Transitional Justice Commission, the BOL also provides for a transitional justice process.[56]

Rights protected under BOL Article X include religious freedom; native titles and indigenous customs; justice systems and indigenous political structures; an equitable share of revenue from natural resources; free, prior and informed consent; political participation; access to basic services (housing, water, power, health services, and education); and freedom of choice of identity without discrimination.[57] Special provision is also made for labour rights, and the rights of women, youth, children, and settler communities.[58]

Legal pluralism is also guaranteed by BOL, Article X, which provides for the Bangsamoro justice system to be administered 'according to the unique cultural and historic heritage of the Bangsamoro people'. Central here is obviously the claim by Muslims that they should be governed by Islamic law, an important aspect of the peace settlement. Since there are also non-Muslim indigenous communities in the BARMM, the BOL deals not just with Islamic law but with tribal customary law too. The BOL determines the critical issue of the extent of Islamic jurisdiction.[59]

Parliament has powers to pass *shari'ah* laws relating to personal, family, and property law; some commercial and civil actions; and minor criminal offences.

[53] Deinla (n 3) 198–99.
[54] BOL, Article IX.
[55] ibid; the BAC (BAA No 13/ 2020) also has 51 sections (in Title XVII, ch I) devoted to human rights and the HRC.
[56] G Radics and J Lamchek, 'Dealing with the past or moving forward? Transitional justice, the Bangsamoro Peace Agreement and federalism in the Philippines' (2021) *International Criminal Law Review* 1.
[57] BOL, Article IV (10).
[58] Article X (10–11).
[59] Deinla (n 3).

These subjects also define the jurisdiction of the *shari'ah* courts, which are given jurisdiction over disputes involving Muslims residing in the BARMM. But these courts (Circuit and District Courts, and a High Court) are also part of the national judicial system, and are subject to the supervision of the Supreme Court of the Philippines on points of law.[60] If one party is non-Muslim the court has jurisdiction only by the voluntary submission of the non-Muslim party.[61] Actions involving property are subject to a maximum value of Pesos 400,000 (about US$7,300); and commercial actions to a maximum value of Pesos 200,000 (about US$3,650).[62]

Consistently with the aim of inclusiveness and recognition of identity, there are also provisions to promote and support the traditional tribal justice systems, conflict-resolution, and peace-building processes of the BARMM's indigenous peoples under their own customary laws, so long as these are consistent with the national legal system and international human rights.[63] It is recognised that encouraging resolution of disputes by traditional customary means is part of recognising identity claims. At the same time the official state courts need not to be marginalised.[64]

V. CONCLUSION

In the transitional process, the design and establishment of a new political entity has so far been successful. But translating that success from legislation and institution-building into lasting peace and prosperity under a flourishing parliamentary democracy is another issue. Politics is still clan-based as elsewhere in the Philippines.[65] There is still a mistrust of institutions as such. It is only a few years since the siege and destruction of Marawi. Bombings still occur, and Philippines forces are still engaged fighting para-military groups in the region.[66] Poverty, underdevelopment, corruption, and injustice are problems that need addressing urgently.

Partly because of the extent of the autonomy granted under the BOL, the BARMM has spawned a debate around the creation of a federal system and wider constitutional reform, for which the BARMM may be seen as a pilot scheme, even though its autonomy is designed to be asymmetric.[67] It does not

[60] The BOL seems not to encompass the possibility of the Supreme Court overturning a decision of qualified *shari'ah* judges on a point of *Islamic law*.

[61] BOL, Article X (1).

[62] Article X (5), (6).

[63] Article X (17).

[64] Deinla (n 3) 205 ff.

[65] MC Macabuac-Ferolin and NV Constantino, 'Localising transformation: Addressing clan feuds in Mindanao through PCIA' (2014) 9(1) *Journal of Peacebuilding and Development* 10. Local clans are known as '*rido*'.

[66] Deinla and Engelbrecht (n 7).

[67] SM Candelaria and ACP Aucheta, 'Minding the gaps: Philippine-style federalism' (2018) 62 *Ateneo Law Journal* 350.

appear that federalism proposals are likely to yield fruit in terms of actual reform, but regional autonomy has become something of a general problem for the Philippines. The current debates concerning federalism proposals owe much to the fact that other regions resent the special concessions to the BARMM, and federalism would offer those regions a similar degree of autonomy. As we have noted, there is some force in this argument, as the BOL confers very extensive autonomy on the region, which is not the only region that can claim to have an identifiable and separate identity. Already in 2018, a new demand emerged for recognition of autonomy for Bangsa Sug, a region comprising other Mindanao provinces that distinguish themselves from the Bangsamoro.[68] There is therefore a possibility that asymmetric regional autonomy may spark demands for a greatly increased and symmetric form of general regional autonomy.

The implementation of asymmetrical autonomy, the ultimate outcome of which still remains to be seen, is not of course without problems. It requires erstwhile enemies at both local and national levels, and politically opposed parties, to work together in a spirit of democracy and compromise. For this reason, there is much emphasis during the current preparatory period on political parties – how they are formed, how they can operate and secure party discipline, and how they can work with each other.[69] The last of these is especially important in a fragmented parliamentary system; and especially difficult when parties are organised mainly along ethnic lines and operate within social structures that are patriarchal and clan-based.[70] And another issue will be intergovernmental relations, where Michael Yusingco has warned, with reference to Bangsamoro, that

> cooperation and collaboration by and between the central government and local governments have yet to be instinctively and consistently practiced despite the fact that intergovernmental relations mechanisms can be found in the nation's charter and in various laws.[71]

In a parallel development, Bill 7778 for an Act Establishing the Autonomous Region of the Cordillera is currently before Congress, and if passed and approved in a plebiscite would make substantially similar provision for that region as that for the BARMM. This Bill follows two previous attempts to provide by law for regional autonomy in that region, both of which failed at the referendum hurdle.[72] The proposed law for Cordillera is directed

[68] 'Isabela city, Bangsa Sug, Reject Bangsamoro Autonomy Law' *Manila Times* (19 January 2019) www.manilatimes.net/2019/01/23/second-headline/isabela-city-sulu-reject-bangasmoro-organic-law/500921/.

[69] N Prieto and F Kayltare, 'Strategic planning on forming political parties in Bangsamoro' (Stockholm, IDEA, 2019).

[70] Macabuac-Ferolin and Constantino (n 65).

[71] M Yusingco, 'Deliberative democracy and the Bangsamoro Parliament' (2021) papers.ssrn.com/sol3/papers.cfm?abstract_id=3791001.

[72] 'Cordillera legislators refile autonomy bill in 19th Congress' (*Philippine Information Agency*, 17 August 2022.

towards similar issues as the BOL, and for similar reasons, but does not provide for a parliamentary system of internal governance. Cordillera has not seen anything resembling the level of violence seen in Bangsamoro, but concerns circle mainly around underdevelopment, environmental matters and despoliation of the majority Igorot indigenous ancestral lands by extractive industries.[73]

[73] Candelaria and Aucheta (n 67) 415.

11

Regional Autonomy III: Sabah and Sarawak

THE SPECIAL POSITION of Sabah and Sarawak within Malaysia's federal system was described in chapter four as the most important issue in Malaysia's territorial governance. This chapter deals with the issue of special autonomy, to be considered alongside the other cases discussed in this Part III of the book. The constitutional status of Sabah and Sarawak will be examined, and the possible solutions to the issues that have led to a sharp increase in nationalist sentiment in those states over the last decade or more. Since the claim is to a great extent an historical claim, we will have to look at the history in more detail than we have done in the other cases.

Special autonomy in Sabah and Sarawak differs from those other cases in two important respects. First, special autonomy was not granted by way of devolution within a unitary state. It was negotiated in 1963 as part of the process whereby Sabah and Sarawak joined the federation via a form of asymmetrical federalism to form Malaysia itself under the Malaysia Agreement 1963 (MA63).[1] It is not therefore an instance where special autonomy threatens in any way the integrity of the nation-state; on the contrary it was a condition for its coming into being. Second, the claim for special autonomy has not been pursued using violent methods but via the ordinary political process. It is a claim resting partly on historical failure to fulfil the terms of MA63, and partly on claims for autonomy that are legitimated prospectively and irrespective of the position under MA63.[2]

The claim of Sabah and Sarawak for autonomy is nonetheless, in some respects, quite similar to the other cases. It is based on ethnic and religious differences, and on overreach of the centre in natural-resource exploitation. It is also evidence of general disaffection, with some groups even expressing a desire for secession.[3] The resolution of the claim is currently being sought in some sort

[1] Kevin Tan and Jaclyn L Neo, *Constitutional Law in Malaysia: Constitutional Principles and Institutions, Text Cases and Materials* (Subang Jaya, Thomson Reuters, 2023) 116ff.

[2] A Harding and J Chin (eds), *50 Years of Malaysia: Federalism Revisited* (Singapore, Marshall Cavendish, 2014).

[3] R Bociaga, 'BorneoExit: Independence for East Malaysia?' (*The Diplomat*, 11 December 2020). This was even recognised by the then Prime Minister Muhyiddin Yasin, when he stated that, 'Some people have long desired secession, and in recent years the drumbeat of separation has only grown louder': ibid.

of devolution of powers, whether one regards such devolution as simply fulfilling the original pact, or else renewing federalism on the basis of subsidiarity or some similar principle.[4] It is also claimed that Sabah and Sarawak were incorporated into the federation without proper consent.[5] The problem of Sabah and Sarawak's status within the federation has in fact been a lurking difficulty ever since 1963, and has become particularly prominent in recent years as a political issue of territorial governance that ultimately could lead to a different form of federalism emerging in Malaysia. There is a palpable sense that the inertia of 60 years of centralisation is gradually giving way to change, and autonomy is an issue on which all parties in Sabah and Sarawak, and now the federal government too, appear to agree.[6]

I. THE MALAYSIA AGREEMENT 1963

MA63 was a way of dealing with what Charles de Gaulle famous referred to as 'the dust of empire'. Other configurations than the emergence of Malaysia in its present form were possible. A vast federation of Malaysia, Indonesia and the Philippines ('Maphilindo') was at one point mooted.[7] The status of not just Sabah (then referred to as 'North Borneo') and Sarawak, but Brunei and Singapore too, was in question. The Philippines' claim for Sabah was an issue. And, in the event, so was Indonesia's non-recognition of Malaysia, leading to '*konfrontasi*' (confrontation) and a brief and occasionally violent rift between the two countries during 1964–66, and an emergency proclamation in Malaysia.[8] In the event Brunei declined to join the new federation, and while Singapore joined under MA63, along with Sabah and Sarawak, it left the federation on 9 August 1965.[9] Indonesian confrontation was faced down by Malaysia (referred to as 'Malaysia's finest hour') and finally ended by the fall of President Sukarno in 1966.[10]

[4] A Harding, 'Devolution of powers in Sarawak: A dynamic process of redesigning territorial governance in a federal system' (2017) 12(2) *Asian Journal of Comparative Law* 257.

[5] See B Welsh, 'Interview with Tan Sri Simon Sipaun' and 'Interview with Tan Sri Sir Peter Mooney' in Harding and Chin (n 2) 50 and 88; J Chin, 'Federal – East Malaysia relations: Primus inter pares?' ibid 150ff; B Simandjuntak, *Malaysian Federalism 1945–1963* (Kuala Lumpur, Oxford University Press, 1969).

[6] As evidenced by the unanimous passing of the Constitution (Amendment) Act 2022, for which see below.

[7] CM Turnbull, 'Regionalism and nationalism' ch 10 in N Tarling (ed), *The Cambridge History of Southeast Asia, vol 2* (Cambridge, Cambridge University Press, 1992) 613.

[8] J Mackie, *Konfrontasi: The Indonesia-Malaysia Dispute, 1963–1966* (Kuala Lumpur, Oxford University Press, 1975).

[9] Kevin Tan, 'Federating for survival: The case of Singapore' in Harding and Chin (n 2) 112.

[10] Poh-Ling Tan, 'From Malaya to Malaysia' in A Harding and HP Lee (eds), *Constitutional Landmarks in Malaysia: The First 50 Years, 1957–2007* (Petaling Jaya, LexisNexis, 2007) 25.

In 1961–63 negotiations leading to MA63 were led by the Cobbold Commission (the Commission of Enquiry, North Borneo and Sarawak, which reported in 1962) and proceeded in an Intergovernmental Committee, which reported in 1963.[11] Referenda were also held in Singapore, North Borneo and Sarawak, the results of which were construed as indicating support for federation. MA63 was signed on 9 July, and on 16 September, following the passing of the Malaysia Act 1963 by the Parliament of the Federation of Malaya and other legal prerequisites set out in the Annexes to MA63, Malaysia came into being.[12]

MA63 is an international treaty, listed with the United Nations, with five parties: the governments of the United Kingdom, the Federation of Malaya, Singapore, North Borneo (to be renamed 'Sabah'), and Sarawak. Accordingly, MA63 is an instrument enforceable in international law.[13]

Despite the sanctity often accorded to it, MA63 is nonetheless a deeply disappointing document. It declares the intention of the parties to establish the Malaysian federation, and provides in detail the mechanism for achieving this as a legal project,[14] but it is deeply flawed in a number of ways. It fails entirely to make clear whether the federation it establishes is a new federation or the admission of new states to an existing federation – a profound ambiguity that has caused serious misunderstandings for the last 60 years. It fails to enshrine the main principles governing the federation. It offers no assurance, nor cites any evidence, that any of the subjects of the federation, including the people of Sabah and Sarawak, consented to the new federal arrangement.[15] It offers the parties no assurances as to their rights and status as they enter into this new arrangement, other than to set out the consequential constitutional amendments. It does not embody the crucial 18/20 Points, agreed by the Federation of Malaya with Sarawak and Sabah respectively prior to MA63, in light of their actual social, economic and political needs and circumstances. These Points were included in the Intergovernmental Committee Report. Referred to in the original documents as 'safeguards', the Points are a summary of the issues and

[11] *Report of the Commission of Enquiry, North Borneo and Sarawak* (Kuala Lumpur: Government Printer, 1962); *Malaysia: Report of the Intergovernmental Committee* (Kuala Lumpur, Government Printer, 1962); J Chin, 'A brief history of the Malay peninsula and northern Borneo' in P Mathews, *The Chronicle of Malaysia: 50 Years of Headline News 1963–213* (Singapore, Didier Millet, 2013) 24ff.

[12] Treaty No UN 10760/1970. See, further, Tan Tai Yong, *Creating 'Greater Malaysia': Decolonisation and the Politics of Merger* (Singapore, ISEAS, 2008).

[13] ibid.

[14] Proposed versions of the Immigration Act; amendments to the Federal Constitution; the proposed Constitutions of Singapore, Sabah and Sarawak within the now federal structure; provisions regarding the public service and the common market, and other incidental matters.

[15] There is evidence that any consent was not real in the cases of Sabah and Sarawak (n 5); and that even the consent of the existing states of the Federation of Malaya was taken for granted. In the case of Kelantan especially, it was clear there was no consent, and the issue was litigated, it being held (see below) that no consent was required.

concerns raised with the Cobbold Commission by interested parties in North Borneo and Sarawak. They were then deliberated upon by the Intergovernmental Committee for possible incorporation into the 'new Malaysian Constitution', which did not materialise. Oddly enough, few of the Points were inserted into the Constitution, and not one was expressly included in MA63.[16] Crucially, MA63, unlike the Intergovernmental Committee Report, does not envisage the drawing up of a new constitution for a new country, but promises only amendments to the existing Constitution of the Federation of Malaya.

It should be noted also that the prior promise of a 'partnership not a take-over'[17] could hardly be fulfilled when one of the partners, the Federation of Malaya, ceased to exist as an entity with its own government and legislature. Sabah and Sarawak merely took their place as two states of the overarching Federation of Malaysia, while the federal government morphed into the government of Malaysia. MA63 was a triumph of what the British constitutional law scholar Stanley de Smith famously termed 'the austerity of tabulated legalism'[18] over political common sense. All of these matters listed are ones that citizens about to become subject to this new arrangement would surely have had a legitimate expectation of being addressed. It is hardly remarkable, in light of these fundamental flaws, that MA63 in recent years has become such a source of increasing controversy.[19] From the perspective of Sabah and Sarawak, Malaysia was a new entity created by the federation of four equal entities; from the perspective of Malaya, it was the admission of three new states into an existing federation. The contradiction could hardly be more marked, and MA63 merely contributed to the ambiguity.

II. THE KELANTAN CHALLENGE AND ITS IMPLICATIONS

The Malaysia project did not find favour in at least one state – Kelantan. And no doubt its reservations stemmed in part from an apparent assumption on the part of the federal government that it was entitled to act as if it were the government of a unitary state, failing even to consult let alone include the state governments in MA63. It was also of course relevant and concerning for those states that the proposal was to admit Sabah and Sarawak on *more favourable* terms than those accorded to the existing eleven states.[20] Kelantan maintained

[16] See, further, Chin (n 11) 27.

[17] *Report of the Commission of Enquiry* (n 11) 237.

[18] S de Smith, *The New Commonwealth and its Constitutions* (London, Stevens, 1964) 194.

[19] J Chin, 'The 1963 Malaysia Agreement (MA63): Sabah and Sarawak and the politics of historical grievances' in S Lemiere (ed), *Minorities Matter: Malaysian Politics and People Volume III* (Singapore, ISEAS–Yusof Ishak Institute, 2019).

[20] Sabah and Sarawak were accorded greater powers, more sources of revenue, and a right to veto constitutional amendments affecting them: A Harding, *The Constitution of Malaysia: A Contextual Analysis* (Oxford, Hart Publishing, 2022) ch 6.

that forming, without consent of those states, a new federation in which three new subjects had a better federal bargain than the existing eleven subjects was a breach of the federal bargain, that is, the Federation of Malaya Agreement 1957, which formed the basis for independence under the 1957 Constitution of the Federation of Malaya. Just six days before Malaysia was due to come into existence, the Government of Kelantan commenced proceedings against the Government of the Federation of Malaya and the Prime Minister for declarations that MA63 and the Malaysia Act 1963 giving effect to it were null and void, or alternatively were not binding on Kelantan.[21] This case is worth examining in some detail because of its fundamental importance in relation to the nature of Malaysian federalism itself, the ambiguity surrounding which appears to have begun before the country even came into being.

Kelantan's case was in essence that the Malaysia Act would abolish the Federation of Malaya, thereby violating the Federation of Malaya Agreement 1957, an instrument to which (unlike MA63) the Rulers of the states of Malaya had been party; and that the proposed changes, by constitutional convention, required the consent of each of the constituent states, including Kelantan, and this had not been obtained. Kelantan asked the court for an injunction that would have blocked the inauguration of Malaysia until the matter could be fully argued.

Exceptionally, in view of the political importance and urgency of the matter, the judge, Thomson LP, proceeded nonetheless to determine the substance of the issues raised. He found that the provisions relating to constitutional amendment had been complied with, a holding which, Jayakumar comments, there is 'very little to quarrel with'.[22] Yet the matter is only that simple if one assumes the conclusion, namely, that the express procedural requirements in Article 159 of the Constitution on constitutional amendment (requiring only a two-thirds parliamentary majority in both houses) exhaust what the constitution demands. It was of course Kelantan's entirely plausible case that further process, by way of the alleged convention, was implied into Article 159.[23] This is to say that, in a federal system, fundamental changes to the structure or the subjects thereof imply a requirement of the consent of, or at the very least consultation with, all the federation's subjects. This issue requires attention not just to the constitutional amendment process but to the entire historical circumstances and all of

[21] *Government of the State of Kelantan v Government of the Federation of Malaya and Tunku Abdul Rahman Putra Al-Haj* [1963] 1 MLJ 355; S Jayakumar, 'Admission of New States: *Government of the State of Kelantan v Government of the Federation of Malaya and Tunku Abdul Rahman Putra Al-Haj*' (1954) 6(1) *Malaya Law Review* 181. Jayakumar points out (182) that this was the very first occasion a case had been brought to have a statute ruled unconstitutional under the federal constitution, and the first time a case had been brought by a state against the federation. It is of course significant that the article is entitled 'admission of new states' and proceeds on the premise that this is what had occurred.

[22] ibid 182.

[23] *cf Reference re Secession of Quebec* [1998] 2 SCR 217, Supreme Court of Canada.

the documentation (referred to above) regarding the federal system. Thomson LP concluded by saying that he could 'not see that Parliament went in any way beyond its powers or that it did anything so fundamentally revolutionary as to require fulfilment of a condition which the Constitution itself does not prescribe'.[24]

In agreeing with this conclusion Jayakumar adopts the theory[25] that '[t]he Federation was not abolished – it continues to exist with additional States and the appearance that it has been abolished is probably due to the change in name'.

This theory is not entirely without merit, but ultimately, it is suggested, it fails when proper regard is had to the history and the agreements concluded prior to MA63, in which it is clear, despite the ambiguity of MA63 itself, that a new federation was envisaged, and not just in name. The admission-of-new-states theory is not even, it seems, consistent with much of the language used in MA63, nor with the separate listing of Sabah and Sarawak in the original (and now amended, under the Malaysia Act 1963, as of 16 September 1963) constitution. Thomson LP's concluding statement is also confusingly at variance with his premise, which is that the power of parliament to amend the constitution is limited only by the terms of Article 159 (that is, it requires a two-thirds' majority in both houses of parliament and the consent of the Conference of Rulers), and that those terms were fully complied with. His concluding statement to the contrary indicates that parliament might conceivably do something so fundamentally revolutionary as to require fulfilment of a condition which the constitution itself does *not prescribe*. In other words, on this latter view the express terms of Article 159 do *not*, contrary to what is assumed throughout the judgment, provide an exhaustive account of what might be required in the event of 'revolutionary' changes. And that in turn is to agree that we have to look at the surrounding circumstances and documentation when we interpret Article 159, the very thing that Thomson LP was disinclined to do.

Another relevant aspect of this discussion is that we are now familiar with the notion of a constitution's basic structure, which cannot be violated even by a constitutional amendment that complies with the expressly prescribed procedure. The basic structure doctrine, originating in the Indian case of *Kesavananda* in 1972,[26] has now spread widely and has been regularly argued and accepted in superior courts and constitutional courts across the world, including in Malaysia itself.[27] In a federal system (as recognised in *Kesavananda* itself) federalism is indeed part of the basic structure, and so, contrary to the

[24] Above n 21.

[25] ibid 186.

[26] *Kesavananda Bharati v State of Kerala* (1973) 4 SCC 225.

[27] Bui Ngoc Son and R Abeyratne (eds), The *Law and Politics of Unconstitutional Constitutional Amendments* (Abingdon, Routledge, 2021).

approach in the *Kelantan* case, the basic structure doctrine supports review of the validity of constitutional amendments affecting federalism which would be invalid if the constitution's basic structure – here, one supposes, the basic tenets of federalism – are violated. This represents a guarantee over and above the express provisions on constitutional amendment.[28] Thomson LP's judgment does not therefore state accurately the rights of the states with regard to changes in the federal structure. It is now clear that the basic structure doctrine can be argued as a limitation on the power of amendment, and it is hard to imagine anything much more revolutionary than a proposal to alter the entire basis and membership of a federation. Of course, the issues raised by Kelantan are water that long ago passed under the bridge of history. But the *Kelantan* case should not be used as authority for changing the federal structure without due consultation with the state governments.

Accordingly, the special autonomy accorded to Sabah and Sarawak, it is suggested, is part of the constitution's basic structure, and can be enforced by the courts if the need arises. In one important sense this issue of federalism as basic structure has already been deliberately conceded. The Constitution (Amendment) Act 2022 recognises the importance of MA63 as a foundational document, and the particular status of Sabah and Sarawak within the Malaysian federation.[29] As was the case prior to a constitutional amendment in 1976, Sabah and Sarawak are now listed separately from the other states and are referred to as 'territories'.[30] This is a considerable step forward in repairing or reconstituting Malaysian federalism, at least at a symbolic level. It also means that the basic structure doctrine implies no less than that fundamental changes in the federal structure need to be negotiated between the federation's subjects in order to be constitutionally valid. This, it is suggested, is the basic norm of Malaysian territorial governance.

Yet, mere recognition of MA63 as a founding document, although perhaps an essential starting point, fails to resolve a number of underlying questions relating to the autonomy of the two states. We now examine this autonomy in more detail, and look at ways in which it might be enhanced. It should first be noted that Sabah and Sarawak are entitled to special constitutionally

[28] HP Lee and Yvonne Tew, 'The law and politics of unconstitutional constitutional amendments in Malaysia' ch 5 in Bui and Abeyratne, ibid. Federalism was specifically listed in *Kesavananda* (n 26) 316 as part of the basic structure in India, and the 2022 amendment to the Malaysian Constitution places this matter, in relation to Sabah and Sarawak beyond debate.

[29] Federal Constitution, Article 160 (definition of 'the Federation'), as amended by the Constitution (Amendment) Act 2022; see, further, Jaclyn L Neo, 'Restoring constitutional equality to Sabah and Sarawak: Do the proposed amendments to the Malaysian Federal Constitution go far enough?' (*ConstitutionNet*, 19 November 2021) constitutionnet.org/news/restoring-constitutional-equality-sabah-and-sarawak-do-proposed-amendments-malaysian-federal.

[30] The Constitution (Amendment) Act 1976, effecting this change, was justified on the basis of a need to create quality between the states, and this ran counter to the entire purpose of MA63: Neo, ibid. For a comparison of the text before and after the amendment of 2022, see Tan and Neo (n 1) 117.

guaranteed grants. They also enjoy special and concurrent powers under Schedule 9 of the Constitution that are not given to the other states, such as powers over personal law, as well as statutory powers over immigration. A separate High Court for Sabah and Sarawak is also guaranteed by Article 121.

III. THE CONSTITUTIONAL VETO

In all federal systems there is a degree of tension between centripetal and centrifugal tendencies. This tension will generally be over resources, legal powers, or divisive political issues such as identity, culture and religion. It requires devices to resolve conflicts in the interests of maintaining the careful balancing act that federalism promises. Malaysia has proved a relatively stable federation, although this stability has been bought, historically, by endorsing a highly dominant federal executive somewhat at the expense of state autonomy.[31] This dominance is now questioned, due partly to the political fragmentation occurring since 2018 at both federal and state levels, and partly to the rise of Sabah and Sarawak nationalism.[32] Attention therefore focuses on constitutional guarantees and the history and status of MA63. From the perspective of these two states, the federal bargain of 1963 has not been honored, and the constitutional guarantees have proved in practice ineffective.[33]

The starting point for this discussion is the veto that protects Sabah and Sarawak from adverse constitutional amendment. Under Article 161E(2) of the Constitution, no constitutional amendment may be made without the concurrence of the *Yang di-Pertua Negeri* (Governor) of Sabah and/or Sarawak as the case may be (acting of course on the advice of the state government) if the amendment is such as to affect the operation of the Constitution as regards a number of specified matters. These matters include legislative and executive powers, parliamentary representation, fiscal arrangements, and cultural issues affecting religion, language, and the protection of indigenous peoples.[34] This veto requirement was given constitutional effect in *Robert Linggi v Government of Malaysia*[35] in 2011, where it was held that Article 122AB of the Federal Constitution (introduced by the Constitution (Amendment) Act 1994, and providing for the appointment of Judicial Commissioners in Sabah and Sarawak) was unconstitutional due to lack of consent by the respective state Governors. It was held that such consent was required as the amendment

[31] This was a prominent theme in ch 4.
[32] See further Harding and Chin (n 2).
[33] Chin (n 5).
[34] See further Harding and Chin (n 2).
[35] (2011) 7 CLJ 373.

affected the constitution of the High Court of Sabah and Sarawak.[36] However, the precise scope of the veto power has not been otherwise tested in the courts. This may change as a result of a case in litigation in which MA63 is being used to argue that the federal legislature trespassed on the territorial sea of Sabah in enacting the Territorial Sea Act 2012.[37]

It should be noted in connection with the veto that the requirement is for consent of the executive branch rather than the legislative assembly. Given the proven ability of the federal government over many years (especially in Sabah) to manipulate government tenure at the state level,[38] the protection afforded by the veto is a paper requirement that has been shown to be easily be satisfied, or even just ignored.[39] Despite the definitional breadth of the veto it is suggested that applying it to all constitutional amendments would afford greater protection. This would avoid technical questions as to these states being 'affected' by an amendment; and in a federal system all constitutional amendments should as a matter of principle be agreed by at least a proportion of states, and certainly by states having special constitutional protection.

IV. THE CASE FOR CHANGE

The emergence of nationalism in Sabah and Sarawak is no great surprise. It is a wonder rather that there was no earlier push-back against the federal overreach that has been witnessed ever since the moment Malaysia was created. So far, we have considered the constitutional status of Sabah and Sarawak against the background of MA63 and the relevant constitutional provisions. But the practical impact of federal overreach on these two states has created a sense of discontent that has fueled nationalism and even spawned calls for secession.[40] What then is the case for constitutional change? Does it relate entirely to MA63?

[36] Similarly, in *Pihak Berkuasa Negeri Sabah v Sugumar Balakrishnan* [2002] 3 MLJ 72 Mohamed Dazaiddin FCJ regarded the 'spirit and intention' of the IGC Report (n 11) and MA63 as relevant to an issue arising under the Immigration Act. And in *Datuk Haji Mohammad Tufail bin Mahmud and 5 Others v Dato' Ting Check Sii* [2009] 4 CLJ 449, which concerned the exclusive right of Sarawak lawyers to practise in Sarawak, the Federal Court treated the same documents as binding.

[37] Admittedly, it is not easy to state what exactly would constitute an amendment 'affecting' either or both of these two states. See, further, A Harding, 'Devolution of powers in Sarawak: A dynamic process of redesigning territorial governance in a federal system' (2017) 12(2) *Asian Journal of Comparative Law* 257.

[38] Chin (n 5) 164ff.

[39] In 1988 an important amendment affecting judicial power (a matter attracting the veto), which precluded the civil courts from exercising the jurisdiction of the syariah courts, was passed without securing the assent of Sabah and Sarawak, but is assumed to apply to them: Harding (n 20) 203.

[40] R Bociaga, 'BorneoExit: Independence for East Malaysia?' (*The Diplomat*, 11 December 2020). This was even recognised by the then Prime Minister Muhyiddin Yasin, when he stated that, 'Some people have long desired secession, and in recent years the drumbeat of separation has only grown louder': ibid.

There is clearly a general feeling in Sabah and Sarawak that MA63 has not been implemented according to the spirit and the letter, and this discontent has acted as a lightning rod for other aspects of discontent, arising mainly from alleged failure to implement the Points that were agreed prior to MA63. More than this, there has been a long and general failure to honour the status of Sabah and Sarawak in terms of intergovernmental relations. The following more specific issues are raised:[41]

(i) There is an economic imbalance between East and West Malaysia, in which Sabah and Sarawak, having the majority of Malaysian natural resources, nonetheless experience a development deficit.[42]
(ii) There has been political interference (often behind the scenes) with the appointment or tenure of state governments (this is apart from the two instances of the use of emergency powers considered above).[43]
(iii) Federal overreach has embraced the exploitation of natural resources in the form of a state royalty of only 5 per cent, and the taking over of territorial sea resources by the federation.[44]
(iv) The enthusiastic granting of citizenship to recent migrants, especially in Sabah, has altered the demographic balance in that state.[45]
(v) Cultural and religious overreach is evident in terms of religious conversions; Malay as the national language; and the lack of protection of the indigenous peoples.[46]

The point is now reached where political parties in Sabah and Sarawak are obliged to take on the mantle of nationalism, and must compete in terms of how to manage the situation. It is, since 2018 at least, no longer the case that these states are any kind of 'fixed deposit' for the dominant party at the centre.[47]

The question then arises, what is the best way forward? While opinion is solid around the reasons for discontent, it varies considerably with regard to how to resolve the issue of autonomy for Sabah and Sarawak. It is important to note that for the most part these possible solutions, secession apart, are not necessarily mutually exclusive.

[41] Chin (n 5) 154ff.
[42] Harding and Chin (n 2) 43.
[43] Chin (n 5) 164ff.
[44] Harding and Chin (n 2).
[45] Chin (n 5) 172.
[46] ibid 179; A Harding, 'Protection of the indigenous peoples of Sabah and Sarawak under Malaysia's federal system' in Harding and Chin (n 2) 187.
[47] As claimed by former PM Datuk Seri Najib Tun Razak prior to the 2018 election, which he lost. See further, A Puyok and PR Sukhani, 'Sabah: breakthrough in the fixed deposit state' (2020) 109(2) *The Round Table* 209; J Samad, 'Unequal Treatment Breeds Secessionist Ideas in Sabah' (*Free Malaysia Today*, 27 September 2023); '60% East Malaysians want to Secede from Malaysia: Kitingan' (*The Vibes*, 8 November 2021).

A. Secession

A question much debated in Sabah and Sarawak has been, could these states secede from the federation?

MA63 makes no provision, nor does the Constitution, for secession. It is easy to see why such agreements and constitutions rarely do so. The danger would be that of secession hanging over every discussion as an implicit threat – not a positive way to build a federal structure. This does not mean that secession is impossible. In fact, in Singapore's case secession was already achieved in 1965, although it should be noted it was not a voluntary aspiration on Singapore's part, and it was achieved by mutual agreement, not unilaterally.[48] The short answer to the secession question is that anything can be achieved by agreement,[49] but a unilateral attempt to secede would be highly problematical in a number of ways. It might spark concerted and even violent attempts to prevent it happening and federal military intervention could not be ruled out. It might well not gain international support. And the necessary negotiation of separation issues would be extremely difficult in an environment of hostility. After 60 or more years of federalism, secession would be painful and problematic, and the future would be uncertain. Nonetheless, there are those whose trust of the federation is so low that they consider this taking of what we may call maximum umbrage the only viable option.[50]

B. Cancellation of MA63

A more radical approach, which we could call the lesser umbrage option, would be to cancel MA63 altogether, in recognition of Sabah and Sarawak's alleged historical right to self-determination, and start over, possibly negotiating a new federation.[51] This approach takes the view, not that MA63 should be fully implemented, but that Sabah and Sarawak never genuinely agreed to be part of Malaysia in the first place, as the referenda were flawed and did not represent true public opinion at the time. There is evidence of lack of understanding, lack of genuine majority agreement, and too much haste to sweep up 'the dust of empire' (as Charles de Gaulle famously called it, referring to Africa) in 1963.[52] But cancelling MA63, as with secession, is also fraught with difficulty.

[48] Kevin Tan (n 9).

[49] According to the Supreme Court of Canada, an expression of a desire to secede would impose an obligation on the federal government to negotiate secession: above n 23.

[50] See Samad n 47. For applicable rules of international law, see M Sterio, *The Right to Self-Determination under International Law: 'Selfistans', Secession, and the Rule of the Great Powers* (Abingdon, Routledge, 2013).

[51] 'Gov't not Considering "Self-Determination" for Sabah, S'wak' (*Malaysiakini*, 25 March 2019).

[52] See above n 5.

Apart from the very unlikely event that the federal government would agree to such a course, it would be necessary to bring a case in the International Court of Justice to invalidate MA63. Those advocating this course have pointed to the 2019 case of the Chagos Islanders, which resulted in a non-binding judgment, supported by a large majority in the UN General Assembly, that the United Kingdom had unlawfully separated the Chagos Islanders from Mauritius in 1965.[53] This finding was based on the Islanders' right to self-determination, which by 1965, it was held,[54] had crystallised under customary international law.

This is not the place to examine in detail the merits of a similar possible claim by Sabah or Sarawak in relation to MA63, especially as such claim has not presently been expressed in clear legal terms. It would presumably be based on the right to self-determination as viewed retrospectively by the ICJ, and seek to find similarity between the cases of Sabah/Sarawak in 1963 and the Chagos Islands in 1965.[55]

Irrespective of these merits, such as they may be, the invalidation of MA63 would face enormous practical obstacles in terms of obtaining international support and mobilising money, diplomatic effort, and expertise to bring the litigation. Even after more than a decade of litigation the Chagos Islanders have not yet been allowed to return to their homeland, in spite of the ICJ's advisory opinion. Even if successful, one could expect such litigation to take at least a similar period, from as it were a standing start, and the problem of autonomy would not be ended. The Chagos case required a resolution in the UN General Assembly supporting the advisory opinion, and it has not been implemented some five years later. The litigation began in 2010, and had been in contemplation, one assumes, for several years before that. Beyond these practical problems, there are several respects in which the facts of the Chagos case differ materially from the facts relating to MA63. In particular, a major obstacle is that only sovereign states are eligible to bring cases before the ICJ. Thus any case brought before the ICJ would require to be adopted by the federal government, who would presumably be a defendant in the case.

[53] 'Legal Consequences of the Separation of the Chagos Archipelago from Mauritius in 1965, Advisory Opinion' (*ICJ Reports* 2019) 95.

[54] In fact this was established by 1960 UN Resolution 1514 (XV), the *Declaration on the Granting of Independence to Colonial Countries and Peoples*.

[55] See the remarks of Robert Pei in 'Sabah, Sarawak, Have Solid Case to Seek Self-Determination, says SSRANTZ' *Dayak Daily* (1 April 2019). An application by 12 Sarawakians against the governments of Malaysia and Sarawak for a declaration that MA63 is null and void was struck out by the High Court at Kuching in 2023, on the basis of the plaintiffs' lack of standing. See the report 'Kuching High Court strikes out suit to declare MA63 null and void' *The Star* (25 May 2023) www.thestar.com.my/news/nation/2023/05/25/kuching-high-court-strikes-out-suit-to-declare-ma63-null-and-void.

C. Fulfilling MA63

A more popular cry is for fulfilment of what was agreed in 1963. And a start has been made in this direction with the constitutional amendment of 2022.[56] The amendment is of course symbolic, but such symbols are often considered important. The listing of Sabah and Sarawak as 'territories' of Malaysia under Article 1, and the listing of MA63 as a federation-defining document in Article 160, mean in effect stepping back in time and agreeing that MA63 was the creation of a new federation, not merely the admission of new states. The knock-on effects of this decisive shift in the theory of Malaysian federalism could be considerable, especially when we consider that the new politics of fragmentation and serial coalition-building give considerable political leverage to Sabah and Sarawak's political parties. We do not yet know where the breaking of the logjam of centralised federalism will lead, but this breaking has created opportunities for fulfilling MA63, and especially renewed attention to the 18/20 Points.[57] The honouring of these points is not only of great practical importance (for example regarding recruitment to the public service, and cultural, linguistic, and religious matters), but is for many people even more importantly a point of honour.[58]

D. Utilising Existing Constitutional Resources

We have seen that one reason for stability in the Malaysian federal system is that, ultimately, powers have not been carefully balanced, but rather heavily tilted in favour of the centre. Another, more positive, reason is that federal-state relations in Malaysia embrace a form of cooperative federalism. This is to say that the constitution contains many provisions that facilitate cooperative arrangements, thereby blurring the line between federal and state powers, as opposed to encouraging both state and federal governments to stand rigidly on their rights, protecting their constitutional turf against all-comers. It is noticed, comparatively, that cooperative federalism tends to provide stability.[59] What this type of federalism entails is that institutions with federal and state representation are established to ensure coordination in shared areas, for example development, environment, and disaster response (especially during the COVID-19

[56] See above.

[57] The demand for fulfilment of MA63 in effect embraces the 18/20 points, even though they are not mentioned in MA63 itself.

[58] 'Malaysia and the non-fulfilment of the 20- and 18-Point Agreements with Sabah and Sarawak' *Malaysia Today* (26 September 2013).

[59] C Saunders, 'Co-operative arrangements in comparative perspective' in G Appleby, N Aroney and T John (eds), *The Future of Australian Federalism: Comparative and Interdisciplinary Perspectives*, (Cambridge, Cambridge University Press, 2012).

pandemic); determination of equitable division of revenues (usually via formal or informal meetings); and development of common policies and uniform laws, where needed.[60]

Malaysia has national councils on finance and local government, and provisions allowing uniformity in some areas like land and local government. In addition, there are, as we have seen above, several constitutional provisions allowing for flexibility and cooperation between the two levels of government.[61] It appears therefore that a great deal can be done to enhance autonomy without even resorting to legislation or constitutional amendment. As an example, we can take the debate in Sarawak about the use of English as the medium of instruction in schools. Changing this medium from Malay to English would require only an order of the minister under the Education Act.[62] The issue is the political decision to make the change, not the means by which it could be effected.

In addition to these resources, Sabah and Sarawak enjoy special fiscal powers and grants under Article 112A-D of the constitution, and special immigration powers (under MA1963 and the Immigration Act). Judicial policing of division of state and federal powers is also, as we have seen, a resource in ensuring there is no trespass by the federal power on states' rights. And of course, Sabah and Sarawak are fully represented in both houses of parliament, in the federal government and cabinet, and in the public service, in addition to their existing powers and government structures at the state level.

It will be objected here that, if all of these resources were really helpful, then the autonomy of Sabah and Sarawak would not have been eroded in the way it has been. The answer to this is that the resources are not necessarily in themselves lacking, but rather it is the failure to make use of them in the past that has contributed to the logjam of centralised power, which, as we have seen, is now breaking up.

There remains, of course, the process of constitutional amendment, which as was seen in 2022, can be deployed to good effect where there is a political consensus. Future constitutional amendment is a matter of pure speculation, but possible areas of reform might be devolution of further powers to Sabah and Sarawak, greater representation in the Dewan Negara (the upper house, or Senate), or a more general decentralisation of powers to state governments. This last may be desirable, but is not likely to satisfy demands for greater devolution of powers in Sabah and Sarawak, which seek, not powers congruent with other states, but powers going beyond the powers of other states.

[60] See eg R French, 'Cooperative federalism' in C Saunders and A Stone (eds), *The Oxford Handbook of the Australian Constitution* (Oxford, Oxford University Press, 2018).
[61] See pp 71–2.
[62] Education Act 1996, ss 8 and 9.

One aspect of devolution of powers makes it more attractive than merely fulfilling MA63. Devolution is open-ended, and so the conferring of greater powers does not close off demand for even greater powers, and can be used in addition to fulfilment of MA63, which has logically a definite end-point. A useful principle to adopt here would be the principle of subsidiarity, under which decisions are to be taken, wherever possible, at the level that is closest to those affected by the decisions. Subsidiarity leads to the question, not what should be devolved, but what should not be devolved.

V. CONCLUSION

The breaking of the logjam of centralisation leads to questions concerning the future of federalism, and it is clear that Malaysian federalism's future does not have to resemble its past. Renewing the federal system will lead to enhanced democracy and greater public participation in the matters that concern them. In the case of Sabah and Sarawak, the legitimacy of Malaysia itself is in question, and addressing MA63 is a necessary but not sufficient step. It is highly arguable that some functions not dealt with under MA63 should be devolved to these states. There seems to be no good reason why, given their natural resources and their desire for more state control over decisions, they should not take on more functions, such as health, education and even policing. But these issues remain for the future. Fundamentally, however, the claim for autonomy is based on the desire of the indigenous peoples and also minority communities for self-determination in a homeland within a federal structure.

Part IV

Conclusions

12

Territorial Governance, Southeast Asia, and Innovation in Public Law

PART I OF this book raised some important issues in territorial governance, and this chapter will state the main findings to which the evidence from Southeast Asia leads. Part II examined five cases of territorial governance in Southeast Asia: three cases of decentralisation; one case of federalism without decentralisation; and one case of arrested decentralisation. In Part III we examined a number of cases of asymmetrical regional autonomy based on ethnic or religious differences. In this chapter the field of territorial governance in Southeast Asia will be briefly subjected to conspectus, critique and assessment. In particular this chapter addresses the question of what lessons can be learned from Southeast Asian experience, in light of the facts that the issues that arise are typical of those arising in other regions, and that there are also special features of the region (not necessarily unique ones) in terms of the internal diversity of the states covered, and the meaning of localism, which were explained in some detail in chapter one.

I. THE RIGHT TO THE CITY AND OTHER LOCALISMS

To begin this discussion, we can start with an interesting finding by Ran Hirschl in his study of the megacity:

> Much of the innovative constitutional thinking concerning megacity governance emanates from the new world of constitutionalism, in particular from Asia, Latin America, and parts of Africa … when it comes to actual constitutional innovation in those areas, it is the world beyond Europe and North America that has taken the lead. Such fresh thinking may be a part of national constitutional transformation … or driven by various central planning factors, intergovernmental considerations, blatant politics, or by a combination of these factors.[1]

Hirschl discusses the global megacity. We will see in this chapter that this claim is also amply borne out in relation territorial governance in Southeast Asia.

[1] R Hirschl, *City, State: Constitutionalism and the Megacity* (Oxford, Oxford University Press, 2020) 103.

Pausing momentarily on the theme of cities, the claims of the city as such have featured prominently in our discussion of all five countries. For example, we have found that the most interesting ideas for the development of territorial governance in Thailand emanate from the city of Chiang Mai, involving citizen assemblies and radical subsidiarity even down to city districts.[2] Cities in fact feature heavily in Southeast Asia's territorial governance systems, enjoying special powers. Jakarta and Yogyakarta are designated special regions as provinces within Indonesia, with elected governors and assemblies.[3] The same is true of Bangkok and Pattaya (although not yet Chiang Mai itself) in Thailand.[4] And in this they are distinguished from other provinces. The Philippines recognises no less than 38 independent cities, having the power of provinces, again with elected governors and councils; and many more that are recognised as cities but are components of provinces.[5] Malaysia recognises 18 cities as having special status, with Kuala Lumpur designated as a federal territory.[6] In Myanmar Naypyidaw has special status as the capital city, while Yangon and Mandalay are designated as provinces. These had elected councils prior to the coup.[7] In this way the city and the megacity are already somewhat empowered across the region.

While Hirschl addresses particular urban phenomena, this book addresses territorial governance at all subnational levels, albeit within a narrower geographical focus. Hirschl goes on to identify reasons why cities have been a source of, or have inspired, innovation. Fundamentally, he finds, it is the factor of necessity arising from urban agglomeration that has driven change.[8] However, necessity is not at all confined to urban issues, and there is of course no reason why innovation should be confined to urban questions. Territorial governance in Southeast Asia, we have seen, owes much to the experience of authoritarianism and militarism.

While cities certainly deserve discussion in the context of territorial governance, one issue with Hirschl's emphasis on the 'right to the city' (inspiring as it is) is that suburban and rural areas surely also deserve consideration. There are also rights – in all geographical areas – to the land and the environment, and rights to identity and democratic, responsible self-government. In Southeast Asia the right to the village makes as much sense as the right to the city, and is actually more in evidence. It is also plausibly the case that cities are already enormously advantaged in terms of infrastructure, facilities, economic opportunities, culture, and sheer political clout, quite irrespective of their constitutional

[2] See ch 7.
[3] See ch 3.
[4] See p.135ff.
[5] See p.111.
[6] See p.68.
[7] See p.99.
[8] Hirschl (n 1) ch3.

status. In Asia government chief executives are, significantly, often former city mayors. The claim that cities need constitutional recognition is well made, and is largely fulfilled in Southeast Asian systems; but does not the same apply to other subnational units?

The field of territorial governance seems in general to be permeated by a curious prevailing silence. Hirschl refers to the 'constitutional silence' concerning cities,[9] while Charles Fombad talks of a 'silent revolution' in African decentralisation[10] – a phrase that could well be applied also to Southeast Asia, where legal scholarship has been largely silent on territorial governance. This silence sits very awkwardly with the importance of the issues raised by territorial governance, which this book has sought to highlight, albeit within a particular geography. It sits awkwardly too with the concerted attempts to deal, by means of innovation, with issues such as under-development, maldistribution, demographic change, inter-ethnic conflict, and democratic or governance deficit. In this book we have seen a proliferation of innovative ideas in Southeast Asia concerning territorial governance. It is therefore worth rehearsing some of the more prominent of these in order to establish the point more clearly. This is undertaken below, but first we need to assess intergovernmental relations and also regional autonomy.

II. POWERS AND INTERGOVERNMENTAL RELATIONS

Decentralisation is usually broken down into political, fiscal and administrative decentralisation, and distinguished from deconcentration, in which central government merely operates at the local level, or uses local governments as agents exercising no discretion over the functions allocated to them.[11] In this book we have paid more attention to the first kind of decentralisation than to the other two. And the formula 'legal/political' is appropriate for this first type of decentralisation, recognising that there are two major elements involved in it.

The first, the legal aspect, is the possession of legal powers regarding certain governmental functions, an aspect that is unpacked in a little more detail below.

The second, the political aspect, also involves two distinct elements. It implies the exercise of discretion regarding the execution of legally granted powers. This involves making political choices subject to democratic controls from below (accountability to an elected council, local elections, and public

[9] ibid ch1.

[10] C Fombad, 'Constitutional entrenchment of decentralisation in Africa: An overview of trends and tendencies' (2018) 62(2) *Journal of African Law* 175.

[11] M Böckenforde, 'Decentralised forms of government' ch7 in *A Practical Guide to Constitution-Building* (Stockholm, IDEA, 2011).

participation in decision-making, for example). Second, it also implicates a system of intergovernmental relations, in which decisions are checked from above by an intermediate local government or the national government, by way of 'supervision' or the like. Critical for local autonomy, as we have repeatedly seen, is the basis on which such supervision is carried out. If it is designed to cancel anything the higher level of government disagrees with, then clearly there is no local autonomy to speak of. If on the other hand decisions are supervised against limited criteria such as illegality, inconsistency, partisanship, or corruption, then local autonomy is preserved, even if in some ways limited, and justifiably so having regard to the purposes of decentralised governance. It will be the task of the judiciary here to act as the guard preventing abuses, or at least to be the guard that guards the guards. There are after all innumerable checking mechanisms ranging from ministry checks on local budgets, to cancellation of unlawful regulations, intergovernmental consultations, and anti-corruption investigations. All of these are powers subject to public law.

One interesting point about accountability from above is that in the five countries discussed in this book there is no instance where a higher level of government has a reserve power to simply take over, or close down, or dismiss an entire local government. There are a few (not many) instances where a higher authority can give binding directions to local governments. This is worthy of brief comparative consideration.

In the United States, the states have control over local government, and will ordinarily have statutory powers to take over a local government and install 'emergency financial management' in the event of fiscal failure.[12] States also assume the right to set minimum standards for school districts, in default of which they can take over education in the district if officials are unable or unwilling to adhere to these standards.[13] In the United Kingdom legislation[14] gives broad power to the government to takeover any local function. Complete takeover of a local government is rare in the UK, but in a notable instance in 2017 the Secretary of State for Communities and Local Government appointed an independent task force to 'support' a local government's recovery from a major fire disaster.[15] Where takeover occurs, in contrast to the United States, it is usually for reasons of service failure or disaster management, rather than because of

[12] A Singla, TL Spreen, and J Schumberger, 'Decree or democracy? State takeovers and local government financial outcomes' (2023) 83(4) *Public Administration Review* 911; A Nickels, S Viswanath and H Lebovitz, 'When states intervene – or don't: Local fiscal distress, municipal distress, municipal takeovers, and the complexities of local control 'ch 8 in RL Hanson and ES Zeemering (eds), *Cooperation and Conflict Between State and Local Government* (London, Rowan and Littlefield, 2021).

[13] DR Berman, 'Takeovers of local governments: An overview and evaluation of state policies' (1995) 25(3) *Publius* 55.

[14] Local Government Act 1999, s 15(6).

[15] See the ministry press statement 'Independent Recovery Taskforce for Kensington and Chelsea council' (*gov.uk*, 5 July 2017), www.gov.uk/government/news/independent-recovery-taskforce-for-kensington-and-chelsea-council.

bankruptcy or other fiscal problems. Yet local government laws across Southeast Asia fall well short of granting such reserve powers to central government. For this reason, powers of supervision are clearly all the more necessary, and the legality and manner of their exercise become of critical importance. Given that courts cannot of course scrutinise every measure in a routinised, day-to-day manner, their power of exercising judgement where there is a serious dispute between different levels of government will ultimately determine the real extent of local autonomy. Despite the absence of the reserve powers we have seen applied elsewhere, this judicial power is the thin thread by which local autonomy ultimately hangs. Nonetheless the absence of reserve powers, in contrast to the territorial governance systems in the USA and the UK, cuts against the idea that Southeast Asian decentralised powers are, comparatively speaking, highly controlled from the centre.

The more fundamental issue in the realm of the legal/political is the actual powers and functions given to local governments. These are often more extensive than the literature often appears to admit. Local governments are frequently described as having few important powers. This is as if to say that physical planning, housing, the environment, social care, and transport are really only details in a system of government where only treasury, defence, and international relations really matter. The absurdity of this is obvious. Constitutions are largely silent (understandably so, given the onerous nature of constitutional amendment process) on the actual powers to be given to local governments, as opposed to their status. Therefore, we have been compelled to put flesh on the constitutional bones of territorial governance by looking, albeit briefly, at the powers granted by the extensive local government statutes that have been passed. What is noticeable is that the range of powers is expressed at considerable length and with great complexity. Usually, around 20 to 70 specific items are listed, many of which are themselves very broad in scope, and could easily be broken down into an even greater number. The basic list is often supplemented by a wide range of ancillary powers, such as that of eminent domain, or imposition of local taxes, and vague general powers such as the taking of measures for the welfare of the inhabitants. Following the example of the Philippines, these powers should be given a broad interpretation in cases of doubt, but even strict adherence to the ultra vires principle allows local governments to exercise powers that are incidental or necessary for the performance of powers that are listed.[16] When they are added up, there is no denying that these powers are very extensive, and that the most important ones have, in this 'silent revolution' been transferred to local governments well within living memory. The idea seems to persist, however, that few powers have actually been transferred.

In order to assess the extent of territorial governance in the region, it is necessary to break down local government powers into manageable portions.

[16] See pp 107–8.

1. *Basic infrastructure.* Almost all local governments the world over are empowered to take care of basic infrastructure, a concept that includes maintenance of local roads and watercourses, including drainage, irrigation, and water supply; parks and public buildings; garbage collection and disposal; and threats to the environment such as public nuisances. These functions are very common but by no means trivial. One suspects they are the functions giving rise to most complaints. Pothole politics is rather widespread.
2. *Regulation.* Local governments are also typically licensing authorities for local businesses, and many other activities, especially ones that impact on public health or safety, such as markets, abattoirs, and polluting industries.
3. *Social services.* Most importantly, and largely as the outcome of decentralisation, local governments are these days involved in delivering important social services that did not previously form part of their portfolio. Prominent examples are housing; transport; social care for the sick and the elderly, and child protection; health services and control of infectious diseases; primary and secondary education; and amenities such as sports facilities, libraries, and preservation of cultural heritage.
4. *Planning.* Significantly for real local autonomy, local governments are given powers over planning, both physical and economic. This enables them to implement the all-important ask of development control under structure and local plans, usually importing elements of public participation; and to promote local investment and employment.
5. *Governance.* All of the above implies local democracy, and many local governments across the region have experimented with new forms of democratic participation and transparency going far beyond electing councillors or mayors once every four years. The important point is that decentralisation and subsidiarity work because they bring government closer to the people.

Looking at these areas of activity and the trajectory of territorial governance across Southeast Asia, what is remarkable is how much greater these powers are now as compared to the pre-decentralisation period. Local government has in general moved from encompassing category 1 functions to embracing functions in all 5 categories. Local governments are therefore empowered to make a real impact on the lives of residents and the environment in which they live. And they do so under governance conditions far more democratic and governed by detailed statute law than was the case previously.

III. RECENTRALISATION?

It has become usual in recent years to look at territorial governance through the lens of 'recentralisation'. Reflection reveals, however, that recentralisation is a highly misleading term to describe what has actually occurred. It appears to imply that powers transferred to subnational units in 'decentralisation' are transferred back to where they came from, that is, to ministries of the central government. However, in policy analysis, 'recentralisation' can be given a different connotation:

> the real goal of reform efforts called 'decentralisation' [is] performance accountability leading to improved outcomes in service provision. It turns out that for accountability to improve from a transfer of authority to subnational units, some central functions will always need strengthening. We call this imperative of strengthening central functions 'recentralisation'. The use of this term does not necessarily refer to transferring functions and/ or responsibilities *from* the subnational government *to* the centre, nor to functions that had previously been transferred from the centre to subnational governments ... recentralisation refers to those aspects of service provision and accountability that central governments must maintain, develop, and reinforce in order to enhance the effectiveness of decentralised reform.[17]

Thus, what recentralisation really refers to is not what it seems. It is not the taking back of tasks by the centre, but rather, increasing the accountability of local governments to the centre as opposed to the local electorate. And in fact, in none of the cases considered in this book has such taking back occurred. Functions transferred have simply remained where they were, but accountability mechanisms have been adjusted.[18] It is suggested that, notwithstanding the narrow, technical meaning that can be given to 'recentralisation', 'supervision' captures the situation better, and is the word generally used in legislation, along with 'review', to indicate this upwards accountability of local government units to the centre. 'Recentralisation' also does not capture a situation where the centre simply continues to exercise existing supervisory powers in spite of decentralisation. In this case we had better simply say that there are limits to decentralisation, not the imposition of recentralisation; and again, administrative supervision or review is the better concept to describe what has occurred. The fact is, that decentralisation is a process involving many conditions and many changes, and difficulties will inevitably be encountered along the way. We have, for example, encountered obstacles such as lack of local expertise; localised corruption; excess of powers; the emergence of clan culture, or little kingdoms ('imperium in imperio'); and inadequate fiscal processes. It is to be expected in this experiment that the emphasis will shift from complete autonomy towards supervision. But this does not of course mean that decentralisation was a mistake or that powers need to be retracted in a sudden centripetal manoeuvre. What the systems of territorial governance have actually tried to do is to find a balance in central-local relations. In Malaysia, for example, a new balance of

[17] AI Gerschberg, 'Decentralisation, recentralisation, and performance accountability: Building an operationally useful framework for analysis' (1998) 16 *Development Policy Review* 405.

[18] See eg p 56.

federal and state powers is being sought in the context of Sabah and Sarawak.[19] A new balance between central and local powers was found in Indonesia's law on regional government.[20]

IV. SOUTHEAST ASIAN INNOVATIONS IN TERRITORIAL GOVERNANCE

In this section we may recall instances in which innovations can be found. Here 'innovation' has two connotations. The first is that laws or institutional set-ups may be innovative in the local context. The second is that they may be innovative in the sense of being without precedent anywhere. Innovation in Southeast Asian territorial governance is of both kinds.

A. Regional Autonomy

Regional autonomy as practised in Southeast Asia represents, as we have seen, a solution that is becoming fairly common across the world. It has had beneficial effects in the region and can arguably make a difference in other long-standing conflicts in Thailand and Myanmar.[21]

The case studies reveal a common pattern in several respects and raise some common issues.

First, issues of ethno-religious identity and history lie at the root of the demands for autonomy, but these are accentuated in all cases by under-development, unequal development, and disproportionality in natural-resource exploitation. Grievances of various kinds naturally often accumulate under a flag once it is raised. Thus development has to be addressed as well as issues of self-determination. Of course, development issues are not confined to ethnic peripheries or enclaves, but uneven development and control of natural resources are clearly typical problems sparking demands for autonomy.

Second, the struggles for agreement on autonomy have often featured, and continue to be punctuated by, violence led by a separatist or autonomy-seeking militarised group or party, with fear of national fragmentation or secession driving the centre's opposition to autonomy for fear of fuelling separatism. The achievement has been to quell this violence, so far at least, in these instances.

Third, the solution in terms of autonomy is expressed in a special regional autonomy law which is plenary in scope and is even constitutionally mandated. This law provides to one extent or another for legal pluralism in terms of local

[19] Ch 11.
[20] Ch 3.
[21] See 102, 140ff.

courts administering local or religious law or doing so to a greater extent than in other regions.

Fourth, regional autonomy leads to various irritants that endanger the process. These involve constitutional issues such as inter-governmental relations, unconstitutional laws affecting fundamental rights, especially equality and civil and political rights, and internal political organisation and representation within the territory. These in turn also raise questions about the equal treatment of other regions within the nation-state. These are issues that are being gradually worked through. They remain to be resolved by a process of implementation or by mutual adaptation of contradictory laws and principles. This can only occur by moving from major to relatively minor but still potentially deal-breaking issues. The important point is that the issues listed mainly implicate the entire nation-state, not simply the region directly affected. In the terms examined in chapter two, the geo-body of the state is called into question in these instances.

One obvious overall conclusion we can draw is that regional autonomy is revealed not as an ideal but as a least damaging solution for instances of continuing violence and/or potential separatism. It has proved very difficult to negotiate these to a state of finality. Typically across these cases, as we have seen, the process has been punctuated by episodes of violence. It would therefore be an exaggeration to say that regional autonomy has become entrenched, accepted, and certain in its parameters. It remains to some extent stuck at the level of experimentation and controversy. Regional autonomy, on this evidence, appears to address the issue of bare adherence to the nation-state, but fails to address the issue of what we may term real-time nation-building. In this matter general decentralisation also has a role to play.

It may be argued that such special autonomy is not peculiar to Southeast Asia, as it features strongly in European precedents such as Scotland, the Basque country, South Tyrol, and so on.[22] Yet the cases of special autonomy we have looked at also differ from those precedents in that in all cases they encompass the significant aspect of legal pluralism. An autonomous region can, as we have seen in all four instances,[23] have its own court and legal system that may differ significantly from the rest of the nation-state, especially, but perhaps not only, in personal law matters. Legal pluralism impacts in the following ways.

First, special autonomy allows for different laws to be adopted from those applicable to the rest of the country. This is of course a feature of autonomy as such, not just special autonomy; but special autonomy generally concedes legislative power over more subject matters than ordinary or symmetric autonomy.

[22] F Palermo and K Kössler, *Comparative Federalism: Constitutional Arrangements and Case Law* (Oxford, Hart Publishing, 2017) 205ff; P Popelier and M Sahadzic (eds), *Constitutional Asymmetry in Multinational Federalism: Managing Multinationalism in Multi-tiered Systems* (Cham, Switzerland, Springer Nature, 2019).

[23] And in the case of Thailand's Southern border provinces: see ch 7.

Second, special autonomy allows for the possibility of adopting an asymmetric system of internal governance, as we saw with Bangsamoro with its parliamentary government system.[24]

Third, it has been argued that special autonomy, necessarily in all of the Southeast Asian cases, implicates legal pluralism, or applying their own law to specific communities that are identified with the region as a homeland. There are many examples of this: Islamic law is applied to Muslims in Bangsamoro, and what might be termed enhanced Islamic law to Muslims in Aceh. Papuan customary law is applied to the Melanesian peoples of Papua; and customary law is applied also in Bangsamoro, and to some extent in the context of dispute resolution to indigenous people at the *barangay* level across the whole country.[25] In Sabah and Sarawak legal pluralism abounds, in that many varieties of *adat* or 'native' customary law apply to the indigenous peoples; Islamic law to Muslims; and Chinese customary law to the Chinese.[26] The important fact about this legal pluralism is not just that it is present, but that it is the most important reason for claiming and fighting for special autonomy in the first place. In this way these cases differ significantly from those of Europe.[27] Myanmar's national races ministers and self-administered areas also offer intriguing alternatives to special autonomy.[28]

B. Localism, Subsidiarity

Regional autonomy prompts us to consider, by way of comparison, general decentralisation and subsidiarity as solutions to issues of localism and identity. We have seen that in numerous ways decentralisation in Southeast Asia caters for issues of custom, tradition, or local identity. We have seen this in *barangay* justice in the Philippines, *adat* villages in Indonesia, and in special statutory or constitutional provisions catering for the customs or political traditions of local communities or indigenous peoples.[29]

There are numerous ways other than through enforcement of personal law that ethnic culture and religion may be expressed: educational medium and curriculum; social care; building, planning and heritage preservation; markets and food regulation; religious buildings and festivals, and public art and symbolism, for example, spring to mind. Even the classic equal-citizen acts of voting and representing communities in the legislature can be culturally inflected or provided for, as we have seen in the case of *noken* voting in Papua, and village

[24] See pp 173ff.

[25] See eg p 177.

[26] The independence of the legal system was one of the main guarantees afforded to those states: see p184.

[27] Palermo and Kössler (n 22) 209–10.

[28] See 95, 96ff.

[29] See pp 110, 114, 117.

household voting in Myanmar.[30] However, general decentralisation has one very important limitation in that, unlike regional autonomy, it cannot cater for legal pluralism. Local governments cannot run special legal systems, and do not have, nor should they have, powers in respect of personal law. One simply cannot have different legal systems at purely local levels that diverge from the national system.

One aspect of intergovernmental relations that stands out is that Southeast Asia embraces the idea of what Indonesians call *tugas pembantuan*, or the duty of assistance.[31] Numerous provisions we have looked at involve cooperation between different levels of government. Examples are the overlapping allocation of powers in the Philippines and co-operative federalism in Malaysia.[32] Malaysia also offers the possibility at least of combining traditional federalism with devolution.[33]

C. Local Democracy

Local democracy has advanced considerably across the Southeast Asian region as a result of decentralisation, and in several respects we can see innovation implanted in the modern, decentralised systems of territorial governance. In the Philippines local democracy is deeply entrenched constitutionally.[34]

In Indonesia local elections have become the norm since decentralisation commenced. One striking innovation is the invention of a special assembly (the DPD) to give localism a voice in national legislative and policy discussions.[35] Local elections are also the norm in the Philippines, Thailand, and (ordinarily) Myanmar, although in Thailand local democracy is limited by the central appointment of provincial and district heads, as well as administrative staff. The role of the General Administration Department in Myanmar, similarly, limits the practice of local democracy. In Malaysia there is strong opinion in favour of the restoration of local government elections, but state governments are already elected and retain responsibility for local government. In several contexts, for example in the alteration of local government boundaries and the creation, abolition or merger of units, a plebiscite or referendum is required.[36]

Of course, local democracy, even if largely an innovation in Southeast Asia, is not in itself an innovation. But democracy is exhibited in various ways other

[30] See pp 168, 100.
[31] See p 160.
[32] See pp 110ff, 71ff.
[33] See ch 11.
[34] See p 37.
[35] See p 52ff.
[36] In Bangsamoro two referenda were held: see, p 172.

than elections, and these ways ensure that the culture of democracy is not simply a once-in-four-years exercise, but is deeply entrenched in the process of public decision-making. Principal amongst these ways is public participation. This may take many different forms, but there are numerous instances of a legal duty to consult the public on various policies and proposals.[37] Planning decisions in Malaysia are a case in point, where such duty exists and is supported by both legislation and judicial review, even though there are no local elections. The public must be consulted in relation to structure plans, which are subjected to extensive scrutiny, and once settled are then binding on the local government in such a way that even minor deviations are subject to the same process. This entire process is then backed by judicial review, in which the courts apply a broad rule of standing in order to allow the public into court to challenge the legality of local decisions.[38] Across Southeast Asia administrative law is developing quickly, and judicial review of administrative actions on the basis of liberal standing rules has become common not just in Malaysia but in the Philippines, Indonesia and Thailand.[39] In the Philippines having a personal interest in a decisional outcome is not an absolute requirement as the judiciary recognises the 'transcendental importance' of a matter. The court may be willing to 'brush aside this barren procedural infirmity [that is, a lack of personal interest] and recognise the legal standing of the petitioner in view of the transcendental importance of the issues raised'.[40] A plethora of local and sectoral legislation requires public consultation on environmental matters.[41]

People's initiatives are also recognised in Thailand and the Philippines, where referenda, recall, and the general duty of consultation apply to local governments. These facilitate demands for legislation and other outcomes, as well as removal of officials who are negligent or corrupt.[42] The *barangay* justice system also has a decidedly democratic flavour,[43] in addition to the fact that the *barangay* also has an assembly of the whole people.[44]

D. Village Law

We have seen that it is at the level of the village that we find traditional forms of governance most represented, and here the innovation lies in replicating, within the framework of the modern state, the traditional role of the village

[37] See eg, pp 21, 64, 116.
[38] See p 83.
[39] Po Jen Yap and H Lau (eds), *Public Interest Litigation in Asia* (Abingdon, Routledge, 2012).
[40] *Kilusang Mayo Uno v Garcia*, GR No 115381 (1994).
[41] W Geera, 'Public participation in environmental governance in the Philippines: The challenge of consolidation in engaging the state' (2016) 52 *Land Use Policy* 501.
[42] See eg p 114ff.
[43] ibid.
[44] See p 116.

head and traditional modes of both local governance and dispute resolution, which is that of acting as intermediary between the village and higher levels of government. In Indonesia a highly democratic innovation allows a village to self-identify as an '*adat* village' (customary village), so as to maintain its traditional local governance. Even where a village does not self-identify in this way, it still normally maintains traditional governance alongside the state-prescribed version. In the Philippines the most important structural innovation is the empowering of the *barangay* as the focus for traditional dispute settlement that emphasises harmony in the face-to-face society. But this village system operates adjunctly to the national system of justice in that its deployment is a compulsory condition for litigation. The *barangay* is also the basic political unit. In Myanmar two village traditions are maintained under modern legislation. One is the role of the village head in acting as both a representative of the village and as a locally-based state official. Another is the traditional voting system for local administrative heads that depends on household voting. If democracy is a culture, not simply something to be desired, then village democracy is its most cultural form in Southeast Asia. Legal pluralism, one way or another, abounds in village law as it does in the legal system.

V. CONCLUSION

The thesis of this book has been that territorial governance should, and can, embrace localism (the local sense of identity) and subsidiarity (the policy of locating decisions where possible at the level nearest to the people). In Southeast Asia (to repeat, the region is not unique in this respect, but it presents a striking case) diversity and a rejection of authoritarian centralism are the most important factors that drive the demand for local autonomy. And territorial governance as we now see it, some decades after decentralisation became a project, attempts to deliver a reasoned and effective response to this demand. It also attempts to satisfy equally important demands for good service delivery as an aspect of development, and in the process redefines development, in empowering local communities, as encompassing far more than the economic bottom line. Territorial governance delivers on the promise of accountability and democracy at all levels. The challenge is for it to make a difference to the lived experience, not just the concept, of development. The law cannot require inspired leadership, or the desire to do things differently, more creatively, or more inclusively. But it can provide a framework that encourages these desirables.

The question has been whether a revolution could be engineered in which considerable powers could be transferred from central bureaucracies to local democracies. To a surprising extent this revolution has been accomplished. But the question now is whether the systems of territorial governance can ultimately generate sufficient confidence to take subsidiarity and localism a stage further.

This book commenced with the strange but in a way inspiring story of a suburban area that suddenly discovered and then reclaimed its identity when it was snatched away by bureaucratic dictat. The hope with which we conclude is that this sense of localism, still for some people raising the prospect of fragmentation, can instead form the basis for a sense of belonging in a notion of citizenship that is expanded to include what is held differently, not just what is held in common.

Index

www.ingramcontent.com/pod-product-compliance
Lightning Source LLC
LaVergne TN
LVHW020200140225
803739LV00003B/92